Ethel

To my wife,
Irene,
with love

LESTER DAVID

Ethel

The story of Mrs. Robert J. Kennedy

WORLD PUBLISHING

TIMES MIRROR
NEW YORK

What though the radiance which was once so bright
Be now for ever taken from my sight,
  Though nothing can bring back the hour
Of splendour in the grass, of glory in the flower;
  We will grieve not, rather find
  Strength in what remains behind;
  In the primal sympathy
  Which having been must ever be;
  In the soothing thoughts that spring
  Out of human suffering;
  In the faith that looks through death,
In years that bring the philosophic mind.

—William Wordsworth

PUBLISHED BY THE WORLD PUBLISHING COMPANY
PUBLISHED SIMULTANEOUSLY IN CANADA
BY NELSON, FOSTER & SCOTT LTD.

THIRD PRINTING—DECEMBER 1972

COPYRIGHT © 1971 BY LESTER DAVID
ALL RIGHTS RESERVED
LIBRARY OF CONGRESS CATALOG CARD NUMBER: 73-145833
PRINTED IN THE UNITED STATES OF AMERICA
DESIGNED BY JACQUES CHAZAUD

WORLD PUBLISHING
TIMES MIRROR

ACKNOWLEDGMENTS
AND SOURCES

To all the men and women whose lives touched those of Robert and Ethel Kennedy—family members, clergymen, teachers, classmates, friends, neighbors, journalists and political associates—my grateful appreciation for sharing their memories with me.

Although it is not possible to name them all, I owe a special debt to some and hereby acknowledge their considerable help.

I thank Jimmy Breslin, the author and journalist, for some nights in a barroom and invaluable first-hand experiences. I thank journalists Frank Mankiewicz, Pete Hamill, Dick Schaap, Andrew A. Glass, Jack Newfield, Joe McCarthy and Kristi Witker for their insights and recollections. I am indebted to old and dear friends of Ethel and Robert, especially K. Lemoyne Billings, Kenneth P. O'Donnell, Bill Barry, Dave Hackett, George Plimpton and Dickie Cummins.

Immeasurably helpful, too, were Ethel's brother, Rushton Skakel; her sister, Pat Cuffe of Dublin; Luella Hennessey, R.N., the staff of the College of the Sacred Heart in Purchase, N.Y. My thanks, too, to T. S. Hyland of Greenwich for permitting me to explore Ethel's girlhood home; to Mr. and Mrs. Johannes Laursen for their remembrances; to the doctors in Los Angeles; the dozens of former Kennedy campaign aides; the clergymen who knew the family well; the staff of the Robert F. Kennedy Memorial.

To Wade Nichols, editor of *Good Housekeeping* magazine; Elizabeth Frank, articles editor, and Ray Robinson, now editor of

v

Seventeen, my deepest appreciation for believing in this project from the beginning and encouraging me during the long hard months of research and writing. To Jim Wade, my editor, particular thanks for his sure and sensitive guidance. And to my wife Irene, a teacher and journalist, my gratitude for her patience, inspiration and invaluable suggestions.

Many publications were consulted, particularly the files of *The New York Times, Washington Post, Washington Star, Chicago Tribune* and *Women's Wear Daily.* Among numerous magazine references, articles in *Good Housekeeping, McCall's* and *The Ladies' Home Journal* were most helpful.

Books that proved invaluable in developing the story of Ethel Kennedy were: *The Next Kennedy,* by Margaret Laing; *Robert Kennedy at 40,* by Nick Thimmesch and William Johnson; *Robert Kennedy: The Brother Within,* by Robert E. Thompson and Hortense Myers; *The Unfinished Odyssey of Robert Kennedy,* by David Halberstam; *Robert Kennedy, A Memoir,* by Jack Newfield; *85 Days: The Last Campaign of Robert F. Kennedy,* by Jules Witcover; *The Founding Father: The Story of Joseph P. Kennedy,* by Richard J. Whalen.

A final note: My book is not a so-called authorized biography nor has it been "approved" by Ethel or any member of the Kennedy family or their representatives. I set out to write the story of a woman who interested me very much and offer it herewith, imperfect surely, but as mine alone.

Woodmere, New York
December 15, 1970

Contents

Part Three

Part Four

Prologue

At 11:30 P.M. on June 4, 1968, the telephone rang in
the bedroom of Suite 511 at the Ambassador Hotel in
Los Angeles. Kenneth O'Donnell, in an exuberant mood,
was calling congratulations from Washington. The California Presidential primary was over and Robert Kennedy
was winning a solid victory over Senator Eugene Mc-
Carthy.

Journalist Jimmy Breslin, a grin on his broad, sweating
face, kidded with Kenny, then handed the phone to Bobby.
O'Donnell, appointments secretary in President Kennedy's administration, was an old football buddy from
Harvard days. Bobby, in shirtsleeves, had been conferring
with his brother, Senator Edward Kennedy, Theodore
Sorensen, Richard N. Goodwin and brother-in-law Stephen
E. Smith. Outside, the large living room was jammed with
noisy campaign aides, newsmen and important local Democrats. "It was a madhouse," Breslin was to say. "The
only way Bobby could have a private conference was to
lock himself in the toilet with somebody."

"You know, Ken," Bobby spoke into the phone, "finally
I feel that I'm out from under the shadow of my brother.
Now at last, I feel that I've made it on my own. All these

ix

years, I never really believed it was me that did it, but Jack."

He paused, then continued: "But I believe it now, and I also believe I can go on and be elected President—on my own."

It was a revelation of major significance. Apparently, Robert Kennedy had been convinced that all he had accomplished, as United States Attorney General and later as United States Senator, had been due in large measure to John Kennedy's influence while he was alive and the upsurge of national sympathy after his murder. Many people had said this, but few suspected Bobby thought so too. Then had come the final stretch of his campaign for the Democratic Presidential nomination, his primary victories in South Dakota and now in California.

Bobby hung up. Accompanied by his wife, Ethel, and their friends and aides, he went downstairs to the Embassy Ballroom where a huge throng waited to hear his victory speech and an assassin lurked in a serving kitchen.

On this night, less than an hour before he was shot, Bobby Kennedy discovered for himself what Ethel Kennedy had believed all along—that he was his own man, with his own greatness and that he could, in truth, "make it on his own."

Ethel Kennedy was totally committed and unswervingly loyal to the man she married almost eighteen years before he was gunned down only sixteen feet from where she stood.

The story of this woman is the story of a remarkable faith in a man, of a life that was, in its beginnings, much like his own, and of a love that was deep and lasting. For Ethel Kennedy had what all women seek—love for a man that was beautiful and strong, and that was returned full measure.

Robert Kennedy once wrote a book called *Just Friends and Brave Enemies,* which he dedicated to his parents and to Ethel. Next to his wife's name, he wrote a simple line: "Ruth, I:16-17."
Look up the Biblical verse. It reads:

> Entreat me not to leave thee, or to return from following after thee: for whither thou goest, I will go; and where thou lodgest, I will lodge; thy people shall be my people, and thy God my God;
> Where thou diest, will I die, and there will I be buried: the Lord do so to me, and more also, if ought but death part thee and me.

What is the woman like, to whom Robert Kennedy paid this tribute? Let us see.

Part One

ONE

Seven Little Skakels and How They Grew

The house is four miles from the center of town, down a road darkened even in blazing sun by arching maples, elms and hickories. A trampled lawn the size of a football field spreads apron-like before a three-story brick mansion. On the heavily wooded ten and one-half acres are a garage with quarters for the help, a teahouse and a conservatory. In the rear is another lawn, which terraces downward toward a swimming pool, in use in all but impossible weather.

On the grounds are dogs and cats, lying down or running about; turtles and lizards, sometimes caged, often not; chickens, ducks, pigs, sheep and even a goat. On the grounds, too, most times of the day, are swarms of children of all ages—those who live in the house and those who are visiting. A father walks unperturbed through the uproar, encouraging the games on land and water and even joining in them. A cheerful mother doesn't even wince when more guests, business associates of her husband or friends of her children drop by unexpectedly, making it eighteen for dinner that evening.

Could this be Hickory Hill, where Ethel and Robert Kennedy whirled in a kind of perpetual motion with their children and livestock during their busy Washington years? It has the unique stamp of Hickory Hill in its informality and its atmosphere of barely controlled bedlam, but this is not McLean, Virginia. It is an estate on Simmons Lane in Greenwich, Connecticut, the girlhood home of Ethel Skakel, where she lived for many years, long before she met Robert Kennedy, became his wife and went to live in a place so incredibly like it.

9 9 9

In this house thirty-five miles from New York City, George Skakel, a darkly handsome, stocky man of Dutch extraction, and his large, attractive, blonde wife raised seven bright and boisterous children. Their first-born was Georgeann, who was followed by three boys, James, George, Jr., and Rushton. After them came three more girls, Patricia, Ethel and Ann.

Their father could have been a model for a Horatio Alger story. George Skakel earned eight dollars a week on his first job as a railway clerk and rose to head his own mammoth company and become many times a millionaire. Born in Chicago to James Curtis Skakel and Grace Mary Jordan Skakel in 1892, he migrated with his family to Iowa, where he attended high school in Sioux City. After several years of railroading, he became traffic manager for a coal-producing firm in Chicago, then served as an ensign in the U.S. Naval Reserve during World War I.

Mother of the improbable Skakel brood was Ann Brannack, of Chicago, whom he met, wooed and married the year the war ended. Inches taller than her husband, she weighed close to two-hundred pounds and was a wonderfully goodhearted person, deeply religious, generous and unfailingly cheerful. She was also a forgiving human being, a trait often put to severe test in her household by her ebullient youngsters, who were guilty of more mischief on any given day than the Katzenjammer Kids. Once her sons, pretending to be bullfighters, had taught Joey the goat to charge like a *toro* at a *corrida*. He learned exceptionally well. Spotting Ann Skakel at the rear door of the house one day, Joey lowered his head and lunged, catching her precisely at her center of gravity and propelling her face down into the house and halfway across the floor. For once, Ann Skakel's good nature deserted her and, thoroughly enraged, she rose to punish the offenders who, of course, were nowhere in sight.

George and Ann Skakel ran a loose ship. "They weren't crabby old parents," Teddy Wahl, the rangy riding master who first taught Ethel to sit properly in a saddle, would remember years afterward. "They believed in letting the kids have a good time." Teddy, who has loved Ethel like his own daughter and watched with pride as she developed into a superb horsewoman, spent many hours on the broad rear terrace of the estate, sitting and drinking and passing the time of day with Mr. Skakel.

Not that George and Ann did not try to discipline their children. Mr. Skakel would try with the tone of his voice, which was not especially successful because he did not like to yell very loud. Ann Skakel would try occasionally by taking a bearing on an errant child and swinging her hand full force, hoping to connect. She rarely did. With their excellent reflexes, combined with superb fleetness of foot, the young Skakels became extraordinarily adept at anticipating their mother's smacks and dodging them. Sometimes, though, she would manage to reach home and then, Rushton ruefully remembers, "She'd hurt too." But there was much love in Ann Skakel and with that Irish humor of hers, she could never stay angry for long.

Whatever disciplining there was did not keep Ethel's two older brothers, George, Jr., and Jim, from becoming the terrors of the neighborhood. Years later, there were still many Greenwich residents who recalled their exploits with some awe and possibly a few shudders. One high police official who knew them well thought they were "headstrong kids," a euphemism. The truth was that they scared hell out of the whole community, out of their sister Ethel and, on more than one occasion, out of the boys who came calling on the Skakel girls. When the mood was upon them, which was frequently, George and Jim would snipe at the unfortunate swains with their air rifles from a high window and their aim was good. (Everyone agrees that the third brother, Rushton, was a good deal better behaved.)

The antics of George and Jim were nearly incredible. They were, for example, great on games, the riskier the better. Once they invented one that went like this:

You take this ancient wooden-sided station wagon you picked up from the first New York World's Fair and park it on the driveway that slopes down past a shallow pond at the rear of the house. Fill it up with a group of young guests, explaining that they will be taken on a tour of the acreage. Start the car, let it roll down the hill. Then, as you pass the center of the pond, give the wheel a sharp twist and dump the station wagon and contents into the water. Rushton recalls: "Jim was usually at the wheel, and he got so good at the game that he could put the car far enough into the pond so that the guests would have to get good and wet to get out. Afterward, they'd winch out the wagon, get it back up the hill and wait for another unsuspecting bunch."

Another game George and Jim played was called "King of the Castle." One boy would climb atop a car while the other drove it around the winding, wooded Greenwich roads, trying to wipe him off by whipping under the lowest tree branches he could find. The youth on the roof would remain King of the Castle until dethroned; then it would be the other's turn. "They were both wiped off plenty of times," says Samuel Meek, Jr., a family friend who became a banker, "but they were tough kids."

Once, on an idle afternoon, the boys thought it might be fun if they tied a rope around one of the younger girls and hung her outside a window. Ethel, who was never afraid of anything, volunteered gleefully. So George and Jim knotted a length of clothesline around Ethel's middle and lowered her from a second-story window. They jerked her up and down like a yo-yo, swung her in a wide arc like a pendulum and finally hauled her up. Ethel, thirteen at the time, thought it was great fun.

The boys were close friends but, like all friends and brothers, would get into fierce squabbles now and then. (John Kennedy too would get into bruising fistfights with his older brother Joseph, Jr. Bobby vividly recalled when, as a small boy, he watched with saucer-eyes as his two older brothers pounded away at each other on a Cape Cod beach.) On one occasion, Ethel and one of her closest teen-years friends, Pixie (for Priscilla) Meek, went to the movies in town. At 11:00 P.M., Mrs. Skakel sent the boys to collect them and drive them home. Pixie Meek remembers the ride home as one of the most harrowing of her life. "One was driving, the other was in the back seat," she says. "Somehow, they got into a fight, so there they were, whacking away at each other while the car was moving fast along a dark road. I was scared out of my wits." After that, only the most compelling reason could get Pixie into an automobile with either of the boys.

Her brothers' shenanigans worried Ethel a good deal.

She would confide her fears to Pixie on their sleep-over dates in each other's homes as they lay wide awake in the dark, chattering endlessly until one mother or the other ordered them into silence. Ethel would defend her brothers, insisting they were just high-spirited and not really all that wild, though she would have drawn arguments there from neighbors and other Greenwich residents who, on a number of occasions, called Mr. and Mrs. Skakel to complain loudly about their sons.

Nevertheless, though some neighbors predicted a dire end for "those Skakel boys," they managed to grow up fine. They all became highly respected business executives and sportsmen.

George Skakel, Jr., was, in fact, a highly unusual man. William F. Buckley, a close friend, was to call him something special, a man who grew up with a lust for life— "the kind of thing great artists and writers and statesmen have had, Michelangelo and Victor Hugo, Thomas Jefferson and Winston Churchill." Ethel was influenced to a considerable degree by this brother; thus it is important that we know something of his character and personality.

George was the kind of man who would ski in Vermont in the morning and fly to New York in the evening to play in an indoor polo match. He was a free spirit who worked hard and played hard and who would knuckle under to nobody when he thought he was right.

Once George was the sole crew member aboard a sailboat skippered by John F. Kennedy, then the United States Senator from Massachusetts, during a race off Martha's Vineyard. At one point Kennedy barked an order to adjust the sheets, an instruction that Skakel was convinced made no sense in light of the wind direction at the time.

"Look, Jack," he told Kennedy, "are you going to keep

screaming at me to trim this sail when I know damned well better than you do how it ought to be trimmed?" Kennedy, who could be equally single-tracked once he had his mind made up, told him curtly to be still and obey orders.

Skakel had enough. Let Kennedy trim his own sail. Though they were two miles off shore, he stood up, dived into the Sound and swam off. The words then spoken by the future President of the United States as he watched George Skakel strike out for shore were mercifully swallowed up by the snapping winds.

George Skakel hated pomposity and officiousness. He was a direct man who believed in straight, direct dealings. One day he demonstrated his irritation with a meddlesome bureaucracy in a *beau geste* that, coincidently, also involved John F. Kennedy, who by this time was President of the United States.

After Kennedy took the oath of office on the steps of the Capitol in 1961, Skakel trailed after the dignitaries, among whom were President Kennedy, Dwight D. Eisenhower, Vice-President Lyndon B. Johnson, Richard M. Nixon and their wives, to the reception room for refreshments before the group went out to review the Inaugural March. Skakel, waiting to be admitted, became irked at the officialism of the bright-eyed young men surrounding J.F.K. With a courtly bow, he handed over a much-prized pass to the reviewing stand to a black porter, and stalked off into the cold January afternoon.

☯ ☯ ☯

The Skakels were a warm, close-knit family, active and athletic, filled with a love and lust for living—and as competitive as the Kennedys.

One observer, related by marriage, says: "Whatever they set out to do, they were going to be best." Rushton admits: "The old man never liked to lose." There was, it appears, the same urge to compete, the same striving to be first and the same conviction that coming in second doesn't count for anything that has dominated the lives of the Kennedy clan. To this day, Ethel herself is a ferocious opponent in sports, asking no quarter and giving none, loving it when she wins, hating it when she does not. She says candidly: "I like competition, but I like to win better."

Teammates at Amherst recall that George, Jr., played football with a savage recklessness, heedless of personal injury. He was the same at polo. "A trophy for a match might be a fourteen dollar cup this big," says a friend, "but he would want it, and if he didn't get it, he'd be mad as hell." Later Jim Skakel was curious to know if a man, armed only with a harpoon, could conquer a sperm whale. He went to the Azores to find out, and discovered that man could—at least a man such as Jim Skakel could. It is things like this that make one wonder what might have happened had a team of Skakels, coached by George, Sr., ever squared off on the playing field against the Kennedys, coached by Joseph P. Kennedy, Sr.

During the years when her personality was being shaped, Ethel was extremely close to her father, deeply respected her mother's devotion to their faith and plainly adored her brothers. Unconsciously, Ethel adopted a number of her father's characteristics—she would gesture the way he did, walk like him, even use his expressions. Rushton would recall afterward: "Dad and Ethel were remarkably alike, even to their magnetism. The old man could come into a room and completely dominate it with the force of his personality. Ethel was very much the same. You always knew when she was around."

Just as her own deep faith came from the influence of her mother, her later independence, her love of life and her physical courage flowed to her from her father and brothers. "For sheer guts I have never seen a girl like her," Rushton would remember. Once, in her teens, Ethel climbed a tree, fell and broke her arm. As soon as it healed, she was back up in the same branches. It was pure George Skakel, Jr., who years later was to demonstrate the ultimate in cool when he was trapped by a man-killing shark in a tiny underwater grotto. Scuba-diving in the Bahamas, Skakel entered the grotto through a narrow opening, discovering with a shock that he had been followed by the shark. Aware that any unusual movement on his part would be disastrous, Skakel remained absolutely still in the little chamber, the shark so close he could reach out and touch him. Minutes later, the big fish slithered out through the opening, and Skakel rose safely to the surface.

It is not surprising that Ethel was to fall in love with a man who possessed the same kind of raw gutsiness, the same love of the outdoors, the same nonstop energy, the same competitiveness, impulsiveness, loyalty and mischievousness as her brother. Buckley once called George Skakel, Jr., a man of "enormous competence, curiosity, charm. He loved danger, not merely social and political, but physical. Every sport that involved personal risk, he devotedly cultivated, shrewdly sizing up the odds, and pressing close to the brink. . . ."

He could have been talking about the man Ethel was to marry.

TWO

The House on Simmons Lane

꽃️❧

Ethel's family is not as rich as the Kennedys but it is rich enough.

The Skakels own the Great Lakes Carbon Corporation, one of America's largest family-owned businesses. It is a multimillion dollar company with 2,700 employees and a dozen plants in the United States, Canada, England, India and Sweden. Its manufactured products include carbon and graphite electrodes, foundry coke, graphite fiber, barbecue briquets, crude petroleum and natural gas.

In addition, the parent concern, through its subsidiary corporations, has vast real estate holdings, owning substantial interests in:

A two-hundred-acre residential and commercial center called Del Amo in Torrence, California, that is dominated by a twenty-acre financial center. Three thirteen-story office towers will eventually be constructed; the first has already been completed;

A 170-acre commercial and residential community, called simply The City, 30 miles southeast of Los Angeles.

The project, about a mile from Disneyland in Anaheim, will have a 200-room Holiday Inn, a shopping center, medical center, high-rise apartments and office buildings;

A Portuguese company that owns and is developing a four-thousand-acre resort and retirement community called Vilamoura on the Algarve Coast on the country's southern tip. Vilamoura has a mile of sandy beachfront on the Atlantic and a championship eighteen-hole golf course;

The Palos Verdes Water Company, which serves thirty-thousand residents of the area twenty-five miles south of Los Angeles. Here too the family, through a property investment subsidiary of the parent firm, had bought six-thousand acres where private developers and builders have constructed single-family homes, co-operative apartments, department stores and other retail and service establishments.

It all began in 1919 when George Skakel, Sr., and Walter Gramm formed a partnership in Chicago and organized a coal and coke business, buying coal wholesale and distributing to retailers. The American economy was just picking up speed for its rush into a decade of unparalleled prosperity, and the new firm began roaring along with it. By the middle of the Twenties, the Great Lakes Coal and Coke Company had become actively interested in petroleum coke and by-products of the oil-refining industry.

Came the stock-market debacle of 1929, followed by the country's cruelest Depression, but the Skakel and Gramm firm, no longer small, continued to do remarkably well. As the crisis worsened for most of the nation, the company opened an office in New York City and, during the early 1930s, successfully marketed several million tons of petroleum coke along the Atlantic seaboard as a solid fuel for domestic and industrial heating.

Steadily the company grew. Then, as the Thirties advanced, a new idea was conceived that made millions for George Skakel. Up to that time, the electrochemical and electrometallurgical industries had calcined, or purified, the petroleum coke essential in their manufacturing process at their own plants. Why couldn't the Skakel-Gramm company do the job itself at plants close to the refineries that produced the petroleum coke? It could sell the purified product at higher prices than the raw material, and the industries, relieved of the calcining burden, would be happy to pay them. Moreover, since purified coke takes up considerably less space than raw coke, a great deal more could be shipped, reducing transportation charges.

It sounded like a good idea all around, and it was. The first Great Lakes calcining plant went into operation in 1935 at Port Arthur, Texas. Sales and profits rocketed. Additional calcining plants were subsequently built at Lockport, Illinois, Wilmington, California, the Calumet section of Chicago and Casper, Wyoming. Today, the petroleum coke output of the company's Carbon Division is sold throughout the Free World, primarily to the aluminium, graphite-products and steel industries.

In 1939 the business was reorganized as the Great Lakes Carbon Corporation and continued to grow, expanding and diversifying through the years. After the United States entered the war in 1941, the firm went into the oil business to help lubricate and power military machinery. In 1944, it acquired the Dicalite Company, a Nevada-based concern, and began marketing a variety of diatomaceous earth products used in industry principally in filtration, for fillers and for heat and sound insulation. When the war ended, George Skakel looked about him, saw a great construction boom shaping up, and took his company into the building-products field. And so it went, each move lifting George Skakel to dizzying heights of affluence.

Ethel was born in the early morning hours of April 11, 1928, in Chicago's Lying-In Hospital, brought into the world by a fifty-year-old woman physician, Dr. Blanche Mayes Elfrink. George Skakel, already a wealthy man at thirty-six, had settled his family in a large rambling home at 5317 University Avenue, in the exclusive Hyde Park section on the Lake Michigan shore.

When Ethel was eight, Skakel decided to move to New York because the bulk of his business was being conducted there. He settled in Larchmont, a suburban community on Long Island Sound. The following year, he migrated ten miles northwest and put down roots in Greenwich, Connecticut, where Ethel spent the next twelve years of her life until she met and married Robert Kennedy.

Greenwich in the 1930s and '40s was one of the country's most exclusive residential communities, the social hub of Fairfield County, and has remained so over the years despite the inevitable problems brought by a changing America. While this area of southwestern Connecticut is not, as some residents are fond of claiming, the richest county in America, it comes close enough. (It is the tenth richest.) Once, a writer and editor who lives there, Lyn Tornabene, was asked on the street by a passing motorist: "Can you tell me where the Rich family lives?" Miss Tornabene was puzzled for a moment, then replied: "I think that adjective would really apply to every family here." Only after the motorist had driven off shaking his head did Miss Tornabene realize that he was asking for the whereabouts of a family named Rich. The story tells something about the place where Ethel grew into young womanhood.

Only twenty-eight miles from Times Square, Greenwich

was then, and is now, a place of surpassing beauty. The homes and grounds are among the best-kept and most carefully manicured in the nation. The hills and woodlands that roll toward the six miles of excellent coastline along the Sound are always lushly green in summer and afire with color in autumn. Swimming pools, many of them Olympic-size, not the kidney-shaped ones mass-produced to cost less than a medium-priced car, are as common as rhododendron bushes, and many homes have stables and corrals for their horses. Miles of marked bridle paths criss-cross the back country, especially in the northern area of grand estates and huge Tudor mansions. Fox hunts are still held occasionally in the area, though not as regularly as they once were. Often the Skakels had twenty or thirty young people asleep all over the place, awaiting the first light of dawn and the call to the hounds.

When the Skakels arrived, Greenwich had 5,981 residents, a population that increased tenfold in the next 30 years. There were fine shops on the elm-shaded main thoroughfare, Greenwich Avenue, many of which would still serve the old established families many years later. The residential areas stretched south and north, down to the coves and bays of the Sound, up through the hilly countryside.

George and Ann went house-hunting, and found a mansion for sale near Lake Avenue, not far from the center of town. Built in the 1920s by the Simmons-bed family, it had been decorated in elegant, eclectic style by Lady Mendl, the former Elsie DeWolfe, a social luminary of the era as well as an interior designer of renown. The Simmonses fell upon temporary hard times in the Depression years and Skakel was able to buy the house, furnishings and all, for two-hundred thousand dollars.

Come for a tour of this magnificent house where Ethel Kennedy grew to womanhood.

Stand between the two towering elms whose topmost branches form a cathedral-like arch on the front lawn and look at the house itself. It has no special architectural style. It is built of brick washed with white, is three stories high, bears a heavy slate roof and rambles the length of a city block. Actually, if you press to pigeonhole it, we will be forced to say that it resembles nothing so much as a cottage, grown to outsize dimensions.

Cross a stone terrace into the portico, walk through the large double doors into the entrance hall with its floor inlaid with pure copper and marble squares. Ahead is the dining room, measuring almost twenty-five feet square, with a massive oaken table and beyond it a large breakfast room that looks out upon the lawns and hills of the estate. Several hundred feet away is an oval reflecting pool. Press a button on the wall of the breakfast room and a forty-foot jet of water springs up suddenly in the pool's center, a lovely sight after dark when multicolored lights play upon the shooting sprays.

To the left of the dining room is a twenty- by fifteen-foot butler's pantry leading into a huge kitchen. There are hand-painted birds on the walls: awkward pelicans, majestic cranes, bluebirds and robins in full flight. Ann Skakel spent a good deal of her time here, sometimes supervising but more often cooking herself for her family and guests. She did it as a child in Ireland, as the wife of a struggling businessman in Chicago and saw no reason why she shouldn't do it now, millionaire's wife or not. She employed cooks but, in H. H. Munro's immortal line, "As cooks go, they went," departing with especial regularity and rapidity in the Skakel household. Partly to blame for the quick turnover was the unwillingness of cooks to share sovereignty in the kitchen. Another reason was the meal-time chaos that customarily prevailed.

In addition to the ordinary gas stove we might expect to find in kitchens, we see a huge coal-burning Aga stove from Sweden, installed by the Simmonses before gas was available and kept by the Skakels. Glance around the kitchen and we can see notes, neatly hand-written by Ann Skakel and tacked up in strategic places. On the door of the lavatory down a small corridor we read: "For cook's use only," this to discourage handymen and little Skakels and their friends. For the guidance of the cook, when there was a cook, we see a schedule of meal hours for family and guests: breakfast, lunch and dinner to be served only at certain specified times. It was a brave effort by Mrs. Skakel to inject a little organization into the household, but nobody paid much attention to the scheduling, least of all the hungry little Skakels who could fast-talk any cook into giving them whatever they wanted, or, on those rare occasions when they couldn't, would filch something out of the refrigerator.

This kitchen was the scene of many adventures, some comic, some exciting.

Once Ann Skakel decided to make her own cream from the milk provided by her two cows. From somewhere she acquired a separator, which consisted of a large bowl, an outlet for cream and another for milk, and an electric motor. The idea was to pour the whole milk into the bowl which, activated by the motor, would spin rapidly, forcing the cream into the midpart of the bowl and the skimmed milk toward the outside. The cream would then flow out through one outlet, the milk the other.

The gadget worked fine for a few moments but suddenly the bowl spun out of control, lurched and shot milk

with explosive force all over the kitchen. Ann tried hero-
ically to stop it but couldn't, and for a few terrible moments remained there under milk fire until she was
drenched and the bowl was empty. The story has been a
family howl ever since.

Another time, when Ethel was alone in the house with
her grandmother, Mrs. Skakel's aged mother, the cook
and the chauffeur got into a furious argument. The cook
grabbed a long carving knife and began chasing the chauffeur around the kitchen and butler's pantry. Ethel, then
thirteen, heard the screams and rushed down. Terrified,
she phoned her friend Pixie and asked her what to do.
Mrs. Meek got on the phone and suggested she call the
police. Ethel did and they took care of the matter.

To the right of the entranceway with its antique European paneling, we find the central hall, where a gracefully
curved staircase leads to the upstairs rooms. Beyond is the
library, the largest and most beautiful room in the house,
fifty-seven feet long with a casement window at the far
end. French doors look out upon the grounds in the rear;
opposite them is a large wood-burning fireplace.

There is a font of holy water in the library and several
priedieux, or praying chairs, for despite its rambunctious-
ness this is a deeply religious household. Ann Skakel may
have been an indulgent mother but she created in her home
a milieu of godliness, not only by her instructions and
counsels but by her sincere and positive examples. Ann's
own faith, stemming from her own devout Irish parent-
age, was generous, warm and joyful. Unfailingly she
drove into town every morning, regardless of weather,
for 7:00 A.M. mass at St. Mary's Roman Catholic
Church on Greenwich Avenue. From the age of four on-
ward, all her children would do the same.

Only George Skakel, Sr., remained outside the Catholic

circle; born a Dutch Protestant, he remained one, offici-
ally, most of his life. During all the time she knew him,
Ann Skakel hoped and prayed to bring him into the faith
that was her's and the family's. Each day, all the Skakels
would include in their devotions a special prayer for the
conversion of their father. Often, Ann would ask her
clergymen friends to pray too. And yet, though she hardly
realized it, Mrs. Skakel had a far greater influence over
her husband than she believed. Although George resisted
taking formal teaching, a clergyman who knew the family
well believes it may indeed be said that he began to receive
"instruction" the day he married Ann. "The home atmosphere she created," he says, "was the living-out, in everyday life, of the truths of the Catholic faith."

Ethel's deep feeling for her religion was bred into her
from earliest childhood by her mother by example and by
teaching. In later years, Ethel was to number among her
closest friends Princes of the Church and parish priests,
religious leaders, educators and philosophers. Her life-
time practice of saying grace before every meal, of wearing a silver rosary every waking and sleeping moment, of
attending early mass daily no matter how late she had
come home the night before—all this and more stemmed
from the religious training Ann Skakel insisted she and
all her children must have.

Return now, to the library, with its ceiling-high shelves
of books, many of them on religious subjects, large comfortable sofas and bright, warming fire snapping behind
the massive andirons in the wall opposite the large windows. It was here that churchmen and educators would
meet regularly, at the invitation of Ann Skakel, to engage
in informal discussions on religious matters. The Right
Reverend Monsignor Michael J. Guerin, pastor of St.
Mary's at the time, recalls these sessions as high-level
intellectual forums that covered a broad range of topics.

Many years afterward, Ethel and Robert Kennedy were to inaugurate a series of seminars at their home, which the press was to label "Hickory Hill University." Here leading university professors would lecture on their specialties and engage in informal discussions with the guests. The likelihood is strong that the idea for Hickory Hill University was born during these sessions held at Ethel's childhood home. "This is what Mrs. Skakel would do in her home," observes Monsignor Guerin, since retired to Sarasota, Florida, "and the logical deduction would be that Ethel, impressed with the example of her mother, carried out pretty much the same thing in later years with her husband in her own home."

Walk out of the library and up the broad curving staircase with its pastoral-scene wallpaper smudged by a hundred hands. Stop on the first-floor landing. To the right is the master bedroom suite, a huge bedroom, dressing room and bath. Surprisingly for such a lavish house, the bath is untiled; its walls are plaster, painted green. Twenty steps to the left of the landing, down a gloomy corridor, is Ethel's bedroom.

It is sunny and cheerful, almost the size of a small classroom, its walls papered in a Chinese motif, its windows overlooking the avenues of elms, the spurting fountain and the swimming pool. Down the corridor and on the third floor were the rooms of the other Skakels. Also on the third floor is a billiard room and a vast, narrow hideaway playroom where Ethel and her friends spent many hours with their games and toys.

Come outside on the terrace. Walk down a broad avenue of elms, past the reflecting pool and see the seventy-five-foot swimming pool behind the hedges. On any reasonably nice day—it needn't be too nice, just a few degrees above absolutely impossible—there are young Skakels in the water. There was rarely a day from spring until late fall when Ethel was not swimming along its length in her clean Australian crawl.

On summer nights, gay parties are held here. Underwater lights give the water a blue and white shimmer; high in the trees rimming the pool are more lights that filter through the leaves and throw a soft radiance. On a raft anchored in the center of the pool, is a dance orchestra. Beautiful young girls in flowing pastel gowns, handsome young men in white jackets sway to the music by the poolside.

It is a lovely setting, a midsummer's idyl—until one of the Skakel boys gets a notion to shoot out some of the tree lights with a .22 rifle.

∅ ∅ ∅

The Skakels had a great deal of money and spent it lavishly. There were always several shiny Cadillacs in the spacious garage, the children were sent to the finest private schools, the best food was bought and served to guests they didn't even know, horses were bought for the girls, cars for the boys. At the same time, George and Ann never forgot that others were less fortunate, giving large sums to charity regularly.

But despite the family's opulent life-style, Ann Skakel had a thrifty streak in her that emerged clearly on occasion. Once Ann decided she was spending too much of her household money on soda pop, which her children and their friends were consuming in huge quantities. She was purchasing pop by the case from a local distributor. Somehow, she learned that private schools receive a special discount by virtue of being educational institutions. So she telephoned the distributor, informing them that the big house on Simmons Lane was a school and could she have the discount, please? She could and she did for a number of months, until the distributor found out and politely but firmly refused to grant the discount any more.

During World War II, when meat was being rationed, Ann decided she should be able to provide items in short supply for her family by purchasing live fowl and animals. Thus, at one time during the war, by actual count kept by Chester Neminski, the Skakel's gardener and man-of-all-work for many years, the nonhuman census was : two cows, four saddle horses, six sheep, two French goats, two-hundred chickens, ten wild ducks, twelve turkeys, twenty-five pigs. There were also eight dogs, fifteen cats and twenty pigeons.

The pigs were the last to be acquired but the first to go. One spring morning, Mr. Skakel was breakfasting on the terrace when he frowned, lifted his head and began sniffing. "Ann," he called out to his wife, "what in blazes is that awful smell?" Mrs. Skakel, sniffing too, answered it was probably the new pigs. "Well, get rid of them!" her husband said, leaving his breakfast to move inside. That day, Ann sold twenty of the pigs locally for two-hundred-and-fifty dollars and had the others butchered for food.

☙ ☙ ☙

Ann Skakel had to work hard to keep the house on Simmons Lane looking elegant but she did not always succeed, for the seven young Skakels and their friends were not sufficiently impressed with the Elsie DeWolfe furnishings to be especially careful of them.

As the years went on, the house began to look lived in, which is to say it was noisy most of the time and somewhat sloppy some of the time. The fine carpeting in the library was wrestled upon by the boys, played upon by the girls and, with some regularity, peed upon by the Skakel dogs who would drift unchallenged into the house.

The Skakel children moved out in 1956, eighteen years after the family arrived. The house remained empty for four years and by the time Thomas S. Hyland acquired it in 1960 it had a kind of Charles Addams atmosphere about it. Mr. Hyland observes: "When we bought it, the place was very run down. Jackie Kennedy would not have walked into it."

No matter. If the house lost its grace and polish during the years of Ethel's girlhood, it was far richer than most in love—love of family, love of life and love of God.

THREE

Of Horses and Tap Dancing

There are some fortunate women who look in maturity almost exactly as they did in girlhood, and Ethel Kennedy is one of these. At forty-two she has laugh lines around the eyes and mouth and her skin has lost its youthful tautness, but the face with its look of an eager child seems the same as when she was eleven. At fifteen, she had attained her full height of five feet, five and one-half inches, and her weight of one-hundred-and-twenty pounds has never varied. The coltish body, lean and muscular and tanned, the short-cut unruly light-brown hair with reddish highlights, the brown eyes that almost literally dance, the low, small-girl voice, all are unchanged.

And she was then, as later, vivacious, energetic and absolutely incapable of sitting still for more than a few moments. "Un paquet de nerfs," Mlle. Figuet, her French teacher, pronounced her as she fidgeted all through class. Mademoiselle had her hands full with her little "bundle of nerves" when she cast her as the Fairy Godmother in

25

a class production of *Cinderella,* performed entirely in French. She cavorted all over the stage at rehearsals but, Mlle. Figuet recalls, settled down to give a fine performance.

In 1936, Ann Skakel, holding nine-year-old Ethel firmly by the hand, walked with her up the worn steps of the ancient red-brick building on Maple Street occupied by Greenwich Academy, and enrolled her in the fourth grade. The school (since moved to newer headquarters, which do not, as these did, resemble an old police station) was one of the three exclusive institutions of learning to which the wealthy residents of the area send their children. (The others are Greenwich Country Day School and Rosemary Hall.)

Here almost at once Ethel formed an inseparable triumverate with Pixie Meek and Pan Jacob. The three called themselves the PEP girls—for Pixie, Ethel and Pan, of course. They played together, agonized together over homework, did assignments together (once they created an enormous painting, each working on a segment like members of a Renaissance school of fresco artists) and confided innermost secrets to one another.

Ethel's scholastic record at the academy was unspectacular, if not downright poor. Pixie's mother, recalling failed tests and bad reports from teachers, says candidly: "Ethel and Pixie had a terrible time there. They were always in trouble with their lessons, both of them."

Pan Jacob: "We were probably a lot brighter than our grades showed. The trouble was we spent too much time being naughty and not enough working."

The PEP girls, for example, often would cut study hall, required periods in the morning and afternoon during which students were expected to apply themselves to homework and other chores, and take long walks around the academy grounds, slipping inside just in time to make their next classes.

But there was one overarching reason why Ethel did not shine brightly in scholastic performance. She was in love.

At the age of nine, she gave her heart to horses and the passion occupied most of her time and much of her mind.

She learned to ride at Teddy Wahl's stable and when she became proficient in the saddle she got a horse of her own, Smoky—black with four white feet—for which her father paid eight-hundred dollars. Later, she acquired Gurmada, whom she called "Gwamy," a chestnut, which cost fifteen-hundred dollars. By the time she went to college, she owned a dark bay named Beau Mischief.

Ethel rarely missed a day on their back. She and Pixie would thud off in the afternoons, returning only at dinner time and often much later. Ethel took plenty of chances on horseback and, as a consequence, plenty of falls. Miraculously, she was never seriously hurt. She and Pixie became so good they picked up a shelf-full each of cups and ribbons at country-club and regional horse shows.

When not winning at shows, the girls were out watching them and, when they became bored in between events, looked around for pranks to play. One afternoon, Ethel and Pixie went to the ladies room at a show, crawled underneath the doors of the pay booths, opened them and left them that way for free access. Quite possibly, this may have been Ethel's first experience as a social activist. Soon Teddy Wahl was receiving an urgent call from the irate manager: "Would you please come up and get these girls out of here!"

Later, Ethel's pranks were to become bigger and gaudier. Once, during a horse show at Madison Square Garden, she slipped into the stall of an Irish mount that was about to be ridden by an Irish rider and painted him bright green with vegetable dye.

The girls talked of horses almost constantly and if Ethel gave any thought to her future in her adolescence, it was not to marry a politician or anybody else but to become a veterinarian. The depth of the girls' enthusiasm for riding can be judged by a poem they once composed for English class, the opening lines of which read:

When I am one and twenty
Of horses I'll have plenty.

When World War II broke out, the PEP girls devoted many hours to thinking up ways to raise money for the Red Cross. Once Pixie sponsored a horse show on her own spacious lawn, charging a twenty-five-cent entry fee for the various events. Ethel showed up and galloped off with most of the prizes.

Besides riding, Ethel excelled in practically every sport she tried, and she tried many because the need for physical action was bred into her very chromosomes. She was then and is now spectacularly good at everything—tag and tennis, skiing and skating, swimming and sailing, field hockey, touch football and even tap dancing.

One day, toward the close of 1969, Ethel attended a rally in a District of Columbia cathedral for striking California grape workers. Glancing down the list of supporters, she noticed that she had been named to the entertainment committee. She whispered to a friend: "What did they expect me to do, a soft-shoe routine?"

With a little brush-up, Ethel could indeed perform a soft-shoe, and probably a very good one, because in her teens she was a whiz at tap, good enough, her teacher said, to have had a successful professional career.

When Ethel was in the eighth grade, Mrs. Arthur Pethick, coach of the Greenwich Academy's athletic teams, as well as physical-education teacher and dance instructor, decided to introduce tap into the curriculum as a change of pace from the classical type of dancing to which the girls had been subjected for so many years. Arched eyebrows greeted Mrs. Pethick's plan. Whoever heard of doing tap in a private school? At a nightclub, yes, but at the *academy?* But Mrs. Pethick, a spirited little woman, stood her ground: She insisted that tap dancing would be wonderful for the girls and their parents would love it. It was and they did.

One of her star pupils was the tanned, slender little Skakel girl who, says the teacher, was soon tapping away as though she had been reared in a vaudeville trunk by theatrical parents. Ethel loved it so much she took private lessons with Mrs. Pethick in the evening.

A few months after the program began, the teacher decided to hold a recital to show the school and the parents how well everyone was doing. At the old Roxy Theatre in New York ("That's where I got most of my routines"), Mrs. Pethick watched a pair of professionals in a dance called "A Boy, a Girl and the Apple," a story of a girl who spurned a young man until he tempted her and won her with his offering. She memorized the choreography and assigned the roles—Ethel would be the Boy, Patricia Grant the Girl.

Onstage before a crowded house at recital time, Ethel spun gracefully around the stage, her taps sharp and clear, flirting brazenly with the Girl, who tossed her head and turned away, tapping out a firm rebuff. Ethel dolefully tapped out her heartbreak, her body seeming to crumple, then there was a brightening as the idea hit. She picked up a huge apple and held it teasingly before the Girl who stole a desiring look at it, turned away, turned back. Now Boy knew. Triumphantly, outrageously, he taunted Girl with the apple, dancing exuberantly around her as he held it out, drew it back, held it out. Finally, the Boy ended his teasing and gave Girl the apple, winning her to thunderous applause. The dance was easily the hit of the evening.

In her childhood, Ethel Kennedy displayed little aptitude for, or interest in, any of the homemaking arts, strange in view of her mother's attachment to the kitchen. She did, however, become an excellent washer of dishes. Dickie Mann, a close friend and later a classmate at college, recalls: "There was never any help in the house and always plenty of people for dinner, and somehow Ethel was always the one who ended up doing the dishes. And you know—never once did I hear her complain about it. She never said, 'Oh, why me again?' or anything; she just did it. It's one thing that has always impressed me. When I tell my children [she is now Mrs. Gerald Cummins and has five] to do something around the house, they always say: 'But I did it yesterday.' Why don't I have an Ethel?"

Boys and dates mattered little or not at all during the active midteen years: horses were all. She was not sexually sophisticated as many young girls are as they approach womanhood and as some of her own friends became, remaining, as Mrs. Meek put it, "somewhat childish about these things." If she had a date or two all through high school, they are not remembered. Her sexual awakening was manifested outwardly only by violent crushes and in common with most adolescent girls, they were directed at men safely out of reach, such as sports figures. For a full month she sighed over a dashing young Celt, a member of the Irish team that came to this country to participate in an international horse show.

❧ ❧ ❧

So it went, a happy childhood unmarred by any real pain, unshadowed by sadness, lived in glowing good health in a houseful of people who loved her and were deeply loved in return—a childhood that lacked nothing.

The years sped by and there were no clouds, not anywhere about—only the promise of even happier times. Soon Ethel would be seventeen and her path would cross that of a frail-looking, serious-faced young man with sandy hair, the seventh child and third son of Rose and Joseph Kennedy.

FOUR

Meeting Bobby, Losing Bobby

❧ ❦

The grim old building on St. Nicholas Heights sat stolidly in the Indian-summer heat, its stones, red when newly masoned, now crusted with the grime of the years. Startlingly like a fortress, it was hardly a sight to ease the anxieties of the young girls trooping up its worn steps into the massive entrance hall.

This was the main building of Manhattanville College of the Sacred Heart, and these were incoming freshmen of the class of '49. Among them was Ethel Skakel, who had driven down from Greenwich on a sticky September day with a car-full of luggage.

Not that the massive structure wasn't a familiar enough place to Ethel. Her sister Pat had been a student there, and many times Ethel had attended the prim little monthly tea dances in Founder's Hall nearby. But somehow, now that she was enrolling here herself and was to spend the next four years in and around its walls, the building seemed just a little more awesome than usual. In the large

inner hall, she joined other excited and scared young
women, was assigned a dormitory room upstairs, un-
packed, rushed down to an orientation lecture, went to
dinner, griped about the food and so began the life of a
Manhattanville student.

The college occupied a cluster of fourteen aged and
aging buildings on seventeen acres adjoining the College
of the City of New York. The setting was rustic, almost
like a picture postcard, especially when snow clung to the
trees in winter, though the buildings were a wild mixture
of tastes and periods harking back to 1841, when the
college was founded. Three years after Ethel graduated,
the entire site was sold to the city and many of the older
structures torn down to give City College more elbow
room. The school moved twenty-five miles north to Purchase, New York, in Westchester, where it now occupies
a beautiful two-hundred-and-fifty-acre campus, once the
estate of Whitelaw Reid, the diplomat and publisher.

Manhattanville is an independent college, although it
is tied to the traditions of the Society of the Sacred Heart,
an order originating in France and traditionally associated
with the education of young girls from socially elite families. Over a span of three generations, thirty young Kennedys have attended convents of the Sacred Heart. Caroline was a student at the Convent of the Sacred Heart on
New York's Fifth Avenue before transferring to the
Brearley School in 1970. Rose Kennedy studied at Manhattanville, returning there on numerous occasions to
attend private functions and make speeches on behalf of
her campaigning sons. Ethel went to the Convent of the
Sacred Heart in a part of the Bronx then known as
Maplehurst after finishing the ninth grade at Greenwich
Academy. Ted Kennedy's wife Joan is a Manhattanville
graduate; she met her husband at one of the college's

famous monthly tea dances in October, 1957. Manhattanville has become linked in the public mind with Kennedys,
sometimes to the exasperation of its officials. In Tulsa,
Oklahoma, one day, Franklin Kneedler, vice president of
the college, was registering at a hotel. When the clerk
noted that he was from Manhattanville, he said: "Oh—
where all the Kennedy's went." "For God's sake, man,"
The New York Times quotes Mr. Kneedler, "so did
6,600 other people!"

The Kennedy name has been memorialized in concrete
and steel at Manhattanville College (the name was short-
ened in 1967). On the campus stands the Kennedy Physical Education Building, the center of sports activities and
social events. The Kennedy family contributed a substantial sum toward its construction in appreciation for the
sound doctrinal training, rigid discipline and all-around
excellent education received by their daughters. (By 1971,
Manhattanville was preparing to admit its first male
students.)

At Manhattanville, Ethel roomed with a dark-haired,
serious-looking girl named Jean Kennedy, the youngest
daughter of the former Ambassador to Great Britain,
Joseph P. Kennedy. Ethel and Jean were inseparable
companions all through school. Jean, who was to marry
Stephen E. Smith, was less bouncy than her friend but
could convulse the girls with hilarious imitations, particularly a takeoff of a pip-pip-old-fellow Britisher from
her recollections of the type during her father's diplomatic service. The lives of the two girls were to become
far more closely linked than either realized, although
almost from the beginning Jean Kennedy felt that Ethel
would be "crazy" about her brother, a skinny, earnest
young man named Robert.

Ethel studied a great deal harder at college than she

ever had before. She majored in English, minored in history, acted in the dramatic club, played class hockey and was, in her own words, "very virtuous." While she was far from a brilliant student, Sister Kathryn Sullivan, "warden," or dean of students during the years Ethel attended, recalls her scholastic achievements as "very satisfactory.

"She was always dynamic, always interested in everything she was doing, whether it was studying or playing or just ordinary conversation," Sister Kathryn recalls. "She was always totally involved and she was wonderful company."

Sister Florence Weston, professor of history and academic dean at the time, says of Ethel: "She was what we call—though I hate to use the word—a very pious girl. She went to mass and Communion practically every day."

Ethel, Sister Florence remembers, "was a harum-scarum person at that age, mischievous in a certain sense but there was never anything about her that was regrettable."

Ethel's free spirit rebelled now and again against the rigid discipline at Manhattanville, earning her an impressive total of demerits. Once, before a big date, she discovered to her dismay that she had collected enough to be confined to the school grounds. Her quick mind, assessing the situation, concluded that if there were no demerit book, nobody could be punished for having too many. Jean, agreeing the argument had considerable merit, joined enthusiastically with her in the "Demerit Book Caper," helping to swipe it from the office where it was kept. Ethel threw the book down the incinerator chute and kept her date, at the same time springing a handful of other girls who could not be disciplined either in the absence of any proof of their errant behavior.

The Tower, yearbook of Ethel's graduating class,

summed up her personality this way: "An excited hoarse voice, a shriek, a peal of screaming laughter, the flash of shirttails, a tousled brown head—Ethel! Her face is at one moment a picture of utter guilelessness and at the next alive with mischief. . . . The 49ers didn't have to search very far to find in Ethel a heart of gold."

The words fit Ethel nicely in 1949. She never outgrew them.

♭   ♭   ♭

The longer she knew Ethel, the more Jean Kennedy liked her and the greater her conviction that she was just the girl for her brother Bobby. It took a little scheming but she finally got them together.

When cold weather came that semester, Jean invited a group of boys and girls to Mont Tremblant for a skiing party, and there, on the sparkling slopes of the northern Laurentians in Canada, lithe young Ethel, then seventeen, first set eyes on twenty-year-old Robert Francis Kennedy.

She saw a slender boy, five feet, ten inches tall, weighing a hundred-and-fifty pounds, with tousled brown hair worn parted on the right side, blue eyes, a firm chin held characteristically low and a serious face that, on occasion would break into a wide grin. They skiied, drank hot cocoa in the rustic setting of a ski lodge and talked a little, though not very much. For Bobby, unlike his older brothers Joe, Jr., and John, was not gifted with the art of making small talk. (William J. vanden Heuvel, once a special assistant to Robert Kennedy in the Department of Justice and a close family friend, has said that "When you're with Bob, the burden of conversation is always on you." Similarly, author Dick Schaap has observed that "In the art of small talk Bobby is, at best, a few steps in front of the late Harpo Marx.")

At Harvard, where he enrolled following graduation from Milton Academy, Bobby had a reputation for being something of a square—he did not smoke, drink or even attend cocktail parties. When he was in prep school, his father promised him a thousand dollars if he refrained from smoking and drinking until his twenty-first birthday. He proudly showed the check one day to his friends and said it hadn't been at all hard to abstain. "What's the use of going to these parties and drinking?" he said. "I'd rather do something else." The "something else" was talking with a small group of friends about sports and politics, in that order.

Bobby, born at his parents' home in Brookline, Massachusetts, on November 20, 1925, was the seventh of the nine Kennedy children—only Jean and Ted were younger. At Milton Academy, he earned only average grades, sometimes less than average, but won recognition and admiration for quarterbacking the football team.

As soon as he reached his eighteenth birthday, Bobby put in for pilot training at Bates College, in Lewiston, Maine, and shortly thereafter was transferred back to Harvard for training as a naval officer, where news came that his older brother, Joseph, Jr., was killed when his bombing plane exploded over England. Bobby, anguished by the tragedy, felt all the more keenly his own inactivity in the war, especially since news of his brother Jack's heroism in the Pacific had been the talk of Harvard Yard. Soon after midnight on August 2, 1944, PT-boat *109*, commanded by young Lieutenant John Kennedy, was sliced in two by the Japanese destroyer *Amagiri*. Kennedy and ten surviving crew members (two had lost their lives) were rescued after a five-day ordeal, during which the young naval officer, despite an injured back, spent five hours in the sea towing one of the wounded men, Patrick

McMahon, to safety. For his heroism and leadership, Kennedy received a citation from Admiral Halsey and was awarded the Navy and Marine Corps Medal.

Bobby insisted on active duty and got it, most fittingly, as a seaman second-class aboard a destroyer newly commissioned the *Joseph P. Kennedy, Jr.* He spent six frustrating months cruising around the Caribbean, though, doing odd jobs aboard ship, many thousands of miles from the scene of the action he wanted. When the war ended, he returned to Cambridge.

As Harvardians before him, his older brothers Joe and Jack had left behind a legacy of significant accomplishments. Joe was president of the Student Council, an excellent athlete, a good student and had a way with the girls. A classmate remembers that he would generally be seen "in his convertible automobile, with the top down and the prettiest girl beside him." John was only a fair student in his early years, made the golf and swimming teams and, as a senior, expanded a thesis into a book, *While England Slept,* which sold eighty-thousand copies and earned him forty-thousand dollars as well as high critical praise. Both graduated *cum laude*.

It was a hard act to follow. Bobby didn't do especially well in academics ("I didn't go to class very much," he said, and his grades were so mediocre he didn't even apply for admission to Harvard Law School) and he was hardly a lady-killer.

But he accomplished something his brothers never did. He won his football letter—though just barely, because Bobby wasn't a very good player. He was neither heavy enough, nor fast enough nor could he dart and dodge with sufficient agility. But he worked with a fierce intensity to perfect his skills, doubtless to prove to the world, and especially to himself, that he was indeed as good in a sport he chose as his brothers were in theirs. Ken O'Donnell was captain of the varsity in 1947 and vividly recalls Bobby's relentless, unflagging efforts to learn football. Despite many post-practice sessions during which the team captain tried to smooth the rough edges, Bobby became only passably good, though hardly for want of trying.

To win the much-coveted H, a team member must participate, even if for just one play, in the annual Yale-Harvard classic. In 1947, Bobby was holding down his accustomed seat on the bench, watching forlornly as the game neared its close. His chances, he felt, were now virtually nonexistent, especially since the coach knew he had injured his leg a few days before. With only a few minutes left in the game, Yale scored another touchdown and led thirty-one to twenty-one. The teams lined up for the kickoff. There was time for just one more play. Coach Richard Harlow glanced down the bench and called: "Kennedy!" Bobby looked up quickly; he was being sent in. He jogged down the field to right end. A Yale man caught Harvard's kick and charged toward Bobby, who tackled him joyously despite his aching leg and earned his letter.

Up there in the Laurentians, a Canadian wonderland of undulating white hills and tall green pines, Ethel Skakel fell in love just as Jean Kennedy had predicted. She thought the shy youth was "divine." And "very handsome." And "a good human being."

A biographer, re-creating the story of that first meeting, aches to be able to write that the bells rang in Bobby's head at the same time. But they didn't. The truth is that Bobby, while he though Ethel great fun and a dandy little athlete, wasn't especially bowled over by the Skakel girl. At any rate, not by *that* Skakel girl just yet.

A short while after the skiing party, he met Ethel's older sister Pat and began dating her regularly.

Pat, three years older than Ethel, was freckled, darkly attractive and as serious about life as her younger sister was bubbly, and perhaps it was this latter characteristic that appealed to the youthful, intense Bobby.

During vacations, Bobby would come to the house on Simmons Lane to call for Pat. Many times he would pass Ethel on the lawn or terrace and call out a "Hi!" She would greet him in return and flash a smile, but he never knew how she felt inwardly. It was a bleak and unhappy time for Ethel and she does not like to talk or even think about it. "We'll pass over that terrible period," she was to say afterward.

What was the nature of Bobby's attachment to Pat? Was he in love with her, did he ask for her hand? Obviously, the only person who could shed light is Pat herself, who married Luan Peter Cuffe and went to live in Dublin. Pat, who has eight children and a delightful brogue, talked about it by transatlantic telephone with the author:

> *Lester David:* Bobby never proposed marriage to you, did he?
>
> *Pat:* Well now, don't be asking everything.
>
> *L. D.:* May I just ask that one question? Did Bobby ever propose marriage to you?
>
> *Pat:* I can't hear you. The line is very poor.

(The line from the author's end was exceptionally clear. However, it might have been fading in Dublin so the question was repeated more slowly and louder.)

L. D.: DID BOBBY EVER PROPOSE MAR-
RIAGE TO YOU?

Pat: I can't hear you. The line is very poor.

*(Suddenly it dawned on the author that the line was
clear enough but Mrs. Cuffe had no intention of replying.)*

L. D.: Oh, I'm sorry.

Pat: (with a laugh) That's okay.

The reader may infer what he pleases because that's
as much information as we are likely to get on the matter.

Pat thought Bobby Kennedy "very pleasant and very
good-looking" but immature. "He was very young," she
recalled. "He was magnificent in the latter part of his
career, but when I knew him he was just a teen-ager."

In Boston she met Mr. Cuffe, nine years older than
Bobby. Cuffe was studying for his master's degree in
architecture under Frank Lloyd Wright at Harvard. She
dropped Bobby and began dating Cuffe, whom she eventually married. "We thought Pat would become a nun,"
Rushton Skakel says. "She surprised us and married an
Irishman."

FIVE

Winning Bobby

❧ ❧

While Bobby was dating Pat, Ethel busied herself with
Massachusetts politics, drawn to the game by the enthusiasm of Jean, Eunice and the rest of the Kennedys
whom she came to meet, know and like. John, who was
twenty-nine, had announced as candidate for Congress
from the Eleventh District, along with eight other hope-
fuls, after the game-cocky James Michael Curley, then
holding down the job, decided that four years of Washington was enough and it would be pleasant to return to
his old job as Mayor of Boston.

Curley, an old and deadly foe of the Kennedys, was
not especially pleased to see a member of the rising generation enter the lists, but there was not very much he
could do about it. The Eleventh, he and everyone else
knew, was originally Kennedy country before Curley had
won it. Patrick J. Kennedy, John's paternal grandfather,
had used it as a launching pad to the State Senate, and
John F. (Honey Fitz) Fitzgerald, his other grandfather,

had swept all the way to Mayor. There was talk that the skinny, handsome young man with the engaging smile could go far, given the advantages of all this family experience plus something his forebears never had—unlimited amounts of money to spend, for the former Ambassador's fortune was considerable.

It was the first campaign for the new generation of Kennedys and everyone worked hard that spring and early summer. The primary, they all knew, meant the election because no Republican would have even a faint chance in that Democratic stronghold.

None dashed around more madly, rang more doorbells or talked more earnestly with the Irish and Italian residents of that predominantly working-class section than the newcomer to politics, Ethel Skakel. Tirelessly she scurried to six and seven neighborhood parties a day, telling all who would listen how grand John Kennedy was and what a "terrific" representative he would make as she handed out the tons of cookies and poured the gallons of coffee supplied by the Kennedy organization.

Curley, who had come to look upon the district as a snug harbor where he could berth anytime he wished when the political storms blew too strong, took a dim view of yielding it up, and to a Kennedy at that. But Curley never hid from the facts; dolefully he predicted Kennedy would win. "How can he lose?" he mused. "He's got a double-barreled name, John Fitzgerald Kennedy, named for two well-known officeholders. His grandparents will be remembered. He doesn't even need to campaign. He can go to Washington now and forget the primary and election."

Curley was right. On June 18, Primary Day, John Kennedy racked up 22,183 votes, twice as many as the runner-up, and was on his way. Ethel squealed with joy,

pronounced the result terrific and went back to school
burbling with the excitement of it all. Nor did it diminish:
Later, she wrote a college thesis on Kennedy's *While England Slept* and was able to pack in enough first-hand research to win an A.

ʚ   ʚ   ʚ

Nearly two years after this fateful primary, Bobby, in
the winter of 1948, began dating Ethel again. He was
now enrolled at the University of Virginia Law School
in Charlottesville.

Bobby would come up on weekends to see Ethel, bound-
ing up the steps of the main building and announcing himself to the nun at the reception room, who would summon
Ethel. Dating regulations were strict: On weekdays, Ethel
had to be in her dorm by 9:00 P.M. while on weekends
the curfew was 1:00 A.M. Lateness would earn demerits.
It is a matter of record that Robert Kennedy helped
Ethel earn a great many.

Bobby took Ethel to the Stork Club, a popular ren-
dezvous for "cafe society" of those days, but nightclub-
bing wasn't much to their liking. Most times when they
were in the city they went to the movies or sometimes
saw a Broadway drama or musical. Frequently, Ethel
would invite Bobby to Greenwich for the weekend and,
just as often, he would ask her down to Charlottesville.

But now a strange thing happened, or perhaps, accepting as we must woman's changeable nature, not so
strange a thing after all. Ethel had been waiting for
Bobby and made no bones about it. "Thank goodness he
came back to me," she was to say some years afterward.
But now Bobby was pursuing her with increased ardor
and, Ethel's friends say, she appeared to be hesitating.

On a number of weekends she would refuse Bobby's
invitation to go to Cape Cod or come down to Charlottes-

ville because there would be a horse show in town at which she was performing. Bobby would come down anyway and watch the show even though such equine performances bored him silly. "I can fight anything," he said at the time, "but I can't fight a horse."

Dickie Mann says: "He loved her so much. He adored her. He was always there. I just knew . . . we all knew that he loved her very much.

"Lots of times I would ask her: 'Does he want to marry you?' She'd say, 'Yes, he does.'

"Then she'd be quiet.

"I think deep down that Ethel always knew she would marry Bobby, if she would marry anybody at all. At one time, she told us she wasn't sure she wanted to marry at all, that she was giving thought to becoming a nun. But I don't think it was a serious thought.

"When you're very happy with life, when you love life, when you're still in college, it's hard to make a major decision like marriage, and Ethel was finding it hard."

By early in 1950, Ethel resolved her doubts.

One sparkling cold day, Dickie Mann went to Ethel's house for lunch. The entire family was there, and Bobby too. He and Ethel were laughing, Mr. and Mrs. Skakel wore huge grins, the other Skakels were smiling conspiratorially. Dickie stared at them, then approached Ethel and Bobby.

"Do you have anything to tell me?" she demanded.

"Yes," Ethel said, and thrust out her left hand. On the third finger sparkled a huge oblong-cut diamond.

"We're going to announce our engagement," Ethel said.

⑨ ⑨ ⑨

The wedding gown lay stretched out on Ethel's bed. She stared at it, then reached down and ran her fingers lightly over the white satin.

It was early in the morning of June 17, 1950, but already the Skakel household was whirling, even more than usual. In his bedroom down the hall, George Skakel was getting dressed for the ceremony. A few young Skakels had already finished breakfast. Ann was outside on the huge back lawn, supervising the preparations for the reception. A great gray tent had been erected there over a vast wooden floor, and the caterers' people were arriving in trucks with enormous quantities of food and liquor for the fifteen-hundred guests. Ann had been worrying for weeks: "What if it rains?" The day was cool and cloudy, but there was no rain, and Ann sighed with relief.

The pace of the past few weeks had been terrifying. With Pixie Meek, Ethel raced around to the fine shops in White Plains, Westport and New York (Bonwit Teller was a favorite), collecting their trousseaux, for Pixie too was getting married almost the same time. The guest list had to be drawn up, the reception planned, the ceremony rehearsed, the fittings fitted in—and finally the day arrived.

In midmorning, with help from her sisters, Ethel stepped into her gown, adjusting the fitted bodice and straightening the bateau neckline trimmed with beaded Pointe Venise lace and panels of pearls. Her veil was full length, of double tulle attached to a cap of Pointe Venise lace held by a crown of orange blossoms. On a chair by the wall were white satin mitts, embroidered with seed pearls; on another, the bouquet she would carry—stephanotis, eucharis lilies and lilies of the valley.

George Skakel knocked on her door and asked if she were ready. She said she was. "Then let's get going," he called. "It's nearly eleven." Ethel affixed a single strand of pearls around her neck, took one last look in the mirror and went out, sweeping down the curved staircase, radiant in her white wedding dress. George helped his daughter into a limousine and drove with her to the church. The others followed.

St. Mary's Roman Catholic Church on Greenwich Avenue, a beautiful stone building set back on a broad plaza, was already filled with guests. On the sidewalk and across the street in front of the library (since torn down and replaced by a five-and-ten-cent store), knots of people had gathered to watch the arrival of bride, groom and assorted celebrities. They had already seen Robert come in with his best man, John Kennedy, the dashing young Congressman from Massachusetts, and his father, the former Ambassador.

Inside, the entire church was banked in white peonies, regal lilies and dogwood. In the sacristy to the right of the altar, Bobby Kennedy in a broad-lapelled, single-button frock coat and striped trousers, had opened a side door and stepped out on a small balcony. He wasn't especially nervous, just warm in the closeness. He reached out and absently plucked a leaf from a branch of a tall maple that almost touched the church.

Bobby was joined by John, and the two brothers talked quietly for a while. Also taking their part in the ceremony were the ushers: Teddy Kennedy, the youngest brother, then only eighteen; Kenny O'Donnell; Kirk LeMoyne Billings (later Bobby's chief adviser during his Senate campaign; the Skakel boys; and assorted husky Harvardians, most of whom Bobby knew from the gridiron squad.

At 11:30 A.M. the big pipe organ in the rear of the church, since removed, pealed and Ethel, solemn for once, came down the aisle on the arm of her father. Behind her, in white Chantilly lace dresses over white taffeta, walked the matron and the maid of honor, Pat Cuffe, in from Dublin, and Ethel's youngest sister, Ann Skakel. Ethel went through a small wooden gate and knelt beside Bobby on a double *prie-dieu.*

The beautiful tenor voice of Michael O'Higgins of the Royal Irish Academy of Music rose in the Nuptial Mass. Proudly, George Skakel gave his daughter in marriage. The Reverend Terrence L. Connolly, curator of the Francis Thompson Collection at Boston College and a long-time friend of the Skakels, imparted the Papal Blessing and made them man and wife.

The reception was one of the most lavish the Greenwich community, known for its large-scale parties, had ever seen. Every type of delicacy, all manner of fowl and fish and beef, were served in abundance, and the liquor supply was endless. "There were all kinds of great people there," Teddy Wahl remembers, "and we all had a grand time." Chester Neminski, the Skakels' gardener, was there too, watching over the flowers he had banked all over the platform. Tirelessly, the young couple greeted the guests as they arrived.

The festivities got under way shortly after noon when the new Mrs. Robert Kennedy swept onto the dance floor in the arms of her new husband. Then John cut in on his brother. After a few whirls, young Teddy Kennedy walked out for his turn with Ethel but Joe Kennedy, who had been waiting impatiently, strode out, elbowed his youngest son out of the way and danced off with his new daughter-in-law.

SIX

Campus Wife

❦ ❦

In the fall of 1950, following a long honeymoon in Hawaii, the newlyweds settled down to a campus marriage in a small white frame cottage near the University of Virginia. Bobby was a student at the Law School and Ethel became the happy little homemaker.

Happy, though as inept as many brides and possibly worse than most. She puttered around the little house, with its three tiny bedrooms, living room with the sagging but comfortable furniture and small kitchen, managing to keep the place reasonably neat and clean. But she would send out the laundry on an erratic schedule, often leaving Bobby without a clean shirt in his bureau drawer. She "didn't know one end of a needle from the other," as one friend put it, bought too much food or not enough and was utterly lost in the kitchen.

Her early efforts at preparing meals were sheer disaster.

She couldn't fry bacon, overcooked everything and was baffled by the simplest recipe. Once she put in a long-distance call to her parents' home in Greenwich, got one of her sisters and wailed that an omelet she was making had collapsed. How do you fix a collapsed omelet, she asked. Another time she determined to outdo herself by giving Bobby a fine meal. She did. She spent hours carefully preparing four fresh vegetables; at the last minute, as a starving Bobby waited, she realized with a gasp that she had forgotten to cook the meat. Small wonder that she would sometimes draft George Terrien, who had roomed with Bobby at Harvard and later at Charlottesville, to prepare their meals. George, who was to marry her sister Georgeann, was passably good with a skillet. Bobby would always throw him a look of gratitude when he saw him coming in.

Finally, Ethel confessed to her friend Dickie Mann: "I've got to get a cook. I can't give Bobby hard peas and tough steak for dinner again." She engaged one and for the rest of their married lives never cooked again except in emergencies.

Every weekday morning, Bobby, notebook under his arm, would trudge off to class. Late in the afternoon, he would return, toss his book and papers on a chair and, hand in hand with Ethel, walk in the other direction to the Farmington Country Club, which they had joined. There they would play tennis and swim until dinner time.

Evenings, Bobby would study in the school library or in their small living room, while Ethel played with their English bulldog or visited with friends. Often Bobby would hit the books until the early morning hours, reluctantly calling an end upon Ethel's urging to come to bed. Terrien recalls: "Bobby was a bulldog-type guy with his studies as with everything else. He was tenacious, diligent, as hardworking a student as anyone I've known."

＠ ＠ ＠

At this point, while Bobby is poring over his law books and Ethel, for once, is quiet, we should turn our attention to a subject Ethel had pondered for a long time: What kind of a wife would she be to a man?

From the beginning, those closest to Ethel have noted, she determined that marriage would be a shared experience for her, not a division of responsibilities. Many young couples begin their lives together by assigning to themselves the traditional roles of breadwinner on the one hand, homemaker on the other, and rarely moving beyond these rigid compartments. Too often, the result is that they grow in different directions. A wife never comes to understand what her husband really does or how he reacts to the people and the problems around him; a husband never gets to know the day-to-day complexities of a woman's life. "Husbands and wives who allow gaps of ignorance to grow between them," writes Dr. Phillip Polatin of the New York Psychiatric Institute, "often end by living together as mysterious, antagonistic strangers."

Ethel took an active interest in learning as much as she could about her husband's job—what he did, where he did it, his problems. Somehow, she would get to meet most of the people with whom he worked and all his superiors. She would rarely miss a speech he delivered or an important appearance in a court or hearing room. "I like to see Bobby in action," she said once. After the children began coming, she would take all but the very youngest with her.

"Husbands and wives who know what is happening to each other and know how these happenings are making

the other feel cannot become strangers," Dr. Polatin
states. "They are more likely to stand loyally ready at
all times with moral and emotional support." Ethel's
every action, from the first days of her married life,
proves that she believed this with all her heart.

👁 👁 👁

At the Law School, Bobby was elected president of the
Student Legal Forum, which brought national figures to
the campus for talks and discussions. With the help of his
father, who knew most of the important figures of his
time, Bobby was able to book star attractions who packed
the Forum sessions. He was careful to choose them from
all shades of political and social opinion. Thus he invited
the liberal Supreme Court Justice William O. Douglas,
Ralph Bunche, the United Nations official who was the
first Negro to win a Nobel Peace Prize, and Thurman
Arnold, President Franklin D. Roosevelt's zealous trust-
busting assistant attorney general. He also brought down
Seth W. Richardson, the chairman of the Subversive Activities Control Board, and his father, whose isolationist
views were well-known.

Bobby's work with the Forum brought home to Ethel
for the first time what it meant to be the wife of a controversial man. There were to be many times afterward
when she was to see and hear the hatred directed at her
husband and, while she would be constantly astonished
and even disbelieving, she would become accustomed to
the attacks. But this initial evidence that people could hate
and vilify must have cut deeply, at once wounding and
puzzling the young bride.

After the invitation to Ralph Bunche was announced,
the segregationist factions in that small Southern university town rose in fury against bringing a "nigger" to the
campus, citing the Virginia segregation law to prove that

Kennedy was acting not only with Yankee-type scorn for Southern sensibilities but illegally as well. The law specifically called for separation of races in all public places. Torrents of abuse were poured on Bobby for having issued the invitation but he fought back hard in what was his first real defense of Negro rights. With other officials of the Forum, he wrote a letter, actually a legal brief, to the president of the university, pointing out that the United States Supreme Court, in a Texas case, had specifically exempted meetings in colleges and universities from a segregation law, and therefore Bunche could not be excluded on any legal grounds. The president agreed this was indeed so and Bunche, who had said he would not appear unless his audience was racially mixed, came down to speak.

Ethel was to hear more invective poured on Bobby after Joseph R. McCarthy was invited. The Republican Senator from Wisconsin, until a year before an obscure freshman legislator, was generating national attention, and alarm, with his charges of Communists in government. He had electrified the country with assertions that members of the Communist Party had infiltrated the State Department, and followed this rapidly with charges that men in high places were guilty of treason, espionage and corruption. This time the liberals on campus rose and howled, but again Bobby rode out the storm.

The question of Bobby Kennedy's involvement with, fondness for, and approval of Joe McCarthy has received considerable attention. At this stage of his career, Bobby believed, as his family did, in the Communist-hunting Senator's aims, a belief that was to become stronger over the next two years. And Ethel, who believed in what Bobby did, was with him all the way.

McCarthy was even then a close friend of the elder

Kennedy, who was to say afterward: "I liked Joe Mc-Carthy. I always liked him. I would see him when I went down to Washington, and when he was visiting in Palm Beach he'd come around to my house for a drink. I invited him to Cape Cod." Part of the Senator's attraction for Joe Kennedy may well have been his views, which, understandably enough, won the overwhelming approval of large segments of the Boston Irish. "I liked the fight he was putting up against Communists in our government," said the elder Kennedy. "I thought he'd be a sensation." Rarely a day would pass during the McCarthy era without at least one lengthy long-distance telephone call from Joe Kennedy to McCarthy during which he would offer copious advice on the conduct of the Senator's investigations.

Widely overlooked, however, was another reason for the Kennedy clan–McCarthy friendship. The Senator possessed the type of physical courage that the Kennedy's admired so much. Roy Cohn, counsel to the Senator's investigating subcommittee, has said: "Even his enemies agreed he was a man of raw guts. He was never afraid of physical injury, nor of sickness nor dying." As a student at Marquette University, McCarthy joined the boxing team, and those who knew him remarked upon his blind courage against much superior opponents. Once the man he was battling wanted to stop a fight because Joe was covered with blood from a beating he was taking. Joe, grinning through the pain, insisted on continuing. At Hyannis Port, he played Kennedy-style touch football recklessly and competitively. A poor swimmer, he nearly drowned one afternoon when the boat he was following outdistanced him, but he never lost his head. "He didn't complain," said Joe Kennedy admiringly. The Kennedys liked this in a man.

Around Thanksgiving, Ethel discovered she was going to have a baby. Neither this first pregnancy nor all the others that were to follow were to make the slightest difference in her routine. She continued to play tennis, run and bounce. Once she leaped into a chair at home while entertaining some friends and knocked it over. Bobby observed dryly: "That's what I like about Ethel. She's such a lady." When warm weather came, she would swim daily at the country club until, her time approaching, the manager became alarmed. One day he took her aside and, flushing with embarrassment, told her he could no longer take any responsibility if anything happened. Ethel went swimming anyway. Says a friend: "She dived into the pool and it seemed as though the water rose two inches."

In mid-June, Bobby graduated from law school, fifty-sixth in a class of one hundred and twenty-five, and the Kennedys left Charlottesville for Hyannis Port. On the Fourth of July, Ethel gave birth to a little girl she and Bobby named Kathleen Hartington. Godfather to the child was Senator Joseph McCarthy.

₰ ₰ ₰

Over the long summer of 1951, Ethel and Bobby swam, sailed and took long walks on the beach at Hyannis Port. Two topics occupied most of their attention—their marvelous new baby and how she was developing, and the direction Bobby's career would take.

After graduation from law school, young Kennedy had interviews with the heads of some prestigious law firms in New York but, he told Ethel, the legal business held no special fascination for him. Neither did wheeler-dealering in the world of high finance, where his father had accumulated his immense fortune. Actually, Joe Kennedy had never wanted any of his children to follow in his footsteps. He had repeatedly stressed the excitement and importance of government service, telling them he had made enough money to free them from the necessity of having to earn a living.

Bobby at length decided that, with his legal training, he would start his career with the Department of Justice. Senator McCarthy helped him get his first job in the Internal Security Division, investigating the records of alleged spies and subversives. His salary was $4,200 a year.

The Kennedys needed a place to live, so Ethel went house-hunting in Washington. "Now remember," Bobby told her as he left for work one morning, "don't pay more than four-hundred dollars a month."

Ethel promised and, with Dickie Mann, scoured the Georgetown section, only a few minutes drive from downtown Washington. In colonial days, Georgetown had been the commercial hub of the lower Potomac; now it was a quiet, tree-shaded showplace of narrow streets and expensive fine homes.

Ethel and Dickie tramped all over, went in and out of countless homes for rent but could find nothing for the limit Bobby had set. She reported her vain search to Bobby, who said he was confident she would find something, but didn't offer to raise the ante.

Finally Ethel found a charming little frame house on S Street, a short, quiet little lane that seemed to have been plucked out of the previous century. It belonged to an Army colonel who was being transferred. The house had four bedrooms, a fair-sized living and dining room and a garden surrounded by a high wall. Ethel fell in love with it at once but, alas, the rental exceeded Bobby's strict limit.

Ethel and Dickie went into a coffee shop to talk things over. "Call up the colonel," Dickie urged, "and tell him you think his house is absolutely divine but you simply can't go over four-hundred dollars. Maybe he'll relent."

Ethel said she would and began rehearsing what she would tell the officer. "Make believe you're the colonel," she told Dickie, and launched into an impressive plea.

Suddenly Dickie caught sight of a man in uniform in the booth behind Ethel. "Ethel," she whispered, "behind you . . . that man. I'll bet you that's the colonel." Ethel whipped around. Hesitating only a second, she asked him if he were the officer who owned the house on S Street.

"Why, yes I am," the man answered.

Ethel grinned. "I love your house, but I can't pay any more than four-hundred dollars a month, and I was just practicing what I was going to say to you."

The colonel was charmed and Ethel got the house.

ᕮ ᕮ ᕮ

Ethel and Bobby lived in Georgetown for the next six years; he rose in importance as a government investigator and she raised babies. Joseph Patrick III came along on September 24, 1952. Robert Francis, Jr., was born January 17, 1954, David Anthony on June 15, 1955, and Mary Courtney on September 9, 1956.

All during these years, Ethel never wavered from the objective she had set for herself: to know as much as she could about the work Bobby was doing. When Bobby was transferred briefly to the Eastern District in Brooklyn to work under United States Attorney Frank Parker, she visited his office in the ancient Federal Building near the Brooklyn Bridge a number of times. Mr. Parker was to remark later that she was exceptionally eager to learn about the tax frauds, bribery and corruption cases the new attorney was investigating.

In the spring of 1952, Bobby resigned to serve as campaign manager for his brother John, who was making a bid to unseat the incumbent Senator Henry Cabot Lodge, Jr., from his Massachusetts seat. Bobby was only twenty-

six, but Joe Kennedy felt that John Kennedy's interests
would best be served by a member of the family, no matter
how inexperienced he may have been for such a key role.
The appointment angered a number of supporters. One
campaign worker was heard to exclaim: "What had
Bobby done up to that time politically? Nothing. Not a
damn thing. And all of a sudden he was there as campaign
manager, waving the banners." In his eagerness Bobby
ruffled many feathers, notably those of Governor Paul
Dever, who was seeking re-election. One day Bobby
astounded Governor Dever by stalking into his office and
bawling him out for what Bobby thought was a tactical
political error. Richard J. Whalen, who tells the story in
The Founding Father, says the infuriated Governor
thereupon telephoned the elder Kennedy: "I know you're
an important man around here and all that," he stormed,
"but I'm telling you this and I mean it. Keep that fresh
kid of yours out of my sight from here on in!"

Ethel plunged zestfully into her second hurrah. Kennedy women are famous for having exerted great energy
in behalf of their office-seeking men at election time but
it is doubtful if any campaigned nonstop throughout an
entire prenatal period, as Ethel did. She raced around
Massachusetts, addressing women's groups, giving tea
parties, writing letters and performing a hundred-and-one
chores almost to the day Joseph Patrick was born. She
talked to a group in Fall River, lumbered out of the auditorium and into a car and drove to Boston to have her
baby. She took only a few days off, then returned to the
campaign trail until Election Day, when Massachusetts
voters elected John Kennedy to the Senate. The baby was
baptized by Archbishop Richard Cushing of Boston, subsequently named a Cardinal, who was a close friend of the
Kennedy family.

There can be no minimizing the help Ethel and the other Kennedy women gave John Kennedy. When Lodge was asked to what he attributed his defeat, he replied: "It was those damned tea parties."

It could also have been a man named Joseph Raymond McCarthy, with whom Bobby and Ethel were to be linked more closely in the next couple of years.

By 1952, Joe McCarthy was an important political force. He had taken the Communist issue into Connecticut and was instrumental in bringing about the defeat of William Benton for the Senate. Millard Tydings lost by a forty-thousand vote plurality in Maryland after McCarthy entered the state, attacking the Democrat for failing to oust Communists from government. Scott Lucas, the Senate Majority Leader, was defeated by Republican Everett M. Dirksen after McCarthy went into Illinois. The elder Kennedy knew all this. He also knew that if McCarthy came into Massachusetts to campaign for fellow Republican Lodge, John Kennedy's chances for election might be seriously harmed.

Joe Kennedy succeeded in keeping McCarthy out of Massachusetts that year, reportedly by making a substantial contribution to the Wisconsin Senator's own campaign and helping to raise money for him in Wisconsin.

Thus, the friendship between the Kennedys and McCarthy was further strengthened. McCarthy was re-elected to the Senate that year and named chairman of the powerful Senate Subcommittee on Investigations of the Committee on Government Operations, the forum from which he was to rock the nation. Late that year, the elder Kennedy telephoned McCarthy and asked him to name Bobby chief counsel to the subcommittee. McCarthy, however, had already appointed a cocky but brilliant young lawyer, Roy Cohn, who was winning a reputation as a

Communist-hunting prosecutor in New York. He would name Bobby to his staff to work with Cohn.

Bobby accepted and went to work for the McCarthy committee, where he met the twenty-seven-year-old Cohn. The two took an almost instant dislike to one another and a feud began that never was to end.

In 1953, the McCarthy subcommittee turned its attention to the Army, charging that a Communist spy ring was funneling secrets to Russia from the Signal Corps Center at Fort Monmouth, New Jersey. A few months later, the McCarthy probers sought to find out why a dentist at Camp Kilmer, New Jersey, one Irving M. Peress, had been granted an honorable discharge despite the existence of a file of so-called derogatory information against him. The Peress case brought McCarthy and Roy Cohn into a violent confrontation with the Pentagon and President Eisenhower, and led eventually to the Army–McCarthy hearings.

The Senate had named a special subcommittee to investigate charges that McCarthy and his associates had sought preferential treatment for an Army private, G. David Schine. Young Schine, a friend of Roy Cohn, was on the McCarthy subcommittee staff as a consultant. McCarthy and Cohn, it was charged, used improper pressure to obtain a direct Reserve commission for Schine. In turn, the McCarthy group charged that the Army tried to force the subcommittee to give up its investigation into Communist infiltration within its ranks.

By the time the hearings began, Bobby Kennedy had turned in his resignation as assistant counsel and deputy staff director of the McCarthy subcommittee, explaining in a letter to the Senator that he planned to enter private law practice. Later, in his book *The Enemy Within,* he wrote that he had lasted only six months with the subcommittee because "with two exceptions, no real research was ever done. Most of the investigations were instituted on the basis of some preconceived notion by the chief counsel [Roy Cohn—ed.] or his staff members and not on the basis of any information that had been developed. Cohn and Schine claimed they knew from the outset what was wrong; and they were not going to let the facts interfere."

Bobby served for a few months with former President Herbert Hoover's commission studying the reorganization of the executive branch of government. Frankly bored by the work—his assignment was an evaluation of the U.S. Weather Bureau—he left after a few months, then returned to the McCarthy subcommittee in February as counsel to the Democratic minority.

The thirty-six-day Army–McCarthy show, with its high drama, suspense and comic interludes, enthralled the nation. More than twenty million persons listened and watched on radio and television sets that were turned on in homes, offices, saloons, garages, factories, shops, halls and even movie houses. Housewives stopped work to watch. Patients cancelled doctor and dental appointments. From Los Angeles came a report that during hearing hours the number of cars on the freeway thinned and attendance at bars and cocktail lounges zoomed.

There was no more avid spectator in the Caucus Room of the Senate Office Building than Ethel Kennedy. Her schedule during those weeks was ferocious. She would sit with her children at breakfast, drive Bobby to the hearings, return to Georgetown to play with the children, then rush back to watch the morning session. During the luncheon recess she would return home to be with the children, then go back to the hearing room, often meeting Bobby after adjournment to take him home.

As minority counsel, Kennedy had been assigned to

write out questions that the Democratic Senators (John McClellan, Henry Jackson and Stuart Symington) would ask of witnesses. Cohn's friend Schine had prepared a plan to sell democracy overseas by creating so-called deminforms to encourage the formation of democratic parties in foreign countries. Senator Jackson scoffed at the idea, aided by Bobby, who fed him questions to ask. "They picked at point after point in Dave's plan, finding something hilarious in each," Cohn said. "And every time Kennedy handed him something, Senator Jackson would go into fits of laughter. I became angrier and angrier as the burlesque continued."

When the session ended, Bobby and Roy Cohn found themselves face to face. Cohn, still angry, upbraided Kennedy. "Tell your friend Scoop Jackson we're going to get him on Monday," he told Bobby, who replied: "Get lost." More words followed and then Cohn said: "Look, apparently there is only one way to settle this," and prepared to swing.

"Two men grabbed me," Cohn said, "Bobby moved away and no blow was struck."

Since Bobby was in excellent physical shape and Cohn has admitted that he was unable to pass the West Point physical aptitude test measuring muscular power and endurance, it was probably fortunate that the fight never came off.

In December 1954, following a hearing by a special committee, the Senate voted to condemn McCarthy for conduct unbecoming a Senator. Thereafter, the awesome power he had wielded quickly faded; he died in 1957 of a liver ailment, a broken man.

Bobby, along with his father, had a personal fondness for Joe McCarthy. "I liked him," Bobby once said, "and yet at times he was terribly heavy-handed. He was a very complicated character. His whole method of operation was complicated because he would get a guilty feeling and get hurt after he had blasted somebody. He wanted so desperately to be liked. He was so thoughtful and yet so unthoughtful in what he did to others. He was sensitive and yet insensitive. He didn't anticipate the results of what he was doing. He was very thoughtful of his friends, and yet he could be so cruel to others."

In 1955, following the censure vote, Bobby showed how he felt toward the Senator. The Junior Chamber of Commerce had selected Bobby as one of America's ten outstanding young men of the year. Edward R. Murrow, the late newscaster and head of the United States Information Agency who had excoriated McCarthy in a television broadcast, was scheduled to attack the Senator once again. During Murrow's address, Kennedy rose abruptly and left the room. When McCarthy died, Bobby flew to Appleton, Wisconsin, to attend his funeral.

Part Two

SEVEN

Her Infinite Variety

The woman Robert Kennedy married is an absolute original. She is exuberant, impulsive, life-loving, cheerful, gutsy and sentimental. She is Funny Girl, Supergirl, Compassionate Girl and sometimes all three in the same hour. She is loaded with money, charm, and *chutzpah*.

Ethel Kennedy, for all her uniqueness, is remarkably similar to her late husband. Like him, she has an abiding love for nature and all living creatures, a profound commitment to her faith, a fierce competitive drive, a capacity to grow and learn and change. Like him, she is an intensely physical person, with a need to move, to feel the exhilaration of putting her body through a punishing workout on an athletic field.

And, like him, born to wealth, accustomed to asking and getting, she has been a little spoiled. Bobby demanded a great deal and stepped on many toes. Ethel, too, can be imperious, calling upon her many friends to help in her activities, heedless of their own schedules or responsibilities, expecting them to attend. When she wants something, and feels she has good and sufficient reason, Ethel will tune out any objections and reach for it.

But there are differences too. Where Bobby was a complex man of many moods who could command blind loyalty as well as make bitter enemies, Ethel has always been direct, easily understood and almost universally admired. Where Bobby was an introspective man and essentially a loner, Ethel has always been outgoing and, hating solitude, insisted upon being surrounded by people. Where Bobby, troubled all his life by an older-brother complex, fought ceaselessly to prove to himself and the world that he could achieve on his own, Ethel has no observable hangups except for a dread of flying, and she has plenty of cause as we shall see.

It was never easy to talk to Bobby. Even with a small group he knew well, the words rarely flowed. Hardly ever would he expound his social or political theories at length; instead, he would sit silently much of the time, listening, asking more questions than he would answer. Ethel is a yakker. She talks and talks: bubbly, informal, slang-larded talk on anything that happens to fascinate her—children, sports, doctors, parties—spoken rapidly in a low, somewhat breathy contralto. She is a complete extrovert: she might do a quick tap-dance routine if the mood strikes her and the gathering is small, and she rarely needs coaxing to get up and sing.

Her mind does not run to abstract reasoning but it is extraordinarily alert. She responds emotionally and intuitively rather than intellectually to people and events. Since Bobby's death her reading has been more diverse, especially in the field of social justice. Where once her taste ran to books about heroes (General Douglas MacArthur's life was a favorite) and James Bond, she now reads about politics and social problems. William Styron's *The Confessions of Nat Turner* engrossed her. Nevertheless, action, seeing things for herself and talking with people, is more her style than reading and thinking.

In an era of relaxing standards, Ethel is considered prim, even naïve. She is shocked by evidences of the new morality, which includes casual sexual affairs. Once on a trip abroad, a man and a woman journalist, married but not to each other, drifted together in a relationship that they did not hide. Ethel was acutely embarrassed; she would go out of her way to avoid them and barely could bring herself to look at the offending individuals. (John Kennedy, on the other hand, was not only tolerant but interested. On campaign trips he would ask journalists: "How are you doing with the girls?")

Ethel never swears and cannot abide profanity now used so freely by many women and most men, including the Kennedy males. Bobby never swore in her presence if he could help it, though infrequently a word would slip out and earn a disapproving frown. Occasionally, she might use a perfectly filthy word or phrase she had overheard someplace, with no idea of its actual meaning. Her friends would double up with helpless laughter, leaving her wondering about their sanity, for they would never tell her.

Smutty stories turn her off completely; double-meaning wisecracks get a deadpan response—that is, if she catches the point, which isn't often. She is thoroughly shocked at the wave of nudity in films and on the stage and cannot understand how actors and actresses can bare their bodies in public.

Washington hostesses have been known to clean things up if Ethel is expected. The wife of a Johnson administration official once matched up dinner partners by distributing nuts of various sizes to the women and bolts to fit them to the men. Men went looking for their partners by trying to screw their bolts in the nuts held by the ladies. The quips engendered by the search turned the air blue. The hostess planned to use the same partner-finding device at a subsequent dinner party until she received an acceptance by Ethel and Bobby. She switched to more conventional place cards.

Doubtless Ethel's religious training at home and school was responsible for her high moral outlook, but equally important was the influence of her father. Her brother Rushton recalls that the elder Skakel, though not a religious man most of his life, adhered to the highest moral standards. "The most embarrassed he would ever be," Rushton says, "was when someone told an off-color story, especially if any one of us would hear, no matter how grown-up we were. He would absolutely die."

While she has become sincerely involved in social-justice causes, she still prefers "jolly, happy things" when it comes to entertainment. She once cornered the playwright Edward Albee after having seen *Who's Afraid of Virginia Woolf* and asked him why he wrote "all those depressing plays." She adored her friend Art Buchwald's satiric comedy, *Sheep on the Runway* and prefers shows like *My Fair Lady,* movies like *South Pacific,* everything by Walt Disney and novels with happy endings. Psychologists, parlor and accredited, can speculate that she has had enough of real tragedy in her life and wants no more in the world of illusion, but the fact is that Ethel has always believed that "laughter is better than tears."

This blithe-spirit facet of Ethel's character is endearing and very prominent. She has always been the comic, the fun-loving Rover, the mischief-maker of her own family and later of the Kennedy clan. She has spent hours, sometimes days, concocting the most elaborate stunts to play on people she likes and, on more than one occasion, those she does not.

◊ ◊ ◊

Ethel's humor has not always been good-natured. "She kids with a sharp needle," Frederick P. Dutton, Bobby's chief campaign manager in his bid for the nomination, once remarked. Thus: When Bobby was named United States Attorney General, he ordered F.B.I. Director J. Edgar Hoover to funnel more agents into the fight against crime and fewer into the hunt for Communists. Hoover resented being told what to do, even by a man who was technically his boss, and a deep freeze developed between the two.

One who rallied to Kennedy's side in the internal tug-of-war was William Parker, the police chief of Los Angeles, who also earned Hoover's wrath. Ethel, fuming at Hoover because he opposed Bobby, marched one day to the F.B.I. headquarters in the Department of Justice Building and deposited a terse "suggestion" in the Director's personal suggestion box. It read:

"Parker for F.B.I. Director—Ethel Kennedy."

As early as 1957, a prank Ethel helped engineer made waves all over the country. In August that year, her brother George and his wife Pat planned a large party at their Greenwich home in honor of Ethel and Bobby, then attracting national attention as chief counsel for the Senate Labor Rackets Committee.

Bobby's repeated and bitter clashes with labor leaders Dave Beck and his son, Dave Beck, Jr., were the talk of Washington. The senior Beck, president of the International Brotherhood of Teamsters, was being investigated on charges of embezzling union funds and subsequently went to jail. Bobby had worked up a deep personal dislike for all his witnesses, whom he later described as "sleek, often bilious and fat, or lean and cold and hard," an attitude plainly evident in his interrogation of the Becks. The antagonism was cordially returned.

Picture, then, the amazement of newsmen when they received an announcement from Greenwich that the Becks, father and son, would attend the party in honor of Bobby Kennedy! One of the guests got the idea to hoax the press. Ethel and her sister-in-law gleefully agreed it would be quite a thing, and recruited one of the couples present to help carry it off by posing as Mr. and Mrs. Beck for the photographers. The spurious "Mr. Beck" had somewhat the same rotund proportions of the original.

When a cameraman from the Stamford *Advocate* showed up, Ethel and Pat solemnly introduced the "Becks" and even helped him set up a group picture. They explained that the elder Beck had been there but had been called away on urgent business. The picture and story were duly published.

The Associated Press sent the story out across the country, raising eyebrows from coast to coast, especially since this astonishing quote was attributed to Dave, Sr.: "Although our policies differ, socially we get along famously."

But Dave, Sr., was in Seattle all this time, a fact quickly established by the AP bureau there, and Dave, Jr., wasn't even married! Editors then took a closer look at the photo and realized they had been hoaxed.

Confronted with the evidence, Ethel admitted: "It was crazy." A contrite Pat Skakel said: "All I can do is apologize." Disgusted, managing editor E. R. McCullough of the *Advocate,* in a blistering front-page notice, apologized to his readers and suggested: "If you have any thoughts on adult delinquency, I wish you'd drop me a note."

And in Washington, Robert Kennedy, who had not

been able to get away to attend, said: "Oh, Eth-ull!" It wasn't the first time he uttered this resigned sigh, nor would it be the last.

In September 1967, the liberal journalist Jack Newfield came to dinner at Hickory Hill. The moment he entered the house he faced a barrage of kidding about his long hair. Jack replied: "I'm not going to cut it until Johnson stops the bombing."

Ethel giggled and disappeared. Three minutes later she was back with a huge button, which she pinned on Jack's lapel. It read: "I won't cut it till they stop the bombing."

Ethel has a button-making machine with which she creates her own slogans. She lugged it along on stumping trips with Bobby during his campaign for the Presidential nomination in 1968 and used it often.

Once she stage-managed an elaborate gag that had the entire six-car campaign train rocking with glee but confused the residents of a tiny Colorado town. Campaign manager Dutton was born in Julesburg, Colorado (pop. 1,840), so when the train reached that portion of northeastern Colorado, Ethel had a stunt all prepared.

As soon as the train halted, Ethel and Bobby, trailed by newsmen and others aboard, jumped off and, wearing huge grins, clustered around the observation car with the gathering townsfolk. Each was sporting a huge "DUTTON BUTTON." Ethel shouted: "Dutton for President!" The local residents stared. Bobby then waved a hand-lettered sign: "Sock it to 'em, Freddie," a takeoff on the catch-phrase then aimed at Bobby himself. Other placards read: "Dutton's brother for Attorney General" and "Make Fred, not war."

Finally the balding, bespectacled Dutton emerged and delivered a "campaign" speech in Boston-accented tones and exaggerated R.F.K. mannerisms, concluding with Bobby's favorite peroration, adapted from George Bernard Shaw: "Some men see things as they are and say, 'Why?' I dream things that never were and say, 'Why not?'" In the audience Ethel bellowed: "Let's hear it for George Bernard Shaw!" The entourage howled its approval, trooped back aboard the train to resume the tour and left the astonished Julesburgers wondering what had possessed them all.

Parties, especially her own, have inspired Ethel to unique levels of comedic performance. One day General Maxwell Taylor, an old and dear friend, came to dinner at Hickory Hill, alighted from his car and was startled to see a parachutist dangling from a tree. Ethel had rigged up a life-sized dummy to make the general, who had chuted into Normandy on D-Day with his 101st Airborne Division, feel at home. When she gave a seventy-fifth birthday party for the veteran diplomat and statesman, Averell Harriman, she spent hours collecting a batch of pictures showing him with world-famous figures and putting outlandish captions on them. She also hand-printed a sign and put it on the front door for his arrival: "Ave for 72." Underneath, in smaller letters, she wrote: "Sorry, Bobby."

Once Ethel, pretending jealousy because a high administration official was chatting with another woman and not paying enough attention to her, picked up a candleholder, called his name and tossed it at him. She drew his attention, as well as a disgusted look from her sister-in-law Jacqueline, who watched the incident.

Still, the official got off better than the youthful member of a European royal family who had the front of his shirt sprayed with shaving cream from a pressurized can by a playful Ethel.

At a Saint Patrick's Day dinner party, Ethel wondered for days how to dress up for the affair with the proper touch of green. When her guests, men in dinner jackets, women in evening gowns, finally sat down to dinner they discovered that the color motif was carried through all the way to the centerpieces at each table, which contained the largest (and of course the greenest) live bullfrogs she could find.

At her birthday party one April, Ethel arranged the seating so that twenty-four women found themselves together at one table while she sat at another with all twenty-five men. A howl of laughing protest went up and the company was redistributed in more traditional boy-girl fashion.

Ethel's off-beat humor was reported in England, France and other foreign countries by their American correspondents. The *Daily Express* in London wrote that she was America's new "knacky baby," the British equivalent for a swinging chick. "Mrs. Kennedy earned her title," the *Express* said, "when she startled Washington party-goers with a stunning quick switch. She turned up at a party carrying a small suitcase. Then she disappeared into a bedroom and emerged in a rhinestone-studded black shift which was way, way above the knees. Ethel explained: 'Everybody was talking about Vietnam and I thought we all needed a change of pace!'"

Celebrities have never awed Ethel, though she may have disconcerted a few. When Robert Frost came to dinner, she distributed paper and pencils to her guests and announced a poetry-writing contest. Another time she drove out to pick up Marian Anderson, who was to perform at a Washington concert, and sang to the famous contralto all the way home. William Manchester, who tells the story, observes that the Kennedys "will compete

with anybody in any field" and that "some of the in-laws
(*i.e.,* Ethel) have just as much moxie (*i.e., chutzpah*) as
the charter members."

During John Kennedy's administration, Ethel's zani-
ness emerged in its most acute form around swimming
pools. The Kennedys have always been impulsive pushers-
into-the-water. In 1963, during a trip to Latin America
undertaken at the President's behest, Bobby and Ethel
were spending an afternoon by the poolside in the back of
the United States Embassy in Buenos Aires. When Andrew A. Glass, a journalist accompanying the couple,
walked by, Ethel rose from her chair with a grin and
shoved. Glass, in bathing trunks but wearing shoes and a
street shirt, toppled into the water.

The Kennedy mania for pool-dunking got out of hand
in June 1962, when Ethel and Bobby gave a big party at
Hickory Hill to celebrate their twelfth wedding anniver-
sary. Some three-hundred important personages were in-
vited, including Lyndon Johnson, the Vice-President; two
Supreme Court Justices (Arthur Goldberg and Byron R.
(Whizzer) White; a clutch of Cabinet members (Stewart
Udall of Interior, Orville Freeman of Agriculture and
Lawrence O'Brien, Postmaster General); the British
Ambassador, David Ormsby-Gore and Lady Ormsby-
Gore; astronaut John Glenn and his wife; and historian
Arthur Schlesinger, Jr., then a Presidential assistant.

Ethel had flung some planks across the forty by sixteen-
foot pool and placed a table and chairs on the improvised
bridge for herself, Glenn and Justice White. Glenn val-
iantly took his place but the Justice did not. Ethel, lovely
in a bright red evening gown, walked out and sat at the
table, opposite Glenn, chatting gaily. Suddenly the bridge
lurched, tumbling Ethel into the water. Seconds later,
Schlesinger and Mrs. Spencer Davis, a close friend of
Ethel's, were in the pool too.

News stories said the eminent historian was pushed, but in his account of Kennedy's White House years, *A Thousand Days,* Schlesinger explained that he and his partner walked out on the uncertain bridge, which shook beneath them. "To our horror," he wrote, "we saw Ethel's chair slide on the wet boards to the edge and then into the water. After a moment, I plunged in after her. We changed our clothes, and the party went pleasantly on." *

Schlesinger was hardly the first celebrity to dip, fully clad, into Kennedy waters. Bobby heaved in his brother's press secretary, clothes, cigar and all. White-maned, dignified Senator Kenneth Keating of New York was also shoved in by Bobby (before the two squared off in their Senatorial election). Small wonder Senator Barry Goldwater observed that the Kennedys' invitations to formal dinners ought to read: "Black tie and snorkel."

Shortly after the much-publicized Schlesinger incident, these water sports at Hickory Hill ended abruptly and mysteriously. Nobody of any distinction was pushed in after that.

It is reported that President Kennedy himself, realizing that the high-spirited play was giving the country a soggy image of the New Frontier, ordered everybody out of the pool.

ᕲ   ᕲ   ᕲ

She is Supergirl.

Her energy and stamina have been almost limitless since childhood. "By any normal standard of human en-

---

*Did he fall or was he pushed? Years later, Lee Udall, wife of President Kennedy's Secretary of the Interior, confessed it was she who shoved the historian. "I was dancing by and he was standing there holding forth and looking so Arthurish," she said (according to *Time* magazine). "I just stuck out my arm and pushed him in and danced away. He never knew."

durance," one awed publication remarked, "Ethel Kennedy should be a wreck." She could perform at least a dozen athletic feats during the day, including bouncing on a trampoline, running races on a beach, swimming, tennis, water-skiing, touch football and baseball, and still be ready for dancing at night. Friends have sometimes come upon her as she leaned wearily against a door frame or wall in a hotel room after a day of rigorous campaigning, and once—just once—a friend heard her remark, "I'm pooped." But she has always bounced back, ready for more action.

In July 1967, Ethel and Bobby, their seven older children and a party of friends took a trip down the Colorado River to the bottom of the Grand Canyon. The party included John Glenn and his wife, Art Buchwald and his wife, singer Andy Williams, author George Plimpton, and James Whittaker, the conqueror of Mount Everest, and his wife. One can emerge from the mile-deep gorge by one of three modes of transportation: aboard a helicopter, on the back of a sure-footed mule or on foot.

The Kaibab Trail from the canyon's floor to the South Rim runs 7 miles. Most in the party opted for the helicopters or the mules—Ethel and Bobby chose to hike. Despite the intense 115-degree heat, they made it side-by-side in 5 hours. (A well-known guidebook has this to say about hiking into and out of the canyon: "Not recommended except for those in sound physical condition because the heat and the 4,500-foot climb back are exhausting.")

Ethel has surprised even nationally known athletes by her ability to perform. Whizzer White, once an All-America football star, stood between Ethel and a touchdown at Hyannis Port. He rushed in for the tag and met empty air. Ethel had darted past him in a dazzling display of footwork. "Attaboy, Ethel!" called out Bobby, who had thrown her the scoring pass. She is what physical-education experts call a natural athlete because she possesses all the essential characteristics: superior muscular co-ordination, stamina, intelligence, resourcefulness and courage.

Ethel must win at games. Once at Hyannis Port, when Andy Williams and Art Buchwald defeated Ethel and Jim Whittaker in a tennis match, she dropped to the court and, in a spasm of fury, struck her head a number of times on the clay. William J. vanden Heuvel, once a special assistant to Robert Kennedy in Washington and a close friend of the family for years, documents Ethel's obsessive drive to win with this story:

"It was a particularly hot and sultry day and everyone was exhausted. I was playing the net position and was walking to the net from the baseline. Ethel came running over to me and whispered—and she was in dead earnest —'Bill, what you've got to do is *run* to your position between games. The other side is tired and if they see you run they'll be demoralized.'"

Like all the Kennedys, Ethel won't waste much sympathy on a player who is injured during a sporting event. "Bad luck" is about the most anyone can expect by way of commiseration for a sprain, gash or even a broken bone. Nor would she accept any but a serious ailment as an excuse for ducking out of an encounter.

Once Andy Williams showed up on the tennis court for a scheduled game, his big toe broken and in a cast. Williams, limping, had reason to expect he would be excused but Ethel told him: "Don't look for any sympathy from us. You're not going to let a thing like a little old broken toe stop you—we need a fourth." Williams studied the other competitors: Senator Ted Kennedy was wearing the brace for his back, broken in an air crash; James Whittaker's leg was still bandaged following vein surgery and Ethel herself was seven months pregnant. He played.

This disregard for injury, her own or anyone else's, was present in her childhood. Once at a horse show her friend Dickie Mann rode Ethel's mount Gurmada but, because of her unfamiliarity with him, was having a difficult time. The horse reared and bucked and almost threw Dickie. The spectators gasped in fright but, busy as she was with the reins, Dickie could hear Ethel screaming with laughter.

If Ethel does not spare others, neither does she coddle herself. She has played with painfully pulled muscles, shrugged off jarring, skin-shredding tumbles and collisions, and once was smashed hard in the mouth by a streaking tennis ball. She continued to play with throbbing, bleeding and rapidly swelling lips. Her sister-in-law Jacqueline once hurt her ankle in a touch football match at Hyannis Port and never played thereafter, observing that "just watching them wore me out." It was a withdrawal from combat that Ethel has regarded with contempt in others. "You don't have to be good," journalist Jack Newfield says, "but you do have to try; otherwise you don't rate very high with Ethel."

Even Ethel's parties have always been action-packed and could be rough on the physically unfit. A Johnson administration official once read that after a dinner she gave at Hickory Hill, Ethel announced to her guests: "Let's have a race!" She flew out of the dining room and ran swiftly and gracefully around the vast lawn, followed by a long line of charging men and women. "Thank God I'm not a Kennedy buddy," he said. "I've already had one coronary. I'm not looking for another." He paused, then added in an astonished tone: "Imagine. *Running* after a big dinner! And those dopes really followed."

Once she was hostess at a three-day party in support of a telethon collecting funds for a children's organization. The guests began partying Friday night, paused for a few hours sleep, attended a rehearsal the next morning, went to Ted Kennedy's place for lunch, drove back to Ethel's for touch football, stayed for dinner and more fun, watched the five and one-half hour show, went to Ambassador Averell Harriman's for midnight snacking, slept a few hours, then finished up at Sunday brunch at Hickory Hill. Ethel celebrated her seventeenth wedding anniversary with a combination party and christening for Douglas Harriman that began at dinner time and concluded after the noon ceremony at church.

Nobody can count the teeth that have been loosened, the bones snapped, ligaments torn and muscles painfully stretched as people tried to keep up with Ethel. Once she persuaded her friend Pat Newcomb, a motion-picture publicist, to ride a horse. Pat had never been astride one before—and hasn't been since. She fell and broke several ribs. Another time Ethel, Bobby and a number of other fitness buffs threw a physical-fitness party at the Chevy Chase Club ice-skating rink. Early on, Edward O. Guthman, director of public information at the Department of Justice, upended, broke his arm and was carried away to a hospital by ambulance. Betty Beale, a society-news commentator, dead-panned in her account of the festivities: "Otherwise the affair went off without a hitch."

Only once in anyone's memory has Ethel Kennedy screamed out in pain and fear. In 1967, her son Bobby, Jr., an avid zoologist, acquired a coati mundi, a badger-sized, bushy-tailed native of South America that can be trained as a pet but sometimes forgets its training. Ethel was showing some visitors her son's basement zoo. The coati mundi was wandering at large. As Ethel turned to describe Bobby's reptile house, the animal suddenly leaped at her, digging its sharp claws into her legs.

Ethel fell face down on the floor. "Get him off me, get him off me!" she screamed. "He's biting me!" Vainly she tried to shake him off but the animal clung and moved to her back, clawing and biting. "He's biting me, oh God, he's biting me!" Ethel screamed again. Dick Schaap, author and former newspaperman, leaped forward, picked Ethel up from the floor and sat her atop a cabinet. The animal's grasp loosened. Schaap kicked the animal away. The others drove the coati mundi into another room and closed the dooor.

Ethel, scratched and bleeding, trembled violently, her chest heaving with each breath. She seemed on the verge of hysteria. In a few moments, as Schaap and the other visitors comforted her, she regained her composure. She smiled wanly and, at her visitors' urging, went to a doctor to have her wounds dressed. Later she made light of the incident in a charming "Dear Dick" letter in which she said it wasn't every day that one is rescued from a mad coati mundi by a knight in a gray flannel suit—or was it blue serge? She expressed her grateful and happy thanks to Dick for removing her right thigh from the creature's fangs, and concluded with "warm wishes and scars."

"She was shook up, no question about it," Schaap recalls, "but her recovery was masterful. In a few minutes the sudden, terrifying incident was nearly forgotten."

ᒉ ᒉ ᒉ

If Ethel won't hand out sympathy to anyone bruised in athletic competition, she will extend the fullest measure of support to those caught up in life's tragedies. She would write long letters to people, some of whom she hardly knew, expressing her sadness at the loss of loved ones and assuring them she would pray for their souls. Always her message would be the same: Those who are bereaved must look to God for help. And always there would be something personal for the individual. When the three-year-old daughter of Ray O'Connell, a friend, was killed in an automobile accident in Mount Kisco, New York, Ethel recalled that O'Connell's late father "must have been lonely in Heaven and now she is with him."

Cruelty and injustice to humans and animals triggers a visceral response. Nothing in her entire life illustrates this more aptly than the time she startled the nation by "stealing" a horse.

On a bright fall day in 1963, Ethel and one of her children were riding their mounts near Hickory Hill when they saw an emaciated horse standing forlornly in a chicken coop. "It was a bag of bones," she said, "the saddest sight I've ever seen." She rode home and instructed her groom, Richard Mayberry, to bring it to Hickory Hill for care. Mayberry did, but despite a heroic five-day effort, the horse succumbed.

Two years later, Nicholas N. Zemo, owner of the horse, sued Mrs. Kennedy for thirty-thousand dollars in damages, alleging she took a valuable animal "without any process of law." In January 1967, during a two-day trial in the Fairfax County Courthouse, Mrs. Kennedy, in a blue maternity dress (she was expecting her tenth), told the jury of seven men that the horse was in "terrible" shape and that she had refused to give it back because the owner was "mistreating" it. Zemo, a sixty-year-old horse breeder, claimed the horse was recovering from an injury and had refused to eat.

After deliberating two hours and twenty-five minutes, the jury acquitted Ethel. She darted to a phone behind the courthouse and called her husband in his Senate office. Relieved, he joked with her: "You're not going to be let out again without your keeper."

Would she ever again "steal" a horse or other mistreated animal, knowing a lawsuit would certainly follow? The question was put separately to Ethel and Bobby:

Said Ethel: "I don't think I could live with myself if I didn't."

Said Bobby: "If you can figure out what Ethel's going to do next, be sure to send me the formula."

One day Ethel, in rare philosophic mood, suddenly turned to Mrs. Scott Carpenter, former wife of the astronaut, and said: "We're placed on earth and somehow given a sense of responsibility to give life and love and to help others." The core of the woman is in those words. It is the credo by which she has guided her life.

EIGHT

Hickory Hill

❦ ❦

Next to the White House, an estate called Hickory Hill
was probably the best known place in America during the
years of the New Frontier. This was where Bobby and
Ethel went to live. But knowing now what we do about
Ethel and her origins, we can see what most persons who
looked with awe and puzzlement at this unique dwelling
and its bizarre goings-on could not: that Hickory Hill
was actually the house on Simmons Lane updated.

A new cast of characters, human and animal, swirled
around Ethel but otherwise there was an almost eeric
sameness. There was the same pandemonium, the same
sense of domestic anarchy, the same unscheduled crises,
the same go-go athleticism, all centering around a lux-
uriously furnished, three-story white-brick building.

Leland Hayward, the theatrical producer, once said
that Hickory Hill in full cry "would make the damnedest
musical comedy the Bradway stage has ever seen." Major
national issues were discussed on chaise longues at the

85

poolside while a jukebox blared and children bounded into the water. United States marshals, back from Oxford, Mississippi, reported on the civil-rights confrontations to a boss in bathing trunks. The President of the United States would slam balls around the tennis court (in active service in all but the foulest weather), then dive into the pool and come up next to a child he never saw before.

At one time or another, most of the glittering personages of the New Frontier and their ladies came to Hickory Hill for lunch or dinner and ended up charging around the rolling lawns yelling for somebody to throw them the ball. It would not be uncommon for a Cabinet member to find himself engrossed in conversation with boxer José Torres, or writer Jimmy Breslin to swap yarns with a clutch of Senators or the wife of a Supreme Court Justice to listen wide-eyed to Carol Channing's stories of show business.

On most nice afternoons, Kennedys and non-Kennedys, would be everywhere, splashing in the two swimming pools (one was for learners) at the back of the house beyond the hedges, leaping on the trampoline, riding in the paddock with its neat little white jumps, climbing into a tree house, swinging from ropes tied to huge tree branches, riding across the lawn in an electric cart or leaping from the top of a shed into the bushes. Ethel, lean and lithe in a bathing suit or shorts, would be teaching a child to swim, refereeing a game or watching and applauding the action. Bobby would take time to coach a youngster who was having trouble with a racing dive, show another how to swivel-hip past an opponent in touch football or rub the head of a third who had taken a nasty fall. Jackie Kennedy once captured the frantic scene at Hickory Hill in water colors and presented it to Ethel, who hung it in her front hall, next to the President's gift to Ethel—a map of the United States with the sites of the campaign speeches she made in his behalf marked in red.

Ethel would have liked to run a neater, tighter ship, but it simply wasn't her way. She would return from visits to Jackie Kennedy's Georgetown House filled with genuine admiration for her sister-in-law. "Jackie's house was such heaven and so supremely well-organized, I always get depressed getting back to this madhouse," she once said.

But the depression generally lasted only until she got caught up in the next crisis. Like her mother, Ethel would never know how many guests would come, and when. Bobby would invite people on the spur of the moment, sometimes forgetting to tell her. He might walk in for lunch with a labor leader whom he literally bumped into in the corridor of the Senate Office Building as the latter emerged from the men's washroom, with a Congressman, a civil-rights leader, a law-school pal or a reporter. Once Bobby came home with a dozen hungry people and was surprised to find the tables weren't set. "Eth-ull!" he yelled from the foot of the stairs. "Are you up there?" She was, but she wasn't expecting guests. Bobby had forgotten to tell her he was bringing company. Worse, she had given the kitchen staff the day off. Turning to Pat Newcomb, who was visiting, Ethel asked:

"Can you cook?"

"No," Pat replied.

"Neither can I," said Ethel. "Let's get lunch."

Between them, they managed to whip up some passable hamburgers.

⊘ ⊘ ⊘

The Kennedy home, at 1147 Chain Bridge Road, is set down on six and one-half acres of rolling pasture lands not far from the Potomac River in McLean, Virginia, a tiny town of less than two-thousand population, westward of Washington. Cross the Key Bridge to the George Washington Memorial Parkway, turn off after five miles on Route 123, drive another few miles and you are at Hickory Hill. Ethel can make the drive in half an hour; Bobby, who would zip along the parkway at eighty miles an hour, did it faster.

It is a fine old Georgian house, architecturally purer than Ethel's girlhood home and less sprawling. History is soaked into its very beams, for it is here that George Brinton McClellan, the moustached and goateed general in charge of the Union Army during the early years of the Civil War made his headquarters.

In the mid-1950s, Senator and Mrs. John Kennedy purchased the house, then 130 years old, for $125,000, planning to make it a permanent home base for the family they hoped to raise. By the spring of 1956, Jackie was pregnant and was supervising the preparation of an elaborate nursery at Hickory Hill. John, busy with plans for the forthcoming Democratic convention, insisted on being kept up to date on all arrangements. When the convention was opened in August, Senator Kennedy's name was high on the list of Vice-Presidential hopefuls; however, although he came within a few votes of success, the nomination went to Estes Kefauver. Jackie watched as her husband rose and asked the convention to make the nomination of Kefauver unanimous.

By this time, Kennedy hadn't slept for three days. He and Jackie had agreed that after the conclave ended, he would fly to his father's house on the Cote d'Azur in France for a brief rest, and she would go to the home of her stepfather and mother, Mr. and Mrs. Hugh D. Auchincloss, in fashionable Newport. They kissed goodbye and separated.

On August 23, Jackie Kennedy was rushed to Newport Hospital, where her baby was born dead following an emergency operation and where Jackie herself, weakened by the exertions at the convention, almost lost her own life. The news was telephoned to her husband at his father's home in Val-sur-Mer on the French Riviera, but he was on a yacht in the Mediterranean and did not learn of the loss of his baby and his wife's serious illness until he docked several days later. He flew at once to Jackie's side.

When she recovered, Jackie returned to Hickory Hill with the Senator but everything had changed. The beautiful nursery, built and completely outfitted at considerable cost, stood empty. The house, despite its size and lovely furnishings selected so carefully by Jackie, now appeared oppressive and depressing; the grounds, with the majestic, centuries-old hickory trees, seemed too big and too lonely. John Kennedy and Jackie, in their profound grief at the loss of their second baby—Jackie had suffered a miscarriage the year before—could no longer bear to live there. They found a furnished house in Georgetown and moved away. The baby now lies beneath a flat slate stone alongside her father in Arlington National Cemetery; on the other side, a similar stone marks the grave of Patrick Bouvier Kennedy, who died of a respiratory illness in 1963, only thirty-nine hours after he was born.

By this time Ethel and Bobby had become cramped for space in their little home on S Street. Three more children had come along—Robert Francis, Jr., on January 17, 1954; David Anthony, June 15, 1955, and Mary Courtney, September 9, 1956. Bobby, now chief counsel for the Senate Rackets Committee and in charge of a staff of 55, was bringing home aides for conferences and tripping—literally—over babies. Hickory Hill was perfect for the growing family, and in 1957 Ethel and Bobby bought the estate from his brother for the original purchase price, $125,000.

If Hickory Hill was a sometime-zoo, it was also the site of a short-lived experiment in the higher education of New Frontiersmen and women, jocularly called Hickory Hill University. Late in 1961, the Kennedys began a series of monthly seminars for about twenty students, including a number of Bobby's Cabinet colleagues and their wives. The original faculty consisted of Arthur M. Schlesinger, the Harvard historian who was serving as a Presidential aide, and Walt W. Rostow, at the time the President's adviser on national security and former professor of economics at the Massachusetts Institute of Technology.

The direct inspiration came from a seminar that Ethel and Bobby attended at the Institute for Humanistic Studies while they were on a skiing vacation at Aspen, Colorado, although as we have seen earlier, Ethel's parents had conducted similar sessions at their Greenwich home many years before. Schlesinger launched the "university" with a lecture on the broad sweep of history, and Rostow followed with a discussion of how democratic institutions might be affected by economic developments.

Ethel was one of the most enthusiastic students and according to Professor Schlesinger, an "undaunted questioner." Schlesinger recalled that one evening Ethel stood up to do intellectual battle with the eminent British philosopher A. J. Ayer, then teaching at the University of London. Ayer, who had expressed impatience in his lecture with all forms of abstract propositions, was challenged by Ethel to explain his rejection of metaphysics. When Ayer asked Ethel to define the term, she hesitated and Bobby, not at all sure how she would fare in an encounter with the redoubtable thinker, called out a warning from his seat: "Now Ethel . . ." But Ethel went in swinging. "I mean whether conceptions like truth and virtue and beauty have any meaning." Ayer responded and a lively debate ensued.

"The seminars," writes Schlesinger, "summed up a good deal of the humane and questing spirit of the New Frontier." Even though two of the sessions were held at the White House, President Kennedy never took Hickory Hill U seriously, a top official of the administration reports. The President told intimates that while he was all for intellectualism, he felt Bobby's strength lay in his hard common sense, incisive thinking and down-to-earth practicality, not abstract reasoning.

As the Kennedy family expanded, so did the house. Ethel and Bobby added a large living room and several bedrooms and built a barn for the horses and a bathhouse the size of a school classroom that also doubles as a movie theater. In the basement, Ethel put in a large freezer room where vast quantities of food could be stored for family and guests. By 1970, the house had nineteen rooms.

Women journalists were always trying to worm out of Ethel the number of people she employed but she wouldn't tell. "We have enough," she would say vaguely. Probably there were between ten to fifteen persons: two cooks, a governess, a laundress, a nurse for the babies, a yard man when they could find one, two or three maids, the same number of secretaries, a groom-trainer for the animals. In the summer months, the Kennedys would engage a young man to teach the younger children to swim and to improve the aquatic abilities of the older ones. Ruby Reynolds, the chief cook who joined the household in 1955, would do all the shopping and daily meal planning. Ethel would make up the menus only on special occasions.

The animal population was large and varied, though

never static and often unfettered. At one time or another there were quantities of ducks, geese, cockatoos, lizards, ponies, horses, a donkey, rabbits, hamsters, guinea pigs, a heifer, homing pigeons and a huge turtle that ate lettuce and tomato sandwiches.

Once Bobby, Jr., received a falcon as a gift to take his mind off a pet owl, recently deceased. A sea lion named Sandy, weighing nearly sixty pounds, lived at Hickory Hill for a while but he kept escaping from his enclosure near the pool and, for some reason, chasing the female guests. At one time he waddled all the way to a shopping center about a mile away before he was recaptured. "He scared most grownups silly," Ethel said, "so we finally had to send him to the Washington zoo."

Ethel once went to the airport to pick up a shipment of iguanas. Somehow they broke loose and she, Pat Newcomb and airport personnel began what surely must have been Washington's first iguana roundup. Another time a few of the young Kennedys blackened some white mice with coal dust and hawked them to their unsuspecting cousins as a rare rodent species.

In December, 1964, Ethel planned to put in a bid for some of the New York City Park Department's surplus zoo animals, which were being sold at auction. Among the items for sale were a hippopotamus, a lion cub, a female yak and baby elk. However, somebody dissuaded her from going through with the bids. Two years earlier, however, nobody could stop her from ordering three miniature horses, each about a yard high, from Argentina as surprise birthday presents for her children.

One day Ethel went down to the basement where some of the caged pets were kept and found her son David feeding fifteen dogs and eight cats. She nodded to him, got what she wanted, then did a comical double-take.

"Those aren't ours,!" she burst out. "No," David admitted. "Where did you get them?" David replied that he had found the strays "around somewhere" over a period of weeks and had taken them home.

Probably the two most famous nonhuman residents of Hickory Hill were Freckles, a shaggy black and white spaniel, and Brumus, an enormous black Newfoundland. Freckles accompanied Bobby on his final campaign and was such a favorite that Senator Eugene McCarthy was moved to remark during the California primary: "I think I can campaign against both the Senator from New York and his dog." The entire household was shaken in 1970 when Freckles was lost. Matthew Maxwell Taylor Kennedy, the ninth child, who was then five, put an ad in the local paper offering a reward. Freckles wandered home after a couple of days and everyone breathed easier.

Brumus too got into the news and even more prominently. In the summer of 1962 Bobby, then the Attorney General, took the huge dog with him to work at the Department of Justice, explaining: "He usually stays at home with the children. But the children are away on vacation and he gets very lonely. So I bring him down here and get pretty girls to take him for walks."

The Newfoundland's loneliness may have been assuaged but his master got into trouble. Arthur Krock (among others) pointed out that despite his human compassion, Kennedy was violating Section 201, Chapter 8, Title II of the Rules and Regulations for Public Buildings, which specifically forbade dogs and other animals, except Seeing-Eye dogs, from being brought upon government property except for official purposes. Brumus, said Mr. Krock, should either "be sentenced to home arrest or Section 201 repealed in fairness to other dogs"; otherwise Kennedy and the administration were inviting the loss of the dog-lover vote in the country. After that, Brumus remained at home.

Kennedy critics would pick on stolid, slobbering, not overly bright Brumus to sustain charges that Bobby and Ethel were arrogant and selfish and refused to respect the feelings of others. Thus Ralph de Toledano would write: "Brumus . . . is treated better than important guests. During meals, he is given the run of the dining room. With no admonition from Bobby, Brumus will demand food of the guests and, if this is ignored, will simply help himself, reaching into a plate with his paw for whatever it is that attracts his whim and appetite." A visitor told de Toledano: "That damned dog was all over me, and Bobby seemed to think that my objections were pretty stuffy if not downright unmannerly. Brumus got most of my meal and left paw marks all over my clothes."

ᗡ ᗡ ᗡ

What was it like to be entertained by Ethel Kennedy and her husband at Hickory Hill during those glittering years? Let's go to a dinner there and, at the same time, we can take the opportunity, as all first-time guests will, to get a close-up view of the famous home, its furnishings and its occupants, and to listen to the conversation.

We will see Hickory Hill on a March evening in 1968 through the eyes of Faith and Johannes Laursen, two amiable suburbanites who, they admit, live in a much less pretentious though comfortable home in Rockville Centre, Long Island, New York. Mr. Laursen is the publisher of two thriving weekly newspapers in Long Island, *Merrick Life* and *Bellmore Life,* and his wife is their editor. The papers are members of the New York Press Association, a delegation of which was attending a workshop session of the National Newspaper Association in Washington that year. The editors and publishers, some thirty persons, had been invited to dinner by Ethel and Bobby.

The political experts have called this a "routine Kennedy dinner" but it turned out to be a moment of history. Bobby Kennedy was faced with one of the most important decisions of his life—and he was to make it this very evening.

Ever since the beginning of the year, Bobby and his political advisers had been agonizing over the question: Should he challenge Lyndon Johnson for the Democratic nomination that summer? Some of the old Kennedy organization leaders, called to duty, had been sounding out political leaders all across the country. Reactions had been mixed. As one Kennedy man put it: "It was modified rapture." Kennedy himself checked off all the negatives: If he entered the race, he would almost certainly split the Democratic Party, perhaps enough to insure a Republican victory. To win, he had to be a candidate in every primary and take each one, and the chances of this kind of sweep were not good. And what about his political future if he lost? He recalled that no incumbent President had lost a bid for renomination since James G. Blaine toppled Chester A. Arthur in 1884.

While Bobby hesitated, Senator Eugene McCarthy, dreaming the impossible dream, had gone into the arena, his candidacy supported by a remarkable display of student power. Being "clean with Gene," five-thousand college students roamed across New Hampshire in the primary campaign, ringing doorbells, arguing McCarthy's cause.

Two days earlier, on March 12, they and McCarthy had pulled off a remarkable upset. Although the pollsters had given him between 10-to-20 per cent of the vote, he won 42.2 per cent to Johnson's 49.4 per cent. With another 5,511 write-in votes from the Republican side, McCarthy received a total of 28,791 votes to Johnson's

29,021. The slim Johnson lead was a stunning defeat for the President.

Immediately a torrent of messages descended on Hickory Hill and the Senator's office, urging him to run. He was besieged by the press, asking if he would. The day before this dinner party, he and Ethel had spent the evening at the Fifth Avenue apartment of Stephen Smith, the Kennedy campaign strategist, going over the question. Returning to Washington, he told a newsman at National Airport that he was "reassessing the possibility of whether I will run against Johnson."

While the country awaited the result of this reappraisal, he and Ethel went home and got ready for company.

Ethel had spent most of that Thursday in Washington, returning home after six. There hadn't been time to get to the beauty parlor and so, as she had done many times before, her good friend Rene Carpenter, former wife of astronaut Scott Carpenter, combed and set her hair. Ethel put on a white minidress of tiered lace, with a high neck, long sleeves and pink sash, slipped into pink shoes, and was ready by half-past seven.

The day had been pleasant enough but toward evening a chill had come into the air as a reminder that winter was not quite ready to yield to spring. The Laursens left their Washington hotel at 7:30 and, shortly before 8:00, drove in a rented car into the paved, floodlit driveway at Hickory Hill.

Bobby, in a dark business suit, was standing inside the opened, bright-red door, surrounded by dogs, children and incoming guests.

> *Johannes Laursen:* There was considerable confusion as we came in. All that yakking and barking. It was pretty hard to say hello because we

had to step over a dog or two and weave our way around them.

Faith Laursen: Mrs. Kennedy came over to greet us. She looked like a pretty little girl in her minidress. I remember thinking she was perfectly in fashion, though not startlingly so. Rene Carpenter was with her, in a striking gown with diagonal ribbon and bow just below the waistline and just above her skirt hem, as mini as Ethel's. With her hair piled on top of her head she looked like a model.

Hats and wraps were stored in a hall closet, which also contained an assortment of athletic equipment and a quantity of shoes, bathing suits and other gear left behind by guests, each bearing a tag with its owner's name. Beyond the center hall, the Laursens could see the broad staircase curving toward the upstairs rooms, with potted pink and white azaleas at the side of each step.

In the foyer, a pretty young girl, a list in her hand, was unobtrusively checking off the names of the arrivals as they entered. She was looking for party crashers, not uncommon at Hickory Hill. Uninvited persons might be asked to leave.

The Laursens were ushered past a small, white-shuttered sitting room to the left of the entrance hall, decorated in pinks and yellows and with a deep, lime-green, diamond-patterned carpet. Beyond was the large living room, which the Kennedys had added in 1963, where two white-coated waiters were serving pre-dinner drinks and canapés from silver trays. Two matching, pale-yellow sofas faced each other at right angles to the huge fireplace, in front of which lay an Aubusson carpet, hand-made in France and worth a small fortune. A green silk sofa that once graced one of the palaces of Francis

Joseph, Emperor of Austria and King of Hungary, stood in one corner; around the rest of the room were rare French period pieces. On the walls hung paintings in the style of the French impressionists. Through a window Faith Laursen caught a glimpse of a fountain playing on a white marble statue.

It was a beautiful home but, looking closely, one could see spots on some of the carpets, nicks on some of the furniture legs, marks and scrapes on parts of the wallpaper. This house, like the other on Simmons Lane, was not only lived in but bounced in and romped in by the human and animal members of the family.

At the reception, the conversation centered around the subject uppermost in Washington and most of the country that week: Would Bobby run? Each clump of guests in the living room had a go at the question. As Mr. Laursen, drink in hand, joined a group in the center of the room, Rene Carpenter was saying heatedly: "He's got to run! We can't stand another four years of Lyndon Johnson." One by one, she began checking off the reasons: Johnson's insistence that the war in Vietnam be settled on America's terms, his alienation of youth, which has polarized the nation, the dread prospect that Richard Nixon might be Republican standard bearer that fall and, heaven forbid, be elected. . . .

Robert Kennedy strolled over and listened. When Mrs. Carpenter stopped for breath, Mr. Laursen asked Kennedy why he was considering making the race. Bobby grinned as he replied: "For many of the reasons Mrs. Carpenter has given."

Kathleen, then nearly seventeen, had a date that night; she came in with her escort, a handsome youth in white slacks, introduced him, chatted a moment and left.

An aide whispered to Kennedy, who excused himself and picked up a telephone in the foyer. It was already the third call in an hour; there were to be at least a half-dozen more that night. Johannes Laursen found himself thinking as he watched Kennedy leave: "All these crucial decisions are being made this evening. A man's entire political career may be hanging in the balance. Why didn't the Kennedys call this whole thing off, saying they have more important things to do tonight instead of entertaining you folks?"

At five minutes before nine, the guests were summoned to dinner. Three tables, each seating twelve, had been set up at the far end of the living room. Ethel Kennedy said grace and, when she had concluded, flashed a pixy grin and murmured: "And may the best man win." Bobby barely restrained a smile.

Oyster soup was served at the tables, then the guests went to a buffet in the dining room for roast beef, roast potatoes, a puréed carrot casserole, scalloped onions, mushroom gravy and hot rolls. Dessert and coffee were served—a chocolate roll for the guests and a huge plateful of ice cream with chocolate sauce for Bobby. Each male guest got a cigar from a gold tray and a book of matches, yellow, with "Hickory Hill" engraved on the cover.

Faith Laursen drew as dinner partners mountaineer James Whittaker and Walter W. Grunfeld, president of the New York Press Association and publisher of the Marathon, New York, *Independent*. Ethel Kennedy was at Grunfeld's right. Whittaker drew howls with his recollections of Bobby's famous climb up Mount Kennedy in the Canadian Rockies just three years before when he and Barry Prather, with Bobby tied between them, hoisted the amateurish but gutsy climber up the rugged rocks to place a copy of John F. Kennedy's Inaugural Address and other mementos atop the peak named for his brother. No one had ever scaled the mountain before; Kennedy had wanted to be the first. Some recalled Rose Kennedy's warning to her son: "Don't slip, dear," and Ethel's own observation that Bobby made the climb "to take his mind off the fact that he's not an astronaut."

At Bobby's table, the talk skipped from drugs to politics. Jack Newfield, the liberal young journalist from New York City's *Village Voice,* argued vigorously for legalization of marijuana and shocked the older guests by candidly admitting he smoked it himself with some frequency. Bobby, overhearing, scribbled a note to Newfield asking that he talk about something else lest he cost him the election before it starts. Bobby signed the note Timothy Leary (the former Harvard psychology instructor well-known for his advocacy of LSD and marijuana). Newfield got off a howler when he was asked if Percy Sutton, the Negro Borough President of Manhattan, had a chance of defeating incumbent Jacob K. Javits for the Senate that fall. "Not unless the Jews riot all summer," Newfield replied.

Faith was seated back to back with Bobby Kennedy, and in between sprawled Brumus. She was unaware of the big dog's presence until she dropped her hand on his hairy coat, drawing it back with a cry of surprise. Whittaker remarked that something similar had happened to him once on a camping trip. In the middle of the night he had reached out in his sleep and grabbed a fistful of thick hair. A much annoyed Bobby Kennedy lifted his head from his sleeping bag and asked what in hell he thought he was doing.

Three times during the dinner, Bobby was called to the phone, extricating himself with the utmost difficulty because Brumus had practically locked him in his seat.

Mr. Grunfeld excused himself and left the room. On his way back, he was waylaid at the foot of the stairs by three young Kennedys, two little girls and a boy, each in night clothes. The boy had a huge holster strapped to his waist and a gleaming weapon in his hand, which he pointed at the smiling Mr. Grunfeld. Wordlessly the boy fired, and Mr. Grunfeld received a stream of water squarely in his smile. He mopped his face and shirtfront with a handkerchief and returned to the dining room, unsmiling. A moment later the gunman and his two sisters came in to kiss their parents goodnight.

After dinner the men returned to the living room while Ethel took the women upstairs. The first room to the right near the head of the stairs, Ethel explained, was her son Bobby's, unoccupied at the time.

Faith: Mrs. Kennedy told us Bobby, Jr., had gone off to boarding school. "One evening," she said, "he announced he wanted to go away to school to get away from this confusing family. So he went. We get him back on weekends, though." [Bobby went to Georgetown Prep, a five-day boarding school in Washington.] On the walls and even the ceiling of his smallish room, Bobby had pasted huge, poster-size pictures of his father, mother, his uncle the President and other members of the family.

Next to it was a room that one time was the master bedroom but it was kind of small, so the Kennedys turned it into a dainty little antique-filled sitting room. We walked through it into Bobby's and Ethel's room, an immense chamber about twenty-five-feet long and almost as wide.

Dominating the room was an enormous emperor-sized bed with a pink-and-white sprigged quilted cover. Around the room were beautiful flower arrangements, also in pink and white. There weren't many chairs, so we all stood around self-consciously until Ethel sat casually on the bed and invited the others to join her. It amazed me that she would allow people to sit on her bed, but it was part of her informal personality.

I found a chair next to a small desk. Mrs. Fred Harris, the young wife of the Senator from Oklahoma, came up and sat on the thick rug near me. We searched for an ash tray but the nearest thing was a small antique inkwell on the desk that neither of us dared to use. Mrs. Harris, who is part Indian, got off on a discussion of the terrible problems the Indians were facing. On the way out, I complimented Mrs. Kennedy on her perfectly lovely floral arrangements and asked where she had learned the art. "Oh, I don't do them," she answered gaily. "I call the florist and tell him what I want."

On the bed, Ethel chatted with the women about children, clothes, shopping. Someone asked her what she felt were the most difficult years in child-rearing and she answered they were all equally delightful. Audrey Grunfeld spotted a few small tears in the expensive coverlet and, glancing around the room, saw a spider hanging by its web from the wall. Under the glass of the night table she saw a typed list of emergency telephone numbers— a doctor, a dentist, the police. "It was comforting to know," she was to say later, "that in some respects this was a home pretty much like one's own."

ß ß ß

By midnight, the party began to break up.
None of the New York editors and their wives were

aware that the climax of the drama had occurred while they were at dinner.

Several days before, Bobby Kennedy had offered to remain out of the Presidential race if Lyndon Johnson would agree to name a high-level bipartisan commission to re-evaluate America's involvement in the Vietnam War. Kennedy himself had visited Secretary of Defense Clark Clifford with his friend and associate Theodore Sorensen to make the proposal. At the meeting, unreported to the press at the time, Clifford asked Kennedy to suggest some members of the proposed commission. Among those Bobby named were Kingman Brewster, president of Yale University; Edwin O. Reischauer, the former Ambassador to Japan; Carl Kaysen, former aide to President Kennedy on the National Security Council; General Matthew Ridgeway, former commander of the United Nations force in Korea; General Lauris Norstad, former commander of the North Atlantic Treaty Organization forces, and Senator Kennedy.

Clifford said he would bring the suggestion to Johnson personally and deliver the President's reply as soon as he received it.

During the dinner party, the call finally came from Clifford. He had seen Johnson. And the answer was no.

At that point, Bobby Kennedy made up his mind to run for President.

NINE

"Old Moms"

❧❦

Ethel will deny that she has a master plan for child rearing or that she follows any set of precepts formulated by any one expert or school of developmental psychologists. She uses her own method, which appears to be a mixture of old-fashioned orthodoxy, loving neglect and liberal doses of permissiveness. She has also received, and for the most part followed, advice on child raising that came in a steady stream from her mother- and father-in-law, Rose and Joe Kennedy. If she has any theory at all on how children should be brought up, Ethel has summed it up in one sentence: "For the first five years, it is so important to give them love—after that everything sort of falls into place."

"Old moms," as Ethel calls herself, may not have read Dr. Milton R. Sapirstein's book *The Unhappy Child,* yet she knows perfectly well how to avoid a pitfall that, he explains, can damage the personalities of children from wealthy homes. Dr. Sapirstein, a child psychiatrist, de-

plores the tendency of upper-class parents to delegate the
day-to-day care of their children to parental substitutes,
such as hired help, neighbors, friends and relatives. Any
one of these, he warns, is "potentially a Trojan horse
within the citadel of the home." Some, he says, are bound
to be misfits, unstable and even vicious personalities.
Moreover, since nurses, maids and governesses generally
come and go with great rapidity, a child may become
"hopelessly confused by a changing procession of guard-
ians, insecure in his attachments and uncertain of his
values." Dr. Sapirstein's observations may help explain
why so many sons and daughters of rich and famous people reach adulthood burdened by a variety of problems
that have destroyed some.

Ethel may have had nurses and governesses over the
years, but every one of her children received unlimited
hours of personal attention. Luella R. Hennessey of
Walpole, Massachusetts, a registered nurse and public-
health adviser who assisted at the birth of twenty-seven
of twenty-eight Kennedy children, including all of Ethel's,
says:

"Ethel has never had any special theory of raising
babies. She's the kind of mother I believe in—just give
them all the close loving you can. All her babies received
so much warm close love, right from the time he or she
entered the world. No wonder they are such a warm, close
family!

"She would hug them to her and whisper to each of
them and be so happy with them. I never saw her prop
a bottle—from the six o'clock feeding in the morning
until ten at night, she would hold them and feed
them, all the time telling them how much they meant to
her.

"Bobby was like most fathers. He seldom fed the babies

but loved to play with them when they were bigger and starting to be fun. But Ethel loved them as little babies."

Ever since Charlottsville, she was up at seven to feed and change them and, when they grew, to breakfast with them. Bobby would always be there too, when he was in town, chattering with his youngsters. Kennedy breakfasts have always been large—cereal, ham or bacon and eggs, hot rolls, and milk or cocoa.

After breakfast, Bobby, Sr., would go off to work and the older children to school. Like any suburban housewife, Ethel would take her turn in the car pools, which would come around often because she had so many riders going to different places. She would get behind the wheel of a station wagon, refuse to start until safety belts were attached and make her pickups and deliveries. The Kennedy children, at one time or another, attended Potomac School, a private institution in McLean; Our Lady of Victory School in Washington; Stone Ridge Country Day School of the Sacred Heart in Bethesda and Sidwell Friends School in Washington. Later, they would go on to prep school. Shortly after three, the children would be back home, friends permitted only if grades were up to par, which was often though not always. From then until about six, the action would begin, fueled by chocolate cake baked that day by Ruby and left in the butler's pantry and by soft drinks from a vending machine (no coins needed) at poolside.

Dinner would always be a family affair in the dining room with the best china and the good silver, because Ethel never believed that children should be given second-best treatment. Ethel would be present and often eating too, though a formal affair might be scheduled for later in the evening. She always kept track of each child's daily activities and problems, an awesome accomplishment as the family kept enlarging. Thus, at the table she would ask one son how he fared on the math exam that day, a daughter how the practice session went for the horse show, another daughter about the rehearsals for the school play.

Ethel and Bobby would always treat their children as adults—not that they expected them to behave as grown-ups, but seriously, as one adult might listen to another. They would never patronize them. They would give their ideas, feelings and problems respectful attention and thoughtful responses.

This did not mean that Ethel would allow a youthful Kennedy to barge in upon older folks on just any pretext. When Michael interrupted a conversation to ask for ice cream just before dinner, she told him he was being impolite. But when Chris, not yet five, interrupted her one afternoon with a question, "How did your mommy and daddy die?" she quickly sensed that worry might have crept into his mind about his own parents. She turned away from her friends, giving the boy her complete attention and discussed her answer simply yet to his complete satisfaction. Bobby, too, would stop a high-level conference to answer an urgent question or help solve a problem. Bobby's pride in his children was demonstrated to the world when he crammed their drawings and paintings into his briefcase, along with important government documents, to hang them upon the panelled walls of his massive office in the Department of Justice.

Robert E. Thompson and Hortense Myers, in *Robert F. Kennedy: The Brother Within,* relate an amusing story that illustrates the point graphically. One day in 1960, while Ethel was being interviewed by journalists at Hickory Hill, Bobby, Jr., raced in with the worried announcement: "Our parakeet is going to die!" Bobby, hardly

seven years old, was already the Kennedy family natural-
ist. Ethel, noting his concern, turned from the reporters
and asked how he knew.

Someone had told him, the boy replied, that parakeets
are unable to survive unless they have mates. "We must
have another parakeet so ours won't die," he said. Ethel,
who had been answering questions on the recent election
of John Kennedy, now turned to the more important issue
at hand: Can a bachelor (or spinster) parakeet make it
without a mate or not, she asked her interviewers, but
nobody knew. Ethel, still as serious as was Bobby, told
her son that she would find out and if the parakeet needed
a mate, he'd surely get one. (The story is an old-wives
tale—not true at all, reports Joseph Bell, assistant curator
of ornithology at the New York Zoological Society.)

The inclusion of the children in their lives has also
meant giving them full run of the house. Once Ethel,
carried away by an urge to redecorate, showed Bobby a
set of drawings by an interior designer who apparently
was planning to remake Hickory Hill into something re-
sembling the palace of Louis XIV at Versailles.

Bobby took one look and winced. "Now Ethel," he
said, "we're not trying to build Grand Hotel. We want
to have children in this living room." He held out a
drawing of an elegant salon at arm's length and asked
her: "Can you picture them in this room?"

Ethel grinned and replied: "I guess you're right." The
designer was instructed to redo her work along much
simpler lines.

Ethel would spank an unruly child, as Rose Kennedy
spanked her son John and all others who misbehaved,
and has evolved a form of punishment that might be
termed creative discipline. An offending youngster would

be banished to his room with orders to stay there and read. Thus, in Ethel's view, the child would be punished by isolation and at the same time be using his time to learn something. (Child psychologists may quarrel with the method on the ground that a child might thereby learn to equate reading with punishment, but few of the Kennedys ever paid much attention to the experts. President Kennedy once told an interviewer to stop asking certain probing questions because "I don't go for the couch stuff.")

But there never was too much of this or other punishment. "I guess lots of mothers would say I'm too easy with the children," Ethel said once, "but I just don't believe a child's world should be entirely full of 'don'ts.' We think it's possible to have discipline and still give the children independence without spoiling them."

If a child would want to ski down a steep slope permission would be granted without a chorus of "be carefuls." Climb up an almost perpendicular mountainside? They may. Try a one-and-a-half gainer, backward, from a high board? Sure, and make it a good one. Go spear fishing, horseback riding on rocky terrain, canoeing in fast waters? Yes.

"I want my children to grow up with as little fear as possible because the less fear, the more they can accomplish," Ethel will explain. "This outweighs the risks."

Risks there are. Kathleen took a particularly bad fall from a horse and broke a leg. When she was fourteen, Kathleen tumbled into the rapids on a Western camping trip and was swept perilously close to the edge of a falls. Joe broke several bones before he was seventeen and was bloodied by a bull's horns one summer. At Hyannis Port, Bobby, Jr., climbed a tree to retrieve a pet falcon, fell twenty feet and broke a wrist. Gashes and bruises were always commonplace. "One of these days," a visitor said, "I'll go to Hickory Hill and there won't be a single child with either a cast or a bandage." It hasn't happened yet.

Nor did Ethel, despite her own personal courage, take these accidents nor the threat of them with equanimity. She would shudder when the going got rough. Once, as Kathleen, performing at a horse show, thundered toward high barriers, Ethel plainly showed her terror by hiding her eyes and gasping. When a child would scale the face of a cliff, she would bite her lip and look away. Knowing this about herself, she would scoff at journalists who wrote about her display of "iron nerves" when her children engaged in dangerous activities. She knew the risks and was clearly afraid for them, but she had the good sense to refrain from transmitting her own fears to her children, and the strength to avoid pampering and overprotecting them. She realized, as many women do not, that mothers who stifle their children's attempts to try their wings never permit them to discover their own abilities to accomplish things and to surmount problems.

Ethel, like Rose and Joe Kennedy, has always believed that one of the key qualities possessed by members of the Kennedy family is the ability to make decisions. Like them, she apparently realizes that the ability to make a choice and stick to it is one of the foundation stones of an individual's personality structure, and that without it he may be severely handicapped in later life. Rose and Joe always encouraged their children to think for themselves and care for their own needs, as far as they were able. Ethel has followed the practice, and it has paid off, for her children, like Rose Kennedy's, have developed self-reliance to the point where one small member of the family was once seen entering a hotel dining room by himself, accepting a table to which he was led, picking up a menu and selecting his breakfast from the items listed. He was barely seven years old!

Religion has been communicated to the children through daily Bible readings at bedtime, grace before every meal and, above all, by discussions that bring God into everyday life and by example. Books on the history of the Church and its people are made available; always around is a small volume of meditations, *Imitation of Christ*.

Ethel would go daily to 9:00 A.M. mass at St. Luke's Catholic Church, the Kennedys' home parish in McLean. The entire family would attend the 6:00 P.M. folk mass on Sundays, driven there in a station wagon by Bobby while he was alive, by Ethel after his death. On the ride back home, Bobby would discuss the service and the sermon with the children, asking questions and explaining; Ethel has followed the practice.

Bobby, the most devout of the Kennedy brothers, would look intently at his children during a service. Once the Reverend Albert F. Pereira, pastor of St. Luke's, asked him why. "I want them to understand the mass," he replied. "It disturbs me when they are restless. I want them to be able to talk about it on the way home—what the priest said, what was in the Gospel and the Epistle."

Children would be brought to church as soon as they reached toddler stage, but would have to remain in the rear until the family nursemaid could report that they were "church broke," that is, able to sit reasonably still without making a fuss.

A number of times Bobby discovered that his children had missed the point of the sermons, whereupon the following Sunday he would chide Father Pereira for delivering messages that were overly complex. "My kids are pretty bright," he once told the pastor, according to the

Washington *Star,* "and if they don't get it, other people won't either." The sermons, Bobby argued, should be more like his own campaign speeches—simple and clear, going directly to the point. Father Pereira remonstrated that the two were entirely dissimilar—"You're selling yourself, I'm selling ideas." Bobby replied: "I'm selling a program—ideas. So are you. You ought to pick just one theme, drive it home." When the clergyman suggested, with a smile, that Bobby lend him one of his speech-writers, Kennedy said:

"I didn't mean to be so intent [*sic*]. But religion is so important in life. I want my kids to like it. You all should not be talking about the God up there so much. I want to know what God is like down here, how He is concerned with what we do here. I want to know how my life should be lived here now."

Ethel would always make a point of instructing her children about what God was like "down here," though she would be careful to avoid sounding moralistic or sanctimonious. As Father Pereira says, "She's afraid the children wouldn't buy that kind of thing."

Ethel Kennedy and Jacqueline Kennedy Onassis did not share the same views on child rearing. Not surprisingly, each was bringing up her children to function in the kind of world each preferred, and the two could not be more dissimilar.

Caroline, daughter of the late President, was being bred for elegance, like a rare camellia, like Jackie herself. At an early age, she was already being taught to walk, talk, act, dress and even eat like a person of exquisite taste and breeding. When Caroline was four, her mother took her to watch a two-hour rehearsal of Moscow's Bolshoi Ballet in Washington. Long before Caroline entered her teens, Jacqueline was educating her palate to

haute cuisine, encouraging her to try the gourmet specialties of René Verdon, Annamarie Huste and other fine
chefs she engaged.* (John, too, was an apt pupil. Once
a visitor chanced upon him in the kitchen of Jacqueline's
New York apartment, preparing his own Wiener schnit-
zel.)

Ethel's children wouldn't know *haute* cuisine from a
goal post and couldn't care less. A typical meal: thick
lamb chops or steak, baked potatoes, a green salad, milk,
ice cream with hot chocolate sauce. They also love
chicken—roasted, broiled and fried—and on Fridays
ample bowls of New England clam chowder.

One day, while reading a Superman comic book, Bobby,
Jr., came upon a story of how the "man of steel" helped
promote the late President's physical fitness program. He
promptly fired off a letter thanking the magazine for remembering his uncle. Mort Weisinger, editor of the
Superman comic books, wrote to the boy's father, asking
permission to publish Bobby's letter. Bobby, Sr., replied
he had no objection.

Nor, apparently, did he object to his son's reading
comic books. Jackie, on the other hand, detests them. Her
children were not permitted to read them, or to watch
television as they grew, except on rare occasions. Bobby
and Ethel's children were always TV fans. (A favorite
show was "The Man from U.N.C.L.E.")

During New Frontier days, observers noted that Ethel
did not send her children to the famous White House

---

*By 1967, the gastronomic education of Caroline Kennedy was
showing some, if not total, progress. During the Christmas
recess that year, Caroline and six of her classmates had lunch
at La Caravelle, in New York, one of Jackie's favorite restaurants, where she ordered artichokes *vinaigrette* as a first course—
followed by steak and french fries.

nursery school set up by the First Lady for Caroline, John and a few select youngsters. Ethel felt it was too far away and, moreover, she did not approve of nursery schools for her children. With so many brothers and sisters around, "they can learn more at home," she said.

♄ ♄ ♄

What kind of children did Old Moms produce? Some are extremely bright, some have their woes with math and the sciences, some are on the shy side, some are shameless extroverts. When not on public display, which is the only time to judge, the children were never any more rambunctious than any other kids. One thing about them: They were never naggers. One day five-year-old Chris asked his mother if he could go out on a boat with his older brothers Michael and Bobby. Since it was too close to his bedtime, Ethel said "No." "Oh, please!" Chris pleaded. Another firm "No," and that ended the matter. Bill Barry, the former F.B.I. agent who was Bobby Kennedy's personal security man in his campaign for the nomination, and his wife witnessed the incident.

"It amazed us," Bill said. "My wife and I looked at each other and I know what we were thinking. Our children—we have five—would start to beg and we would explain our stand for five minutes and maybe end up reversing ourselves. But not Ethel. Her answer was final, and the children listened."

There would, however, be lapses from time to time that guests have noted, some to their discomfort. They have been jumped upon and clung to, smitten with pillows, wetted down with water guns and, on at least one occasion, lassoed. Perhaps the children were not at fault. Bobby would wrestle with them on the rugs and over the furniture, stage pillow fights with them, chase them up and down the stairs, permit them to leap upon him, pummel him, yank at his necktie and send him sprawling. In such an uninhibited atmosphere, it is often difficult, sometimes impossible, for a child to draw the distinction between accepted horseplay and just plain rudeness.

There were bound to be problems. In 1968, one of the boys, with a friend, threw rocks at a passing car and broke a windshield. The Kennedys and the other boy's parents paid damages, the boys apologized and a police complaint filed against them was dropped. In August 1970, Robert Kennedy, Jr., and his cousin R. Sargent Shriver III, both sixteen, appeared in Juvenile session of the First District Court of Barnstable County in Massachusetts on charges of possessing marijuana. Judge Henry L. Murphy sent both boys home after lecturing them, saying the charges would be dismissed after a one-year period if there were no further difficulties. Ethel and Shriver issued statements expressing their distress and their faith in their sons.

Almost three years after Robert Kennedy's death, it was still too early to predict the direction in which the children would move. Joe had already delivered a major public address in the nation's capital at the dedication ceremonies for the Robert F. Kennedy Stadium, the sports arena named for his father. He spoke easily and made a graceful figure on the stand as he told the thousands who had gathered of his father's concern for children of deprived families and his lifelong devotion to physical fitness. Kathleen was a quietly intelligent Radcliffe student. After graduation from Putney she had taken a summer job teaching Navaho children at the Rough Rock Demonstration School in Arizona.

None of the Kennedys would make any comment on the record about possible political careers for these or the other young males and females who comprise the brood. Ethel and Bobby agreed that the children must choose their own lifework. Hackett says: "If Bobby, Jr., wants to run a zoo, she would be perfectly happy." With their heritage, however, it would be a major surprise if the next generation of Americans does not see a Kennedy, or several, somewhere on the political scene.

TEN

Ethel and Bobby

❧ ❧

What kind of a marriage did they have?

Their love was strong and deep. They admired and respected one another, which is an important part of marriage. They were powerfully attracted to each other, which is another important part. But they also *liked* one another as human beings and thoroughly enjoyed being together, which is perhaps the most important part.

They hated to be apart for long. Whenever he traveled, he would call her at least once a day, often twice, to talk about his business, ask about the children. Kenny O'Donnell observes wryly: "Plenty of times on trips Bobby got me in trouble with my wife because I sure as hell didn't call every day. Ethel would get in touch with Helen after she had heard from Bobby and tell her everything was OK with me. I used to get it plenty of times from Helen: 'If Bobby can call every day, why can't you? He's busier than you are!'"

If Bobby found he would be away an extended time, he

would send for Ethel; she would pack and be there the same day. Nor would he remain any place longer than was absolutely essential. A friend says: "They would fly anywhere just to be together." For preparation of critical documents, he chose Hickory Hill, where she was, instead of his office at the Department of Justice or the Senate Office Building. In January 1963, when Bobby, as Attorney General, was preparing to argue his first case before the United States Supreme Court—a complex case in which the government sought to overturn the county unit-voting system in Georgia—he did two weeks of intensive work at home. (At the debut, the Kennedys, including Ethel and four of their children, outnumbered the Justices.) In 1967, when Bobby decided to break with President Johnson and call for a halt to the bombing of North Vietnam, much of the drafting of his historic Senate speech was done at home with his aides. Throughout Kennedy's public career, home was where he would confer frequently on all manner of problems with United States marshals returning from Mississippi, with Cuban refugees reporting on Fidel Castro, with speechwriters, constituents from New York, other members of the Cabinet.

Ethel and Bobby always vacationed together, taking along as many of the children as they felt were old enough to travel and enjoy the things they did. It was on these trips, away from social and political pressures, that Ethel and Bobby demonstrated, unashamedly and artlessly, the depth of their affection for each other:

They would sit together at night by a campfire and hold hands. On skiing trips, Bobby would wait for Ethel at the lift and they would go up together, his arm around her. They would ice skate hand in hand at resorts in Canada, the Far West and even in Rockefeller Center, New York, and do it without a trace of self-consciousness. They would

stand, hands clasped, by the rail of a steamer cruising
down the Amazon in Brazil, taking their first awed look
at the dense jungle of coconut palms, mangroves, kapok-
bearing ceibas and other exotic trees along the shore, ex-
claiming in surprise at the parrots, heron and other tropi-
cal birds they could spot.

There were many endearing moments—trivial incidents, perhaps, but artless little tendernesses and gestures
between husband and wife often reveal much about their
relationship.

On their trip into the Amazonian "green hell," during
Kennedy's Latin America tour in late 1965, Bobby and
Ethel were assigned a small, stuffy cabin, which they
abandoned after a few hours. In the morning, the accompanying journalists and assorted Brazilian officials found
them asleep on the fantail, rolled up in blankets like a
couple of papooses, Bobby with the sleeping mask he always wore.

One night at a party in Chile the orchestra struck up
what Bobby called "bull-fighting music." Stamping his
feet and simulating horns with pointed index fingers at his
temples, he called out to Ethel and rushed toward her.
Ethel, catching the spirit, performed an elaborate pass
with a scarf. The guests formed a circle and watched in
delight as the Senator and his wife played bull and mat-
ador for several minutes.

One freezing, snowy February day in West Berlin,
Bobby rose to deliver an impromptu talk before 180,000
persons jammed into the vast City Hall square. He had
lost his overcoat and wore his father's, which had been
sent over to him. But it wasn't an especially warm one and
Bobby, who had been driving in an open car, was shaking
so hard with the cold his words would barely come out.
Ethel, watching him closely, rose quickly and stood by his

side. Unobtrusively, she slid her hand under his coat and began to massage his back, circulating the blood and providing the warmth needed to finish his brief remarks.

Dickie Mann Cummins says: "Watching them, you could feel the happiness they felt, and the love of life, the love for their children, the love for each other."

Their constant companionship was not lost on President Kennedy, whose wife Jacqueline could pursue her own special interests with her friends independent of her husband and who frequently holidayed alone. The President once remarked wistfully to a friend: "Ethel is always there."

Other members of the Kennedy family had this to say about the marriage:

Eunice Shriver, Bobby's older sister who married Sargent Shriver, former director of the Peace Corps, later Ambassador to France: "Bobby was a lonely, very sensitive and unfulfilled youngster. He met Ethel, and all the love and appreciation for which she seemed to have an infinite capacity came pouring down on him. How he blossomed."

Ted Kennedy: "It was an extraordinary relationship. With Ethel and Bobby, everything just clicked all the way."

Bobby himself was to say it best. On the campaign trail, he was asked by a reporter what he thought was his greatest achievement. Bobby didn't hesitate a second.

"Marrying Ethel," he replied.

⊙ ⊙ ⊙

"If you ever knocked Bobby in her presence, I think she would come over and hit you."

So says Kenny O'Donnell about the extent of Ethel's commitment to Robert Kennedy. It was total. She was not her husband's severest critic nor a critic at all; she was his protector and defender. And if she would not actually swing a punch at someone who said mean things, she would hate, scold, lecture and snub him, even if he were the President of the United States. She has done each of these things.

From the start she was alert to any criticism of Bobby and would not let it pass. When young Kennedy was chief counsel for the Senate Labor Rackets Committee, following his service with the McCarthy subcommittee, Willard Edwards of the Chicago *Tribune* wrote a Sunday magazine article assessing the political future of the two Kennedy brothers. While the piece was generally extremely favorable, Edwards could not resist weaving into his discussion a veiled barb at Bobby. "One could envision," he wrote at one point, "Senator John Kennedy as the fiery declaimer, the persuasive seeker of votes for his office (the Presidency is definitely his goal), while the younger brother performs the maneuvers behind the scenes so essential to political success. He has tireless persistence and a sufficient amount of guile to qualify him for such a role."

Bobby, reading the good parts, was delighted with the article and told Edwards so, but Ethel was not and she told Edwards too. During a recess at the rackets hearing, she came to the press table and scolded: "I read between the lines and I think you were trying to imply something unfavorable." Edwards says: "She was much more sensitive to criticism because that's precisely what I was trying to do."

One evening she was watching a Huntley-Brinkley newscast at Hickory Hill and heard Chet Huntley say something about Bobby she regarded as unfavorable. Immediately after the show, she called him long distance and bawled him out. At a writer's luncheon, Laura Berquist of

Look magazine asked Kennedy a tough question about Vietnam, which he fumbled. Ethel glowered at her. Later she grabbed Miss Berquist in the ladies room and angrily snapped: "I thought you were a friend of my husband's."

During the campaign for the nomination in 1968, Ethel was surrounded by newsmen, one of whom said that many of her husband's colleagues considered him "worthless" and did she have any comment? Later, the horrified journalist confessed to a slip of the tongue: He had intended to say "ruthless." Ethel, her face pale and hands visibly shaking, replied in a tight voice she could barely control: "I've never heard anyone say that about my husband. I would use 'brilliant' to describe him myself because that is what he is."

One day, more than a year after her husband's death, she encountered Senator Eugene McCarthy, who had opposed Kennedy for the nomination, in a Washington restaurant. As she passed the table where he was seated, McCarthy rose, smiled broadly and held out his hand to her. She took it quickly, murmured something and walked on. "It was like walking through a receiving line," a witness said. "She didn't even pause. It took about a second-and-a-half." At her husband's graveside in Arlington, President Johnson moved to kiss her as he offered words of consolation, but Ethel averted her cheek. Lyndon Johnson had said harsh things about Robert Kennedy. Bobby hated *The New York Times* because it had opposed his appointment as Attorney General in 1960 and his bid for the nomination in 1968. He had even felt the newspaper was anti-Catholic, saying it went out of its way to publish unfavorable stories about nuns and priests. So Ethel hated the paper too. She called up Jack Newfield after he had sent her a copy of his book *Robert Kennedy, A Memoir,* and told him: "I always knew you were going to get even with Johnson and McCarthy, but when I saw you were giving it to *The Times* then I knew the book was going to be great."

Ethel was genuinely astounded that some people would call her husband ruthless. She knew, of course, about the severe attacks upon him—she winced when she read that Gore Vidal had called Bobby "dangerous"; she shook her head when she heard of the other characterizations: vindictive, cynical, opportunistic. She never understood why. For her, there was only one Bobby and he was a devoted father, compassionate, God-loving human being and considerate husband.

Bobby, who could be brusque with aides and associates and downright ferocious with foes, was always gentle with Ethel. Once he was in the midst of a meeting with his staff in his Senate office when Ethel called. Kennedy had been excoriating in a cold hard voice opponents of a measure he was sponsoring. Abruptly his tone changed. His voice quality became much softer, his face relaxed, he smiled. Andy Glass, who witnessed the incident, says he sounded as though he were talking to a little girl.

Bobby always feared Ethel would commit a political gaffe, for he knew that despite her sensitivity to criticisms and determined efforts in his behalf, she was actually naïve about politics and unschooled in its complexities. The Kennedys were political animals but Ethel was merely competitive, and there is a difference. Like a nose for news, there exists a sensitivity for what will win or lose votes and Ethel did not possess it. During the 1960 campaign, John Kennedy would almost instinctively avoid priests and nuns, fearful he might be photographed with them and thereby ignite the Catholicism issue. Kennedy would worry about the large amount Jackie would spend on clothes and furnishings, not because the sums would dent his finances but because it was poor politics. During his Senate campaign, Bobby took his late brother's son to visit the house in upper Manhattan where the boy's grandparents once lived, knowing the sentimental journey would generate sympathy that could be translated into votes.

Ethel never developed this fine vote-gathering instinct. She took some of her older children to Indiana and California, but not to show them off. She knew their father missed them and that they missed their father, and she wanted them to be together.

The extent of her inability to "think votes" was astonishing. On the cruise down the Amazon, the guests were served a mushy rice and aromatic chicken for Sunday breakfast, a Portuguese dish that hardly tickled the palates of the Americans. Andy Glass, who was sitting with Ethel, sighed and said it would be nice if they could have some lox and bagels instead.

Ethel asked: "What's that?"

Glass's head snapped up. "Ethel," he said, "you must be kidding. You really don't know?" Ethel replied that she did not know about the dish—smoked salmon on a hard doughnut-shaped roll, a favorite Jewish delicacy.

"Ethel," Glass said in astonishment and reproach, "you mean you're the wife of the Senator from New York State, whose constituency includes about two million Jewish people, and you never heard of bagels and lox?" He explained and invited her to sample some at his home some Sunday morning.

Another time, Ethel mused that while she had traveled to many parts of the world she had never been to Egypt. She would love to visit the ancient land of the Pharaohs, see the great Nile, the Sphinx, the pyramids. Again Andy Glass was shocked. "Ethel," he told her, "you can't go to Egypt!"

Ethel was surprised. "Why not?" she asked. Glass explained. "Your husband," he said, "has too many Jewish constituents and they would hardly look with favor upon a visit you might make to Egypt, where you would be welcomed by Nasser." She finally understood.

She could ask in a puzzled tone following Bobby's defeat in the Oregon primary: "Is fifteen thousand much to lose by?" It wasn't much mathematically, but almost everything psychologically, particularly since it was the first time a Kennedy had ever lost an election in twenty-six campaigns. This had not occurred to Ethel, and even when it was explained she found it difficult to understand.

It may well be that her daughter Kathleen has the kind of political acumen Ethel lacks. When she was only eleven years old, Kathleen was overheard at a ski resort warning her younger brother Joe, who was being mischievous, to behave himself. "Do be quiet!" she ordered. "You are losing votes like this!"

Politically, Ethel thought in terms of absolutes. It was their side against our side and no such thing as a middle or neutral group. She never could understand why a journalist who was personally friendly to Bobby and to her could write anything unfavorable. "I thought you were one of us," she said to Glass one day after he had written an appraisal that bore some unflattering references.

To Ethel in the years her husband was alive and politicking, politics was a game of touch football.

๑ ๑ ๑

The one thing in his life—perhaps the only thing— from which Bobby excluded Ethel was his relationship with his brother's widow after Dallas.

Robert Kennedy felt bound by a strong moral commitment to act as surrogate father to her children, John, Jr., and Caroline, and to help their mother over the period of her bereavement. Himself possessed by grief and despair, he could know the depths of Jackie Kennedy's anguish. As often as he could, Robert Kennedy would go to Jackie's home in Georgetown after she had moved from the White House, play with the children and have dinner with Mrs. Kennedy. After she moved to New York, he would leave his apartment at 860 United Nations Plaza, taxi to Mrs. Kennedy's apartment at Eighty-fifth Street and Fifth Avenue and remain for several hours.

He did this so often that, for the few times in the relationship, Ethel became irked with her husband. One evening shortly after the President's assassination, Bobby and Ethel were invited to a friend's home for the evening but, en route in the car, he decided to spend the hours comforting Mrs. Kennedy. He ordered the driver to proceed to the Georgetown house, stepped out and told Ethel to go on without him. She remonstrated; Bobby insisted: Would she *please* go without him. Finally she went.

A few days later, again left alone for the evening, Ethel remarked to a guest that Bobby was probably right— "He's got to comfort Jackie." But she did feel, friends have said, that he was with Jackie too much. She knew how the assassination had all but shattered Bobby and it is not unlikely she wanted her husband exposed to life and cheerfulness rather than reminders of tragedy.

Bobby, however, felt almost passionately protective toward the woman who had glittered so brightly in the life of the brother he idolized. He felt Jackie had suffered so much that she should be shielded from further hurt and granted what he called a "free ride" from that time on. He meant that the world, and particularly the American people, should not raise questions or offer any criticisms about her actions but respect her right to the privacy she had always sought.

Once he expressed himself pointedly on the subject. During an airplane flight on his final campaign, he had had several drinks with a journalist and was asked: "Didn't Jackie want it both ways? She insists upon her right to be left alone, but goes continually to public places and especially restaurants that she knows are patrolled by gossip journalists who will see to it she gets her name in the papers. Why doesn't she adopt the simplest solution—avoid those notoriously newsy places and eat at the many restaurants where the problem of exposure is not nearly as great?"

Bobby replied: "I don't see why the public cannot be courteous and give her the same right to eat where she pleases and go where she wishes as anybody else." Bobby, who never felt comfortable in the role of idolized, poked-at, spied-upon, pulled and tugged public figure, could sympathize with Jackie's wish to be left alone.

For her part, Jackie grasped at the support Robert Kennedy offered in those terrible months. Every widow knows that after the death of a husband, especially a sudden death, there is a blessed numbness, during which one can function reasonably well, followed by grief that can be close to physical pain. There is an intense loneliness, a loss of equilibrium. To the grieving, "the world is a dreary wasteland," Joshua Loth Liebman has said. Jackie felt the pain and the despair. She needed a strong hand and gratefully accepted Bobby's.

The question arises: Why did Bobby exclude Ethel from this time of healing with Jackie Kennedy? The probability is that he did so intuitively because he must have realized it was Jackie who was shutting out Ethel. It was apparent to him that they were two different people: one was as elegant as the other was informal, as regal as the other was simple. Friends of both knew that

Jackie looked upon Ethel as a "bit of a country bumpkin" and a "plain little Catholic schoolgirl." Jackie was always polite to Ethel but the two women never became close friends, mainly because they were so unlike. In any event, Jackie did not allow for any role for Ethel in her relationship with Bobby after Dallas.

Because she did not, and because Bobby did not include Ethel either, a rumor arose that Jackie and Robert Kennedy had developed a romantic relationship. There was no basis in fact for the whispers but they persisted for many months during the time that Bobby and Jackie were together so often.

Inevitably, the story reached Ethel. She was amazed and hurt that anyone would actually spread such a tale. Robert Kennedy too was astonished and angry. Says one close friend: "I am certain that this rumor wounded Kennedy more than any other story spread about him in his life. He could accept philosophically almost any other kind of personal attack against him, his beliefs, his religion, his character, but this was too much."

A second rumor, considerably more widespread concerned Robert Kennedy and the famous sex goddess, the late Marilyn Monroe. One small booklet, published soon after Miss Monroe's death and purporting to tell the inside story, was in such demand on the West Coast that copies sold for fifty dollars. An eighty-page soft cover book, *The Strange Death of Marilyn Monroe,* by Frank A. Capell, former chief investigator of the Westchester County, New York, sheriff's office, went through six printings. In his biography of Marilyn Monroe, *Norma Jean,* Fred Lawrence Guiles details the star's purported involvement with a "married man" in the last month of her life, asserting that the alliance was surprising and shocking to her friends. Guiles refers to the man as an "Eastern lawyer." *

Let us examine the story and the "evidence."

On May 18, 1962, Marilyn Monroe, in a shimmering white floor-length gown, sang a throaty "Happy Birthday" to John Kennedy at a Democratic rally in the old Madison Square Garden in New York City and was publicly thanked by a smiling President.

On that trip, Marilyn Monroe met Robert Kennedy for the first time. Later, back in Hollywood, they met once more at the home of actor Peter Lawford, then married to Patricia Kennedy, Bobby's older sister. Bobby was in the movie capital for discussions with the late producer Jerry Wald on the filming of his book *The Enemy Within*. Bobby reportedly visited Marilyn's Brentwood home frequently, talked with her on the telephone many times and met her by arrangement at the home of friends. At one point, Marilyn was reported to have expressed the fear to a friend that she was "too dumb about politics and such things" to interest Kennedy, whereupon the friend, the daughter of a physician, began coaching her in national and international affairs.

On the evening of August 4, the story continues, Marilyn Monroe received a telephone call from a friend in-

---

*In a private communication to the author, Guiles has stated:

"I have been asked many times in interviews and privately if the 'Eastern lawyer' mentioned in my biography of Marilyn Monroe is not one of the Kennedy brothers, John or Robert. I have consistently answered that the decision to delete the identification of this public figure from the text was an ethical one and not based on legal or libel law factors.

"I prefer not to compromise either the book or myself by supplying the name on request."

viting her to dinner at his home. Robert Kennedy would be there. Miss Monroe refused, pleading she was tired. Between 10:00 and 11:00 that night, she is supposed to have called the friend to tell him she feared she had taken too many pills. The friend called Mickey Rudin, Miss Monroe's attorney, but was unable to reach him. The star's body was discovered early the next morning, the phone still in her hand. She had died, the coroner subsequently reported, from an overdose of barbiturates that may have been deliberate or accidental.

Those who claim to have investigated the circumstances cite the following as evidence:

1. Marilyn made a number of long-distance calls to Kennedy during that last summer of her life. Because of direct distance dialing, a record is automatically made of every long-distance call. However, the telephone-company records were impounded by Los Angeles police soon after Miss Monroe died and were never released. When Police Chief William H. Parker died in 1966, a check showed the records were no longer in the department's files. *Was someone interested in causing these records to be obliterated?*

2. Patricia Newcomb, Marilyn's personal press agent and a close friend, who was the last to see her alive, was suddenly whisked away to Hyannis Port a few days after the tragedy, then went to Europe for six months and wound up working for a while at the Department of Justice, near Kennedy's office. *What did Miss Newcomb know and were the Kennedys attempting to silence her?*

3. Marilyn and Kennedy were seen together in June and July by neighbors of the star and other

persons, including a police officer who reportedly observed them at a wild party in Santa Monica.

Friends of Robert Kennedy claim it is absurdly simple to punch gaping holes in this "documentation":

1. The alleged disappearance of the phone records hardly proves anything. It is known that Miss Monroe met Ethel and Robert Kennedy a number of times, once at a party at Peter Lawford's home, and there well might have been social communication. (One critic discovered Miss Monroe had sent a "personal message" to Ethel and Robert Kennedy on June 13, 1962, in the form of a telegram addressed to Hickory Hill. He did not know the text of the message but implied something sinister. A Kennedy friend says: "June 17th is Ethel and Bob's wedding anniversary. It doesn't require much of an imagination to figure out that this 'personal message' must have been a wire of congratulations.")

Nor was there ever any mystery about the call Marilyn received the evening before she died. Peter Lawford said a few days later that he phoned the actress, who had been a close friend of the Lawfords, about 7:00 P.M. "She said she was sleepy and was going to bed," he related. "Thinking she was lonely, I asked her to have dinner with me and some friends. But Marilyn decided not to come along." Among the guests were Milt Ebbins, a friend and business associate, and his wife; television producer Joe Naar and his wife, and George (Bullets) Durgom, a theatrical agent.

2. Pat Newcomb had met Ethel Kennedy in 1960 and was a member of her intimate circle of friends.

Before *and after* the death of Miss Monroe, she visited Hickory Hill many times as a guest of the Kennedys. She rushed there the day President Kennedy was assassinated to help take care of the children. She was invited to spend a weekend with the Kennedys at Camp David. It hardly seems likely that this closeness with Ethel Kennedy would have continued had Miss Newcomb been privy to damaging private information linking Bobby with another woman.

3. Kennedy friends say it is entirely unfair to accept the word of unidentified persons who "claim" to have seen the two together. Joe Wolhandler, who knew Marilyn well and was her public-relations counsel for years, says: "I've heard the rumor two-hundred times and I have always asked: 'Show me proof.' Nobody has ever come up with anything but undocumented gossip."

Those who knew Robert Kennedy believe it would have been wildly out of character for him to have had an extra-marital affair. He was never a girl-chaser, even as a young man. George Terrien traveled through the south of France in the summer of 1948 with Bobby and John Kennedy. "Jack and I went girl-hunting quite openly," he recalls. "But while Bobby had dates, he wasn't lustful. He wasn't the roué."

Nor did he change with the years. "Bobby had a Calvinistic moral sense," says Andrew Glass. "He really believed in absolute right and wrong, and this strict code guided his moral life."

Glass continues: "I was with him in as personal circumstances as I know and I really believe he had a deep, continuing and abiding romantic love for his wife and that it would never falter. In the middle of huge crowds and motorcades, he would always look around and ask, 'Where's Ethel?' If he was ever separated from her in a crowd or a social setting, he would always inquire where she was and he would move over to her.

"I attended a Hollywood party once with Bobby. There were plenty of movie stars and starlets there, wildly attractive unattached women, some of whom made a play for him. I watched him carefully and I saw he wasn't the least bit interested in any of them, fantastically beautiful and shapely though they were. He wasn't just pretending, either . . . there was no covert interest. He was completely aloof from them."

Dick Schaap believes that Bobby had a strong Puritanical strain, bordering on the self-righteous. "He seems to have an utter faith in himself," Schaap has stated, "complete trust in his own morality. He even kids his own Puritanism. 'It isn't that I'm a saint,' he once said, 'it's just that I've never found it necessary to be a sinner.'"

Kenny O'Donnell says: "I knew this man as well as anybody. I was intimately associated with him for years and knew everything he ever did, and I know for a fact that this Marilyn Monroe story was absolute horseshit."

What was Bobby's reaction? Ethel's?

He joked about it with O'Donnell. The story flattered him, he told Kenny. He said he didn't think he was "that good." Discussing it one day, he recalled his reputation as a "square" at Harvard and said he must have come a long way if he could be linked with the world's reigning sex symbol.

Ethel never took the rumors seriously. Friends report she wasn't hurt or angry, merely amused. Said one: "Ethel knew her Bobby. She was as certain of him as a woman could be of a man. She knew that people in the public eye are often targets of gossip and innuendo and that other Kennedys had been victims of similar malicious untrue talk." (There had been a story that Jacqueline Kennedy wanted to divorce John prior to 1960 and that Joe Kennedy, fearing the destruction of his son's Presidential chances, reportedly offered her a million dollars to remain his wife.)

Part Three

ELEVEN

Mrs. Kennedy
Goes to Washington

❧❧

Ethel slipped easily into her new life as mistress of
Hickory Hill and wife of an up-and-coming young man in
Washington.

The babies kept arriving, almost one every year. To
the four she brought with her to Hickory Hill, Ethel
added Mary Courtney on September 9, 1956; Michael
LeMoyne on February 22, 1958; and Mary Kerry on
September 8, 1959. Four others were to come in the
decade following.

As a member of the capital's active social set, Ethel
kept up a whirl of parties, sporting activities, Bobby-
watching and, not the least important, shopping trips.
Ethel spent a great deal of money decorating and re-
decorating Hickory Hill, and on clothes, often to Bobby's
dismay.* He respected a dollar more than she, a domestic

---

*Like all persons who spend freely, Ethel can show the human
trait of economizing on trifles. The British journalist Margaret
Laing reports that one morning Ethel bolted down a cold fried
egg because she didn't want it to go to waste.

situation common in many young families—including that of John and Jacqueline Kennedy. In her memoirs, Mrs. Mary Barelli Gallagher, Jackie's private secretary, reports that President Kennedy hit the ceiling when he learned the First Lady had spent $125,000 annually, much of it on clothes. (In just one 3-month period, Mrs. Gallagher wrote, Jackie spent $34,887.25, nearly half on clothes.) In the first year of her marriage to Aristotle Onassis, author Fred Sparks has reported, Jackie spent an estimated $1,250,000 on "personal expenses," which included clothes, furs, cosmetics, cosmetic care, minor jewelry and gifts.

While Ethel hardly approached these extraordinary expenditures, she didn't stint on her own purchases. "Ethel knows how to spend money," a close member of the family says. Her extravagance is an in-joke among her friends. Stephen E. Smith, who manages the family finances, once ruefully observed that his job consists of "keeping up with Ethel's bills."

She has always bought expensive clothes from the finest shops. "No Saturday morning SA side doors for her," commented *Women's Wear Daily,* trade publication of the women's apparel industry, referring to a well-known Seventh Avenue practice of selling garments at wholesale prices to certain customers after the close of the business week. One day she dashed into the Cardin ready-to-wear boutique on the third floor of Julius Garfinckel and Co., an ultra-fashionable department store near the White House, and selected a navy coat and dress that bore a $450 price tag. Another time she purchased a Mollie Parnis dress and jacket in white brocatel with white mink—price, $450. One afternoon she spent an hour at Jacques Tiffeau in New York, selecting a fall wardrobe that included an A-line gray wool flannel dress and jacket

($295) and a white-lace tunic with navy silk pants ($375).

Where Mrs. Onassis is high fashion, Ethel is fashionable and there is a difference. Ethel is not chic, not a stylesetter or innovator. Unlike Jackie, she is not a darling of the Parisian *haute couturiers*. "She buys good American clothes and wears them well with innate breeding and good taste," comments *Women's Wear Daily*. "She is the All-American girl. Mollie Parnis, Oscar de la Renta, Originala, Dior–New York, Ben Zuckerman, Donald Brooks—they are Ethel's babies." When she needs a special gown in a big hurry, she will telephone Madame Paul, who runs a small but exclusive shop in Georgetown also patronized by Joan Kennedy, Jean Smith, Eunice Shriver and Mrs. Hugh Auchincloss, Jackie's mother.

Unlike Jackie, who takes her time, Ethel is a quick shopper. She may stay less than an hour in a department store or specialty shop and order four, five or more outfits. Often, she would telephone the New York office of Pierre Cardin, a special favorite, and announce she'd like "a cute little dress" or something nice but "not too flashy." One would be sent out immediately, sight unseen. She prefers bright colors, generally reds, greens and blues, and swings between a size eight and ten. On the other hand, Mrs. Onassis would spend three or more hours at a Paris salon, studying the models, trying on dresses, and then, after she had made her selections, giving detailed instructions on how they should be redesigned for her. "Everyone from Valentino to Cardin," observes *Women's Wear Daily*, "has felt the designing hand of Madame O."

Ethel would usually be seen at functions in miniskirts, often above booted legs. Although some campaign advisers felt her somewhat daring display of tanned thigh might raise eyebrows in Bible Belt areas on campaign trips, Ethel refused to drop her hemlines. And she got away with it. During the Indiana primary in 1968, *The New York Times* reported, women of industrial towns in nondescript dresses would stare at her white *point d'esprit* hosiery, slim, hard-lined dresses three inches above the knees, low-heeled shoes and tasteful but expensive gold-and-diamond earrings. "But there was no animosity, no disapproval. They would nudge each other and say, 'Isn't she just darling?' or 'She's so cute' or 'She sure don't look like she's had no ten children.'"

☙ ☙ ☙

Watching Bobby in action as his career advanced took up a considerable portion of Ethel's time, and every moment enthralled her.

For three years, between 1956 and 1959, Bobby was chief counsel for the Senate Rackets Committee, which brought him into national prominence for the first time. He conducted what amounted to a running cops-and-robbers show during which he locked horns with such tough, hard-eyed labor leaders as James Riddle Hoffa and Dave Beck of the Teamsters Union. The intermittent hearings on union corruption, televised from the same chamber where the Army–McCarthy charade enthralled the country two years earlier, drew an even larger audience.

Only a disaster, or a birth, could keep Ethel away. Every morning, she would drive to the old Senate Office Building, arriving well before 10:00 A.M., race up to Room 318, the high-ceilinged, marble-walled Senate Caucus Room where the hearings were held, and slip into a front-row seat that a Senate policeman reserved for her daily.

Facing the six-sided, twenty-six-foot conference table

at the front of the seventy-four-foot-long room, she would wave hello to Bobby, already there with his mountains of documents. Reporters, photographers, television technicians, lawyers and visitors jammed every inch of space in the chamber designed to accommodate only three-hundred persons. Senator John F. Kennedy, a member of the committee, would generally be seated to Bobby's left. To his right would be dour, file-voiced Senator John L. McClellan, the committee chairman. Once in a while, Senator Kennedy's darkly beautiful wife, Jacqueline, would join Ethel; young Teddy Kennedy, then a student at the University of Virginia Law School, would come often. Once old Joe Kennedy himself came down to watch.

Ethel listened intently, often leaning forward in her chair as the investigations disclosed tales of beatings, murders and extortion under Bobby's questioning. Characters who might have come straight out of central casting sat under the glaring television lights, facing the slim young prosecutor. Anthony (Tony Ducks) Corallo, Big and Little Helen, two "businesswomen" from the West Coast; Joe (Caesar) Di Varco, John (Johnny Dio) Dioguardo and others equally colorful sat a few feet from her. Once the dark, handsome, slick-haired Johnny Dio punched a cameraman in the room. Hoffa and Bobby clashed repeatedly, on and off the stand.

Ethel reacted strongly to the unfolding drama.

She paled when Edward Bennett Williams, counsel for Hoffa, taunted Bobby, who had asked for an explanation of a complex point. "I don't understand," Bobby had said. "I do not expect you to. I think the lawyers on the committee will," Williams shot back, jibing at Kennedy's lack of legal experience.

She chuckled at the Damon Runyon dialogue:

Kennedy: Did you know Cockeye Dunne?

Barney Baker, a Hoffa organizer: I didn't know him as Cockeye Dunne. I knew him as John Dunne.

Kennedy: Where is he now?

Baker: He has met his Maker.

Kennedy: How did he do that?

Baker: I believe through electrocution in the city of New York of the state of New York.

Kennedy: What about Squinty Sheridan? Did you know him?

Baker: Andrew Sheridan, sir?

Kennedy: Yes.

Baker: He has also met his Maker.

Kennedy: How did he die?

Baker: With Mr. John Dunne.

"Isn't Bobby great?" Ethel would ask practically every day, and apparently the country agreed, for before either of them knew it he had become a popular hero. An embarrassed Bobby, observed by a giggling Ethel, had to fight his way through swarms of squealing teen-age girls (bobby-soxers, they called them in the Fifties) on his way out of the hearings. Thousands of letters poured in from all over the country, some of them love notes from women of all ages, many expressing gratitude that at last somebody was fighting toe-to-toe with the cynical, vicious labor racketeers of the day.

There were some who felt Bobby wasn't all that great. A professor at Yale Law School, Alexander Bickel, afterward wrote in *The New Republic* that the youthful investigator and other committee members engaged in a "relentless, vindictive battering" of witnesses, citing this exchange with one Joey Glimco, who headed a Chicago local of the Teamsters Union:

> *Kennedy:* And you defraud the union?
> *Glimco:* I respectfully decline to answer because I honestly believe my answer might tend to incriminate me.
> *Kennedy:* I would agree with you.
> *Senator McClellan:* I believe it would.
> *Kennedy:* You haven't got the guts to answer, have you, Mr. Glimco?
> *McClellan:* Morally you are kind of yellow inside, are you not? That is the truth about it?

A Republican member of the Democrat-dominated committee told a newsman: "The witnesses are all gangsters and you can't defend them. Even so, a lot of the things that are done are unfair. For example, staff investigators will be put on the stand and will make statements without any proof. These statements become part of the record, but often they are nothing more than the investigators' belief. There is no effective rebuttal. The effect is that some witnesses who might testify if they got a fairer chance take the Fifth Amendment."

Bobby bristled at the criticisms. "What am I supposed to do," he once exclaimed, "when a man like Dave Beck takes the Fifth when I ask him if he knows his own son!"

When he resigned from the committee in September 1959, to run his brother's campaign for the Presidency, Bobby had concluded two-and-one-half years of hearings, with five-hundred open sessions. He had scored some impressive victories, chief among them the downfall of the rotund Dave Beck as president of the Teamsters. Beck was convicted of stealing union funds and eventually went to jail. The committee discovered evidence of corruption in fifteen unions and fifty companies. One large union, the Bakery and Confectionery Workers, was expelled from the AFL-CIO; leaders of a number of others, whose activities were exposed, were forced to resign.*

---

* Kennedy's arch-foe throughout the hearings, Jimmy Hoffa, escaped unscathed—for then—but Bobby was to pursue him with all the dogged determination he displayed when he was trying to learn to play football. Hoffa, who railed at Kennedy as a "young, dim-witted, curly-headed smartaleck," was finally sent to jail in 1967 on a charge of jury-tampering, after exhausting a long string of legal appeals.

TWELVE

"Do Japanese Cats Have Tails?"

❧ ☙

Following the election of John F. Kennedy to the Presidency in 1960, Bobby Kennedy became Attorney General of the United States, the first person in history to serve in the Cabinet of a President-brother. He resigned in September 1964 from the Cabinet of Lyndon Johnson to run for the Senate in New York, defeating the incumbent Republican, Kenneth B. Keating, the following November by more than 700,000 votes. For his brother, for President Johnson and on his own, Bobby Kennedy traveled all over the globe, and nearly always Ethel went along.

Business leaders, professors, clergymen and specialists from the State Department were called in to brief the couple well in advance of any foreign mission. For more than a month before they set out, Bobby and Ethel held "seminars" every Saturday at Hickory Hill, starting at breakfast and running through lunch, drilling themselves on the politics, geography, culture and language of each nation on the itinerary.

"I read whatever I can on a country before I go," Ethel once told an acquaintance. "I go into the whole bit, the history, the poetry, the novels and all the great things the State Department gives you. Actually, they really are good, and some of the things they give you are terrific. I mean some things are better than others, although I have to keep bringing out a map."

"It was very impressive, to me, the number of books he read and the number of people he talked to," said one expert on African affairs. "And that applied to her as well. They both asked a lot of penetrating questions."

In August 1961, Bobby set forth with Ethel on his first good-will mission for President Kennedy. Their destination was the Ivory Coast, a West African nation celebrating its first birthday, and before the plane engines had warmed up, the Attorney General had scrunched down in his seat for some last minute boning up on the French language and African culture.

At Abidjan Airport, Bobby gamely gave the first of his speeches in French after he and Ethel were greeted by Ivory Coast officials and watched a tribal dance performed by grass-skirted natives. From the beginning, Africans of all ranks were fascinated by Ethel's warmth and boundless energy, and Bobby's "young movie-star's physique," as one newspaper put it.

For most of their three-day visit, they were on the go, driving from village to village, applauding singers and dancers and watching local troop units go through close-order drill. In one hamlet, Ethel learned the subprefect had ten children and observed: "I'm jealous. I have only seven." Everywhere they went they brought a breath of the New Frontier, and some tangible evidences as well: Bobby pinned PT-boat tie-clasps on every official he met whether he wore a tie or not, and Ethel clamped Kennedy campaign bracelets on the wrists of their wives.

Five months later, the Kennedys were off on another junket that was to span half the world, from the Far East to Western Europe.

Their first stop was Tokyo, where hundreds of university students in black uniforms and stiff celluloid collars greeted the couple with enthusiasm and banners that dropped one "n" from Kennedy's name. Moments after his plane landed, Kennedy, with Ethel by his side, stepped before a microphone and, like a man plunging into an ice-cold shower, waded through a short speech in Japanese that left his listeners pleased, if a bit puzzled.

As soon as the formalities were over, Ethel, in a red suit with black trim and matching hairbows, set off without Bobby for a tour of Tokyo. She stopped first at the University of the Sacred Heart, whose superior, Mother Anne Stoepel, had been a teacher at Manhattanville College of the Sacred Heart.

Addressing the girls of the upper school, Ethel declared, "I always thought that the United States was more liberal than this country, but it's not true. At Manhattanville in my day, we were very virtuous. I understand now that you are allowed to get married." The gray-uniformed girls applauded her warmly, but some seemed a bit bewildered by her train of thought.

Leaving the convent, Ethel sped on in an eleven-car motorcade to a hospital for crippled children, then on to Tokyo's Zen Buddhist Temple of the Green Pines, where she gave her hosts a demonstration of Kennedy inquisitiveness and fortitude. She knelt on a grass mat before a low table all throughout a three-hour, thirteen-course all-vegetable lunch during which she asked questions that caused considerable confusion among the Japanese.

"I read that your cats have no tails," she said suddenly. "Is this true?"

Failing to get a reply, she switched to another subject. "Do the Japanese use snuff?" she asked.

After a whispered consultation with his associates, Yasuhiro Nakasone, a Japanese political leader, finally replied: "We don't use snuff. We use incense. It's more civilized."

The kneeling posture finally began to wear on Ethel and she asked a Japanese woman luncheon companion, "Are your legs getting tired?"

"No, are yours?" was the reply.

"I can do it as long as you can," said Ethel grimly, and she did.

At the end of the meal, Ethel was presented with a set of Munakata prints and seven pairs of bamboo stilts for her seven children. "I can see a summer of broken legs and broken arms," she sighed.

Returning to the Embassy, Ethel rested briefly, then appeared at a party for two-hundred-and-fifty Embassy wives and women employees. "I'm so happy to see that you're all living out the President's inauguration speech and deepening American–Japanese relations," she told the women. "You've really gotten your lights out from under the barrel."

That night she appeared on the Japanese television program "What's My Secret?" The secret, her identity, fooled nobody.

The mood of enthusiasm and Asian courtesy changed suddenly when Bobby and Ethel visited Tokyo's Waseda University and ran into a contingent of the tough Zengakuren leftists who had forced cancelation of President Eisenhower's plans to visit Japan two years earlier.

While Ethel struggled through the crowd with the aid of two newsmen, Bobby jumped on the platform and plunged into his speech reviewing his brother's policies.

Jeers and shouts from the rear of the room drowned out his words.

Soon the strategically placed leftists took up an organized chant "Cuba—Okinawa—Go Home."

An exuberant cheerleader, egging on the mob, accidentally struck Ethel in the stomach at one point with his flailing arm. She paled visibly, but managed a weak smile and remained at her husband's side. Embarrassed by the incident, United States Ambassador Edwin O. Reischauer said the hecklers were "a small group of hard-core Communists, and I don't believe they were from Waseda."

The next day the Kennedys arose early to watch a group of Japanese workers stage an exhibition of the Japanese art of self-defense.

Kennedy wisely turned down an opportunity to investigate first-hand the Japanese sport of aikido—akin to judo—but Ethel decided to match her skill with a Japanese woman expert. A moment later, she let out a surprised yell and slipped halfway out of her seat when the woman applied sudden pressure to her wrist.

The instructor then approached Kennedy and reached for his wrist. "I'll take your word for it," said the Attorney General hastily.

There was a trip to Osaka and dinner in a geisha house. For the Kennedys, whose taste ran to steaks and chocolate ice cream, the fare was exotic, featuring such delicacies as dried seaweed and sea slugs.

The graceful geishas made a fuss over Bobby, but showered even more attention on his wife. In a country where political prominence is won late in life, the Japanese were constantly amazed over the youthful appearance of Bobby and Ethel.

"Mr. Kennedy seemed such an easy man to talk to,"

said one pretty geisha. "He appeared as a young man, not an Attorney General."

The Kennedys sang the Waseda University song as their contribution to the evening's entertainment. The gathering seemed delighted, even if Bobby sang in his usual monotone and Ethel, throatily and off-key.

In the waning hours of their six-day visit to Japan, Ethel struck a final blow for international friendship by handing out candy and toys to twenty children at the Futaba Nursery and Orphanage and once again raising her voice in song, this time "Twinkle, Twinkle, Little Star," in Japanese.

From Tokyo the Kennedys flew to Hong Kong where they promptly captured the hearts of thousands of fugitives from Red China in a hectic tour of the British Crown Colony's teeming resettlement area. Bobby skipped rope with refugee children while Ethel helped pass out noodles to the needy and sampled the free milk and cookies. Both asked scores of questions and shook hundreds of hands.

After attending Sunday mass, the Kennedys drove to the Wong Tai Sin Refugee Resettlement, one of the most densely populated square miles in the world. Bobby, face reddened by the Asian sun, and Ethel, pert and fresh despite the heat, waved to hundreds of refugees jamming balconies strewn with washing. Security men tried to shoo away the children who swarmed about the Kennedys, but Bobby waved them back, even though the crowds soon swelled to a huge size.

The following day, Ethel attended a fashion show in Saigon. From there they went on to Thailand, where she nearly fell into a canal while climbing aboard a boat. In the excitement, the local United States Information

Service press chief, William Weeks, lost his balance and landed neck deep in the water.

Two days later, the Kennedys were received at the Vatican by Pope John XXIII, who presented Ethel with a pearl-and-gold rosary and Bobby with a gold medal commemorating his pontificate. There were also rosaries for the Kennedy children.

But the memorable incident in Rome was Ethel's adventure aboard a motor scooter, a gift from foreign correspondents who hosted a luncheon for the couple at the Tuscan restaurant on the Piazza Fontanella Borghese. To the dismay of fellow diners, Ethel revved up the motor inside the restaurant. "Wouldn't it be easier to ride outside?" an English woman asked wonderingly.

Moments later, the scooter whizzed out of the restaurant with Ethel precariously aboard and began orbiting around the piazza to the cheers of entranced Italian bystanders.

The newsmen became concerned when Ethel grazed a slow-moving car and bruised her leg. Finally her hosts caught up with the machine and held it back by force.

On to Berlin and the biggest ovation of all from ecstatic crowds who lined the streets shouting "Bobby, Bobby, Bobby," and greeting Ethel with wolf whistles.

Wherever the young couple went, Berliners waved and cheered. While Bobby made speeches pledging that Berlin's airlanes to the West would be kept open, Ethel went out on the town. Wearing a mink coat over a chartreuse wool suit, she shopped for her children, but regretfully turned down a gift of seven children's bicycles because they were "too big for the boys."

At a German-American community school, Ethel let slip the fact that her husband had flunked the third grade.

As the Kennedys finally headed for home, Ethel gave her appraisal of the trip. "We've had fun," she declared with a tired but happy smile.

"Bobby made the speeches," said one of the newsmen who accompanied the party, "but this was Ethel's trip."

ᴉᐧ ᴉᐧ ᴉᐧ

In January 1964, two months after the assassination of John Kennedy, President Johnson asked Bobby to visit President Sukarno of Indonesia in Tokyo to persuade him to stop his sabre-rattling threats against the newly formed Federation of Malaysia. Sukarno, the strutting marauder of Southeast Asia, had already taken over West New Guinea two years before, with Russia's backing. Now, the pro-Communist Indonesian was hungering for more territory.

The arrival of Ethel and Bobby in Tokyo touched off a thunderous ovation from crowds of Japanese. It was partly a tribute to the memory of Kennedy's slain brother and in large measure a recognition of the vivid impression the attractive couple had made on their visit two years earlier.

Authorities at Waseda University, where Bobby had encountered the ourburst of hostility in 1962, appealed to him to pay another visit so that the students could atone for the earlier display of rudeness.

This time the reception by the students was almost reverential. Tears welled up in Ethel's eyes as her husband recalled that John F. Kennedy "was not only President of one nation. He was president of young people around the world."

Bobby accomplished little more in his diplomatic joust with Sukarno other than widening his culinary horizons by breakfasting on dried seaweed with the Indonesian leader. "To tell you the honest-to-goodness truth, it didn't taste bad," he told correspondents later. Bobby had two meetings at Tokyo's Imperial Hotel and a third five days later in Jakarta, where the Indonesian leader agreed to hold discussions with Tunku Abdul Rahman, the Malaysian Prime Minister. President Diosdado Macapagal, worried over the possibility of having a pro-Communist neighbor, also was to attend. The talks were scheduled for a week hence.

Nobody really expected Sukarno to keep his word and he did not. Hardly had Bobby and Ethel taken off for London when Sukarno delivered an impassioned oration to "crush Malaysia." His guerrilla raids along the Federation's borders resumed in two weeks.

In June 1964, Bobby made a semi-official visit to West Germany to see Chancellor Ludwig Erhard and former Chancellor Konrad Adenauer. A side trip to Poland caused some apprehension in Washington circles since it coincided with a visit to Warsaw by Yugoslav President Tito.

In West Berlin, Bobby unveiled a plaque at the Free University commemorating J.F.K.'s memorable "Ich bin eine Berliner" visit. When Bobby spoke, recalling what his brother had stood for, the response was overwhelming. From seventy-thousand Berliners came the ringing cry "Kenn-needee! . . . Bob-bee!" while Ethel gazed pridefully at her husband.

In Warsaw, huge crowds turned out when Kennedy arrived with Ethel, their three eldest children and sister-in-law Princess Lee Radziwill. Bobby, flanked by Ethel and the youngsters, stood on the roof of a slow-moving Soviet Volga limousine waving to the crowds like an American political candidate. He and Ethel entertained the crowds with a rendition of "When Polish Eyes Are Smiling."

The performance was not appreciated by United States Ambassador John M. Cabot of Boston, who sat glumly inside the limousine while Ethel and Bobby disported themselves on the roof. Finally the Ambassador grumbled to a Kennedy aide: "Would you please tell the Attorney General that the roof is falling in?"

Cabot's displeasure was mild compared to that of Polish officialdom. That evening, a member of the Foreign Office bluntly told Bobby that Polish party leader Wladyslaw Gomulka never played up to the crowds in such a manner. "Well, maybe that's the problem," Bobby retorted breezily.

The climax came when Bobby arranged a meeting with Poland's Roman Catholic Primate, Stefan Cardinal Wyszynski, after authorities had warned him that such an interview would be ill-advised.

The Kennedys may have ruffled the feathers of the Communist hierarchy in Poland but they left a lasting impression on the people.

Ø Ø Ø

In 1965, Ethel went to Saks Fifth Avenue in New York and selected a travel wardrobe that went in heavily for mint, pistachio and almond-greens. Soon afterward, she and Bobby set out on a twenty-day, twelve-thousand-mile trek through Latin America that was part vacation and part education. A formidable entourage accompanied the couple, including colleagues in the former Kennedy administration, newsmen, photographers, advisers, experts and family friends. The party included John Seigenthaler, a former Justice Department aide; Richard Goodwin, a specialist in Latin American affairs and William vanden Heuvel, a long-time Kennedy friend and also a former Justice Department official. Ethel invited two close friends, Judy Harris, a former schoolmate, and

Mrs. Frederick Ames Cushing, who worked in Bobby's New York office.

Only a small crowd was on hand when the party landed at Lima. Stressing the need for security precautions, the United States Embassy staff had waited until the last moment to make Kennedy's visit public. The suspicion crossed some minds that United States Ambassador J. Wesley Jones had deliberately kept news of the visit a virtual secret to curry favor with Lyndon Johnson.

Ethel set out on a tour of schools and hospitals; Bobby boarded an unpressurized DC-4 for a flight over the mountains to the Peruvian town of Cuzco. He was greeted by two-thousand villagers who, seeing him approach, burst through police lines, broke down a barbed-wire fence and rushed at him. The Senator emerged with a cut on his right cheek and torn pants.

Back in Lima, Ethel cornered Andy Glass, who had flown over the mountains with Kennedy, and William vanden Heuvel and Adam Walinsky. "How did he make out?" she asked.

"Bob made quite an impression," Glass replied.

"Oh, aren't you nice to call him 'Bob,' " Ethel said. "I don't think it's dignified for a man who's nearly forty to be called 'Bobby.' I wish everybody would call him 'Bob.' "

Glass was amused. It might help, he pointed out, if she would stop calling her husband "Bobby" each time she referred to him in public. Ethel was surprised. She explained that she had *always* called Bobby Bobby. Ethel turned away and Glass shook his head to clear it.

From Peru, the party pushed on to Chile, where Bobby and Ethel relaxed for a day at the home of United States Ambassador Ralph Duncan, a colleague from New Frontier days. The following day, they toured Santiago's slums, distributing PT-boat tie-clasps to Chileans who had probably never worn ties in their lives. Standing atop a car, Bobby raised Ethel's hand in the traditional prize-fight victory salute and said proudly: "I give you the mother of nine children." The Chileans were impressed.

At the University of Chile in Concepción, Ethel Kennedy underwent an agonizing experience: She watched in growing horror as her husband was vilified, pelted with garbage and spat upon by a group of frenzied, Communist-led students. One cannot doubt that she will never erase the terrible scene from her mind.

Chilean security men warned the United States Embassy that there would be trouble if Kennedy attempted to address the students. The Communists and Marxist Socialists were strongly entrenched in Concepción, third largest city in Chile. They viewed Kennedy as a representative of a country whose hands were "stained with blood." His advisers, knowing that his audience would be dominated by hard-core Reds and that, following Latin American tradition, the police could not enter the university grounds to protect the Senator, strongly advised him to cancel the speech. Even the director of the university felt Kennedy should not appear.

Bobby listened to them all, then gave his answer: "I've got to go." Ethel said: "I'm coming along." Bobby looked at her and said nothing. He changed his shirt and in a few minutes the party set out for the university.

More than two-thousand spectators jammed the stands in the gymnasium, the largest place available for the meeting. The gym floor itself was empty; at one end, a speaker's platform had been set up. Kennedy, accompanied by Seigenthaler, Goodwin, Vanden Heuvel and a newsman, entered, circling the floor toward the stand. Ethel, who had entered with her husband, was led to a seat in the stands and remained with Embassy officials.

Suddenly, a group of about a hundred Communists rose from their seats and, setting up a howl, hurled a heavy barrage of garbage, eggs, small stones and refuse at the incoming party. Andy Glass was hit many times; Vanden Heuvel caught several eggs. Kennedy, however, was untouched.

A sickening scene unfolded. On the platform, Kennedy's words were drowned by the students' shouts and chants. "I believe in freedom," he yelled into the microphone, his words translated by an interpreter at his side. "I believe in free institutions. And I *will* speak tonight."

His words were inaudible. "Go home, go home, you Yankee son-of-a-whore," they shouted at him. "Assassin!" they screamed. They hurled the vilest obscenities at him.

Unable to be heard, Kennedy leaped from the platform and made his way toward the noisiest sector where the Communists were concentrated. Someone pushed a chair toward him and he mounted it and offered to debate any of the Communists on the issues. A student, from a yard away, spat upon him and the spittle struck his right eye. Kennedy descended from the chair, wiped his eye with a handkerchief and told Vanden Heuvel: "Let's go."

As Ethel watched the ugly drama unfold, the Communists in the stand set fire to an American flag. An Embassy man with the Kennedy party giggled nervously at the spectacle; Ethel, who had not said a word up to then, swung toward him in anger. "Don't you laugh when the American flag is being burned," she snapped.

She joined Bobby in the car and drove back to the hotel.

In São Paulo, Brazil, Ethel arranged a birthday party for her husband at the home of Henry and Mildred Sage, old friends who had moved to the Brazilian city. After all, she felt, reaching the age of forty deserved some kind of recognition.

To mark the event in proper fashion, Ethel had composed several outrageously satirical songs on the Kennedy trip and its imagined impact on United States political figures. After the singing, the group filed in for dinner and Ethel passed out favors, among them a toy plane, which she described as a U-2 that Lyndon Johnson had dispatched to spy on Bobby's progress.

Through the slums of Brazil's cities the Kennedys went, through mud and open sewers where the stench was so foul that at one point their Brazilian security guard fled. Women held out their naked children for Ethel, who talked to them softly and patted them on the head.

Between stopovers in Rio and Caracas, the Kennedys decided to pay a visit to Brazil's Amazon jungle.

Flying to Manaus, the river port where the Amazon begins its thousand-mile course to the Atlantic Ocean, they boarded a paddlewheel boat. At a leisurely ten knots they threaded their way up the Solimões, a main tributary to the Amazon. The heat was so intense, however, that at nightfall, Ethel and Bobby abandoned their stuffy stateroom and dragged their mattresses onto the deck. Others in the party slung hammocks on the afterdeck.

The next day the party headed inland through the bush until they came upon a picturesque lake. While a crowd of curious youngsters watched, Kennedy doffed his sweaty clothes and plunged into the water. After a leisurely swim with others in the party, the Senator emerged and was told by nervous local officials that the lake was actually a branch of the Solimões River and therefore infested by flesh-eating piranha fish. Bobby mulled over his apparently narrow escape, but then remarked cheerily, "Piranhas have never been known to bite a United States Senator."

One day in Manaus, Bobby was offered, and grabbed, a chance to visit the interior of Amazonia. The only way of getting there was aboard a single-engine, 1939 plane that took off and landed on water. Muttering, "I must be crazy to get on this thing," Bobby kissed Ethel good-bye and vaulted into the cockpit, next to Goodwin and two reporters.

Bobby was not underestimating the risk. The rivers of the region were rock-strewn; a bad landing on water could leave them stranded or worse. And what would happen if the plane's one engine failed? Later, the journalist William V. Shannon was to tell Kennedy that "crazy" was precisely the right word for what he did, especially since he was the father of nine children. Kennedy, reflecting a moment, replied: "Perhaps it was not the wisest thing I've done."

It wasn't, but Ethel showed no outward fear. No one could tell, of course, how she felt inwardly as she watched her husband fly off in the twenty-five-year-old craft into the jungle; but it was apparent that she had made her peace with the idea that Bobby was this kind of man: that he loved the thrills of being involved in personal danger, that he could not turn away from challenges, no matter the risk. (When Bobby set out on his climb to the top of Mount Kennedy, especially dangerous in view of his inexperience, Ethel said good-bye at Hickory Hill with a cheerful: "Have a good time, Bobby.")

Nevertheless—it is perhaps significant that after he flew off into Amazonia, Ethel spent the evening visiting a nunnery, where she remained for several hours in the company of persons who had given their lives to God.

In Caracas, on the way home, there was a rousing welcome and some disturbing news. A guerrilla revolution was raging in the hills, and from time-to-time bombs exploded in the city. Once a smoke bomb was hurled into a labor hall where Bobby was speaking. The C.I.A.'s antennae picked up reports that Communist elements were threatening to machine-gun Bobby in the streets and kidnap Ethel. Extra security guards were placed around the couple until, after a lengthy and peril-filled journey, they finally took off for the United States.

ᕫ ᕫ ᕫ

Perhaps the most controversial of Kennedy's journeys was the one in June 1966 to South Africa, where the racial situation was explosive. Accompanied by Ethel, Bobby flew to Johannesburg and promptly harangued a group of citizens on the most sensitive subject he could have picked—South Africa's official white-supremacy policies.

"Where men can be deprived because their skin is black," he told the uneasy audience, "in the fullness of time, others will be deprived because their skin is white."

At the University of Natal, Bobby posed a question for students: "Suppose God is black," he said. "What if we go to heaven and we, all our lives, have treated the Negro as an inferior, and God is there, and we look up and he is not white. What then is our response?"

The Kennedys were struck by the look of fear in the eyes of so many of South Africa's blacks when they tried to speak to them in front of white officials, as though terrified that they would be the target of reprisals later on. Ethel told a friend after their return: "About South Africa, the thing that strikes you most is how it must have been in Nazi Germany in 1937. The sad thing is people don't realize, they don't wake up. . . ."

Ethel sincerely felt, however, that her husband had gotten his message across to the Bantu millions of South Africa. "Bobby really got through to the people," she declared, "and he really opened up the minds of people who never thought about such questions as apartheid before."

In Kenya and the Congo there were ovations for Bobby and admiring salutes for his wife. They also managed to see the spectacular African countryside and its amazing wildlife.

For years afterward Ethel liked to talk of the few days they were on safari, away from politics and milling throngs. "We flew in a little plane," she said, "and watched the migration of water buffalo, zebra, giraffes and wild boars and elephant and tigers and cheetahs. . . ." She would close her eyes in recollection.

"We were in the Serengeti, one of the largest animal preserves in the world, and I just found it like taking a deep dive down to the bottom of the ocean. It's so refreshing to see the elephants standing and dusting themselves off, and seeing the giraffes move gracefully and the lions disdainfully ignoring you. Something so regal, and so noble.

"It's a whole new world when you don't sit in Bobby Kennedy's back yard."

THIRTEEN

Helping Bobby Recover

❧ ❧

At 2:30 on a still-warm afternoon in late November, Ethel Kennedy telephoned Mother Odeide Mouton, head-mistress of the Stone Ridge Country Day School in nearby Bethesda. Kathleen, then twelve, and Mary Courtney, seven, were students there.

Ethel's voice was low but completely controlled.

"Mother," she said, "the President is dead." She paused. "The announcement hasn't been made yet to the country. Please tell Kathleen and Courtney. I'll come out and pick them up."

Mother Mouton's usually soft voice was now barely audible. "But you needn't," she told Ethel. "Couldn't I make some arrangement for someone to take the children home?"

"No," Ethel replied. "It's my day for the car pool. And would you also please tell Maria Shriver [daughter of Sargent Shriver and the former Eunice Kennedy, Bobby's sister]. I'll pick her up too so that her mother won't have to come out."

Fragmentary reports were coming in from Dallas. The nuns, listening to radios and watching television newscasts, knew only that the President had been shot in a downtown street during a motorcade and taken to Parkland Memorial Hospital. Nobody knew how badly he had been hurt.

Mother Mouton had instructed the nuns to take the older students into the chapel to pray for the President's recovery. After talking to Ethel, she went to the lower school herself to fetch Courtney.

She held the little girl and gently said to her: "Your uncle has been shot."

Courtney looked puzzled, then brightened and said: "You mean he got a shot, here in the arm?"

Mother Mouton replied: "No, dear, not that kind of shot." She paused. "Your mother is coming to get you," she said.

Ethel arrived at 3:15 and went at once to the chapel, still filled with the students. She knelt in the back and remained there for many minutes. Then she rose and, outside the chapel, she took Kathleen and Courtney aside and told them their uncle was dead. A moment later, Maria Shriver was led to her, and she told her too. She spoke briefly with Mother Mouton, then entered the car and drove back to Hickory Hill.

Mother Mouton, watching them leave, marveled at Ethel's self-control in this moment of anguish.

It had come suddenly, stunning them all on this late-fall day. Though already November 22, the temperature was in the sixties, warm enough for a swim and a poolside luncheon. Bobby's guests at Hickory Hill that day were United States Attorney Robert M. Morgenthau of New York and Silvio J. Mollo, head of the criminal division. They had been discussing the fight against organized crime when the phone rang. Ethel, closest to it, answered and held it out for Bobby, surprise in her look. "It's J. Edgar Hoover," she said. Hoover had never called at the house before. Bobby put the phone to his ear. The F.B.I. Director told him his brother had been struck down by an assassin. Hoover said: "I think it's serious. I'll call you back when I find out more."

Bobby put his hand across his mouth. "Jack's been shot!" he cried out. Ethel ran to him and put her arms around him. His face was contorted with horror.

Bobby rushed into the house to dress, Ethel following. He would go at once to Dallas. The phones were never silent, calls coming from friends, officials of the government, asking information, contributing a little. Bobby had asked John McCone, Director of the Central Intelligence Agency, to come over and McCone arrived as Bobby finished dressing. In the upstairs library, the direct line to the White House rang again. Captain Tazewell Shepard, President Kennedy's naval aide, who had been funneling bits and pieces of news to Bobby, now had the climax. He had just heard from the hospital that John Kennedy had died of his wounds.

Cradling the receiver, Bobby said softly: "Oh, he's dead."

Ethel embraced her husband. They remained there, locked together, his face showing his pain but in full control of himself. His first words were: "He had the most wonderful life." Hers: "Those poor children." Caroline was six, John three.

Ethel, Bobby and John McCone went downstairs where the visitors were watching developments on television. "He died," Bobby told them. He and Ethel started to walk outside when the telephone rang again. It was Hoover at the F.B.I. confirming the tragic news. The

Kennedys talked quietly together for a moment. But there was no time for private grief. Bobby, suddenly become head of the family, had to take charge of all arrangements. Ethel had her family. She picked up a phone and called Stone Ridge about the children. . . .

When the great calamity of his life struck, it was Ethel who sustained her husband and helped him overcome the grief that, for a time, threatened his emotional stability. For Bobby was more seriously affected than was generally realized at the time.

He functioned briskly, efficiently, in the days immediately following the assassination. "We don't want any gloomy faces around here," he told David Hackett, a friend since prep-school days, as he took hold of the reins. He made arrangements for the arrival of the President's body, cleared the way for the swearing-in of Lyndon B. Johnson, sent Teddy Kennedy to Hyannis Port so that old Joe Kennedy, speechless and unable to walk following a stroke, would hear the news only from a son. He even thought about safeguarding John Kennedy's personal files; McGeorge Bundy, special assistant to the President, ordered the combinations on the locks changed immediately. He took his children across the rolling lawn and talked with them quietly under the leafless trees. At 5:00, a little more than two hours after the President's death was confirmed, he drove to the Pentagon, conferred with Secretary of Defense Robert S. McNamara for twenty minutes, then left by helicopter for Andrews Air Force Base to meet Air Force One, coming in with the body of his brother.

Ethel's friends converged on Hickory Hill: Pat Newcomb rushed over from the Department of Justice, hugged Ethel and busied herself with the children. Sue Markham, wife of Dean F. Markham, then the head of the United

States Narcotic Commission, came. Journalist Anne Chamberlain, a close friend, arrived; so did Marion White, wife of "Whizzer" White, the Supreme Court Justice. Soon the house was crowded with friends.

Dave Hackett took Ethel to Bethesda Naval Hospital where the body of John Kennedy was to be taken for an autopsy. Hackett, at the wheel of Bobby's official Cadillac, was so upset he drove the entire distance with the brake on. In the seventeenth floor VIP suite, Ethel embraced Jackie, newly arrived from Dallas, still wearing her blood-stained stockings and pink suit. For Ethel, thoughts of God and her faith are never far away when tragedy occurs. She whispered to Jackie that she was sure her husband had been taken to heaven. Jackie replied: "I wish I could believe the way you do."

₪ ₪ ₪

Weeks afterward, the long funeral rites over, the family details attended to, the reaction set in for Bobby Kennedy and an ordeal that was to last for months began for Ethel.

Before her eyes, Bobby started to slip into a depression. The hurt showed plainly in his face, his lusterless eyes, the droop of his shoulders, his loss of interest in old excitements. He didn't return to work for a while and when he did, associates would find him staring across the room, or he would simply rise and leave, taking endless walks in the great courtyard of the block-square Department of Justice Building and out into the street. There was always a dazed look in his swollen eyes. He was living, as Hugh Sidey was to write, in a "shattered personal world," with the pain of his loss still "soul-deep."

"What happened to Bobby after his brother's assassination was not so strange," Lem Billings says. "Any man would be affected emotionally by the death of a brother, of course, but Bobby not only lost a brother he loved very much, but he had tied up his whole life with that of John Kennedy. He had subordinated his own self, his own career, to that of his brother. He had been totally involved, totally dedicated to helping and furthering the work of John Kennedy." Looked at in this light, it is little wonder his friends remarked that a light had gone out inside Bobby Kennedy after November 22.

Concern grew into alarm as the months passed and the depression seemed to deepen. Late in March, four months after the assassination, Walter Sheridan came to him with news that his long-time foe, Jimmy Hoffa, had at last been convicted on two counts of jury-tampering. Surely this would elate Bobby, who had put Sheridan in charge of a fifteen-man "Hoffa Squad" charged with nailing the Teamster boss. But Bobby merely said: "Nice work, Walter."

Experts in human behavior know that sadness is a normal emotional response to a grievous loss. Usually, the emotional wound heals by itself within a reasonable time period, and the individual, though still remembering tenderly, recaptures his zest for life. Occasionally, however, grief persists for months, even years. The individual is in the grip of a "reactive depression," overwhelmed by sadness, unable to function as he once did.

As the winter passed into spring and his normal spirits still did not return, friends began to fear this was happening to Robert Kennedy.

There can be little doubt this was in Ethel's mind too as she watched her husband wander desolately from room to room, flop in chairs with his hands deep in his pockets, rise and stare out of windows, sit again and look vacantly. December came and Bobby's despair deepened despite two short vacation trips, one to Hobe Sound, Florida, for swimming, the other to Aspen for skiing. Gratefully, Ethel learned early in January that President Johnson had assigned him to calm down Sukarno in the Far East.

But the two-week journey proved only a momentary distraction; Bobby was still like a man in shock. "There was no spring in his step, no light in his eyes," says a journalist who saw him regularly.

Slowly, Bobby Kennedy emerged from his gloom, and the person most responsible, in the opinion of many close friends, was Ethel Kennedy. "Without her," an intimate friend says, "Bobby might well have gone off the deep end after his brother's assassination."

She was the strength he lost temporarily. She was the support he needed to maintain his stability until his spirits revived.

How did she sustain him? In these ways:

By communicating to him her abiding religious faith. "Ethel is as religious a person as I have ever known," says Dave Hackett. "In that time of great sorrow, she reached out to him and kept reminding him of his own strong faith." Ethel, aware that Bobby was the most devout of the three brothers, knew that ultimately he would derive comfort and courage from his religion, once the edge of pain had passed.

By making certain that life went on, that her household functioned normally. "She did not fall apart, nor did she withdraw herself," Hackett says. "After a period of initial sorrow, she went back to a normal routine. Bobby, feeling himself in the midst of normalcy, surrounded by the people he loved, was thereby reinforced."

By banishing sadness from her home. "She simply refused to allow anyone to be sorrowful in Bobby's presence," Dickie Mann Cummins remembers. "She disliked long silences; when the talk stopped, she would say something, anything, to keep it going. She would not allow any morbid dwelling on the event in Dallas or its aftermath." Ethel made certain the house would be filled on weekends with the people Bobby knew and liked best, that there would be plenty of things to do for grownups and children. "She wanted jolly company around Bobby," says Dickie. "And as for herself, she was bright, she was lively, she was Ethel."

Bobby was to bear emotional scars for the rest of his life. Three years later, on the anniversary, Ethel once again saw the glazed look in his eyes and the sagging shoulders after they had returned from a visit to the grave. She distracted him by telephoning friends to play tennis with him. He developed a fatalism never apparent before. In 1964, while talking about his forthcoming campaign for the Senate in New York, he suddenly stopped and burst out: "I don't know that it makes any difference what I do. Maybe we're all doomed anyway." In 1968, he told a friend: "I can't be sitting around here calculating whether something I do is going to hurt my political situation in 1972. Who knows whether I'm going to be alive in 1972?"

He emerged from the shadows with these bitter legacies, but the important point is that he *did* emerge, and Ethel was the one who led him out.

Part Four

FOURTEEN

The Last Hurrah

ﷺ ☙

When it came to seeking the Presidential nomination, there were many questions in Bobby's mind but none in Ethel's. "In politics," Dave Hackett says, "Ethel operated mainly on instinct, and in this case her instincts told her he should get into the race. She felt strongly, overwhelmingly, that this was the thing to do."

Apparently, Ethel's instincts began twanging, or whatever it is instincts do to attract attention, long before Lyndon Johnson stunned the nation by removing himself from the race. While the President's popularity had declined sharply toward the end of 1967 as dissent rose over his conduct of the Vietnam war, few political experts figured anybody had much of a chance to wrest the Democratic nomination from him that summer. Johnson was holding most of the cards, *i.e.,* delegates, and delegates were the key to the nomination. Ethel was not impressed by the formidable odds, mainly because she did not know very much about the intricate mechanics of politics.

173

But she did know one thing better than anyone else—
her husband. She knew about *his* instincts, that they were
essentially activist and combative; she knew he held deep
feelings about the war in Vietnam; and she knew that, in
the main, he would have been a profoundly unhappy man
if he had *not* run. Accordingly, she began conducting a
campaign of her own to convince him, as the following
incident makes abundantly clear:

On December 28, 1967, Jack Newfield, a recognized
spokesman for the New Left and a close friend of Ethel
and Bobby during these crucial months, published a sting-
ing article, as rough a piece as any friend of Bobby's
had ever written.

"If Kennedy does not run in 1968," he wrote, "the
best side of his character will die. He will kill it every
time he butchers his conscience and makes a speech for
Johnson next autumn. It will die every time a kid asks
him, if he is so much against the Vietnam War, how come
he is putting party above principle? It will die every time
a stranger quotes his own words back to him on the value
of courage as a human quality.

"Kennedy's best quality is his ability to be himself, to
be authentic in the existential sense. This is the quality the
best young identify with so instinctively in Kennedy. And
it is this quality Kennedy will lose if he doesn't make his
stand now against Johnson. He will become a robot
mouthing dishonest rhetoric like all the other politicians."

A week after the article appeared, Kennedy spotted
Newfield at a function and strode up to him. "I thought
he was really pissed off and was going to pick a fight,"
the journalist says. "Instead he told me: 'You know Jack,
Ethel loved that article so much she had it Xeroxed and
sent it to fifty friends.' "

Apparently, she had recognized an ally in Newfield,

viewing his article not as an attack on her husband but a means of convincing him to follow his own basic feelings.

During the winter and early spring of 1968, Bobby was a tormented man, playing Hamlet, as David Halberstam put it—"thinking about the race constantly, wanting to make it, being led there by his emotions again and again, only to be brought back from the brink by the cold words of his closest advisers."

Hackett reveals that Bobby and Ethel talked the dilemma over many times in private. "Bobby always took her judgments into consideration," he says. "On matters that were technical or politically complex, she did not have much knowledge. In these, her judgment is not necessarily better than anybody else's. But on the broader issues, she would fall back on her basic inner feelings and was often proven right." Bobby knew this and listened.

There were meetings all over, in Bobby's luxurious apartment at 860 United Nations Plaza, Steve Smith's apartment at 1030 Fifth Avenue, in the Senator's office, at Hickory Hill, in automobiles and on airplanes. Through all the talk, Ethel, heeding those instincts that were sending through the clearest of beeps, stuck to her guns and worked on Bobby. As a friend said: "She had to live with his agonizing and kept telling him he had to do it."

During the months of indecision, Bobby would say: "The only people who want me to run are Ethel and Jesse Unruh." Unruh was the Speaker of the California State Assembly and a power in national Democratic politics. His statement wasn't exactly accurate because Adam Walinsky, Frank Mankiewicz and a few more of "the Kennedy guard" were pushing with fervor. Others, though, held different views. Kenny O'Donnell was lukewarm, though he said that if Bobby announced at 12:00, by 12:01 he'd be fighting on his side. Ted Sorensen, President Kennedy's speechwriter and adviser, and Lawrence O'Brien, his Postmaster General, felt that an attempt to dethrone a President had to be regarded as windmill-tilting no matter what the circumstances. Arthur Schlesinger, Robert McNamara and Walter Reuther shook their heads, and so did Ted Kennedy. While Ted sided with his brother in his criticism of the war, he argued that entrance into the lists at that point would open Bobby to charges, not easily refuted, that a challenge to Johnson would be regarded as ruthless opportunism. Everyone knew that John Kennedy had inscribed a cigarette case to Bobby: "When I'm through, how about you?" It was no secret that Bobby had hopes of some day occupying the Oval Room. But was this the time to seek it?

When March blustered in, Bobby was still undecided. "Only the most emotional people are really for my doing it, like Ethel, my staff and all my sisters," he would say later. The apparently unconquerable Lyndon Johnson was still there, looming like Everest. True, his situation had worsened as the winter wore on. Dissent over his policies raged so fiercely he dared not make personal appearances for fear of triggering riots. His popularity was ebbing fast. But still, he was the President, and Presidents control the levers of elective power. And, so far as anybody knew, he was still in the race. Nobody had any inkling that, when March ended, he would take himself out. (When he finally did, Ethel summed him up succinctly: "Well, he never deserved to be President anyway.")

Gene McCarthy was up in cold New Hampshire with his army of college students, trying hard, but Kennedy sincerely doubted that the Senator from Minnesota would make a good President. "What has he ever done for the ghettos or the poor?" he asked. He did not endorse McCarthy's New Hampshire race for this reason.

On March 12, McCarthy pulled off his extraordinary victory and the pressure on Bobby became intense. Nearly a hundred telegrams an hour, practically all of them urging him to run, were deposited at his Senate office. Bobby, who had spent the day of the primary in New York with Ethel, returned to Washington on Wednesday and, cornered by reporters at the airport, told them: "I am actively reassessing the possibility of whether I will run against President Johnson." That brought the kettle to a ferocious boil: Newsmen wouldn't let him out of their sight, waiting for the result of the reassessment.

On Thursday, after another day of conferences and nonstop telephone calls around the country seeking advice, Bobby went home to Hickory Hill for his dinner date with the Laursens and the other New York State weekly newspaper editors described in Chapter Eight. Before midnight, he had decided to go in, though he still wondered if he were making a mistake. "You think I have a right to run, don't you?" he asked Newfield after the editors had gone. "Tell me if you think I'm being unfair." Newfield replied: "No. You have a right to run and you should run."

Next day he flew to New York for more conferences about his candidacy and a tour of Long Island civic and political organizations. Before he left, he instructed Mankiewicz to make arrangements for press and TV coverage of his declaration. With him on the plane were Newfield and Haynes Johnson of the Washington *Star*. He talked frankly with them. He knew that to announce then, after McCarthy had shown Johnson was not unbeatable after all, would open himself to charges of cowardice and ruthless opportunism. In his book *Robert Kennedy, A Memoir*, Newfield quotes Bobby's painful appraisal of his situation:

"This hasn't been an easy decision for me to make. A

lot of people who have been my friends will be distressed. It is going to make things very difficult for a lot of people. . . . It is a much more natural thing for me to run than not run. When you start acting unnaturally, you're in trouble. At least now I can start reacting normally to events and issues. . . . I have to face myself. I couldn't be a hypocrite. Not to run and pretend to be for McCarthy, while trying to screw him behind his back, that's what would really be ruthless. Making speeches for him, while I'm secretly trying to get delegates for myself—that's ruthless. I'm trusting my instincts now and I feel freer. I know my brother thinks I'm a little nutty for doing this, but we all have to march to the beat of our own drummer. . . ."

Shortly after 9:00 on Saturday morning, Ethel piled 9 of her 10 children into a station wagon (the baby, Douglas Harriman, just a week short of his first birthday, was too young to go) and took them all to the Senate Caucus Room. By 10:00, they were all seated with 450 others watching and listening to Bobby as he rose to say:

"I am announcing today my candidacy for the Presidency of the United States."

Ethel tried to listen and, at the same time, keep her squirming younger children under control. Watching her shushing them and prying them apart when they clashed, few in the audience there and before television screens could suspect that Ethel—as Frederick P. Dutton, Bobby's principal campaign adviser was to say afterward— "without question" was a "major factor" in the decision her husband was announcing to the country.

After his brother's murder, Bobby slid swiftly from the pinnacle of power. Once he had been consulted by the President on almost every major move. Only he and Vice-President Johnson were permitted to enter the Oval Room unannounced through the rear door facing the garden. He had run his Justice Department like "Gangbusters" but had been so closely involved with the White House and its problems that the New Frontiersmen called him the country's Number-Two Man. But now President Johnson, after the first hard months of readjustment, never summoned him for advice or counsel. And—a small matter but revealing—J. Edgar Hoover, whose boss he was at Justice, no longer reported to him directly but to the President.

It was a time for hard rethinking. The one excitement was gone from crime-fighting. The Vietnam war seemed to offer a greater challenge. When Henry Cabot Lodge announced his resignation as Ambassador to Saigon, Bobby wrote a letter to Johnson asking for the job. He could grapple with new challenges and, besides, get out of Washington. But Johnson said no, it was risky business out there and the country didn't want to take a chance on losing another Kennedy.

More to the point, Johnson didn't want to risk being accused of sending Kennedy out of the country during the nominating convention. For a grass-roots movement to swing the Vice-Presidency to Kennedy was taking shape. Many of Bobby's friends and advisers began to generate a good deal of enthusiasm for the idea. It would keep a Kennedy in the executive department, and high up there. It would, moreover, put him in the best possible position for a step-up in 1972, assuming Johnson was elected for two terms.

Bobby, however, wasn't keen on the notion. "There isn't anything you can do in the Vice-Presidency," he said. "Not one damn thing that you are not told to do." And to be told what to do by Lyndon Johnson, who was resented by the entire Kennedy faction, would be galling.

Nonetheless, the movement continued to grow. Richard

Daley, the politically powerful Mayor of Chicago, backed him, along with Governors and State and Party leaders from the Midwest and Northeast. Ethel was ready to spring into action; Jackie Kennedy, vacationing in Yugoslavia, was reported ready to return to "help Bobby."

But one man, and one man alone, picks the Vice-President, and Lyndon Johnson did not want Bobby. He knew more than anyone else that Bobby had become for millions of Americans the living symbol of the bright and beautiful days just past, the hope many cherished that days like them would come once again with Bobby at the helm. A proud and imperious man, Johnson wasn't about to become an interlude between two Kennedys if he could help it, and the clear fact was that he could help it. He could deny Bobby a place on the ticket, and he did.

Late in July 1964, Johnson summoned Bobby to the White House. "I think I know what you want," the President told him. "You want to lead the country some day." When the time came, he said, he would assist all he could, but the subject under discussion that afternoon was the Vice-Presidency and he was sorry that he could not offer Bobby the post. "You have a bright future, a great name and courage," Johnson said, "but you have not been in government very long. I have given you serious consideration, but find it inadvisable to pick you."

Bobby, Johnson said later, swallowed hard as he heard the rejection. On the way out of the Oval Room, Bobby turned and told the President: "I could have helped you a lot." The next evening, Johnson told the country via television from the White House: "I have reached the conclusion that it would be inadvisable for me to recommend to the convention any member of my Cabinet or any of those who meet regularly with the Cabinet."

Nobody was fooled by the transparent maneuver to avoid angering the millions of Kennedy supporters, least of all Bobby. Addressing a group of Congressional candidates early in August, he told them: "I must confess I stand in awe of you. You are not members of the Cabinet, and you don't meet regularly with the Cabinet, and therefore you are eligible for Vice-President. I decided to send a little note to Cabinet members in general, saying: 'I'm sorry I took so many nice fellows over the side with me.'" *

Riding home to Hickory Hill a few days later, Bobby turned to a friend and commented: "I don't think there is much future for me in this city now."

They had been beckoning to him from New York State, and it was there he turned his attention. Months before, friends had suggested he run for the Senate against Kenneth Keating, the genial, G.O.P. incumbent. He had allowed a boomlet to develop while he mulled over the idea but finally, in late June, he had announced he would not take on Keating. He explained he was not a New Yorker and hence would be vulnerable to charges of carpetbagging.

But announcements such as this are hardly final. Steve Smith, his brother-in-law, read Bobby the results of several

---

*A different version of the Kennedy–Vice-Presidency episode was given by Kenneth P. O'Donnell (*Life* magazine, August 7, 1970). Bobby, O'Donnell wrote, decided in May he would not try to be Johnson's running mate. He planned to resign from the Cabinet and return to New York. However, O'Donnell said he persuaded Kennedy to keep his decision a secret until sufficient strength could be built up for Hubert H. Humphrey. O'Donnell argued that Humphrey was the best man around who "represented our views" and that "we owed it to ourselves, and to those who supported his (Bobby's) brother, to make sure we were represented by someone in the Government." If Bobby pulled out then, O'Donnell argued, Humphrey supporters would lose their leverage with Lyndon Johnson and "he would feel free to pick anyone he wanted, a nonentity."

private polls that sounded promising. Endorsements kept coming in from Democratic and Liberal Party leaders, and ultimately from Mayor Robert F. Wagner of New York, who had been reluctant to share political power with Kennedy. Finally, in late August, Bobby stood on the steps of Gracie Mansion, the Mayor's official residence, and, as Ethel watched, declared his candidacy for the Senate. To qualify as a New Yorker, he had leased a $250,000 twenty-five room mansion in Glen Cove, Long Island, for $1,000 a month and taken up residence at the ultra-fashionable Carlyle Hotel on Madison Avenue, where his brother had stayed frequently during New York visits.

On September 1, Ethel, noticeably pregnant, journeyed down from Cape Cod with seven of her children and sat in the balcony of the 71st Regiment Armory, a huge pile of ugly red stone on Manhattan's Lexington Avenue. On the floor below, the State Democratic Convention nominated her husband on the first ballot as its candidate for the Senate.

Each of the children wore large campaign buttons reading: "Let's put Bob Kennedy to work for New York." The voters did, despite the carpetbagging charges he had anticipated and the even more widespread criticism that Robert was coldly using his brother's martyrdom to win a springboard to the White House for himself. He beat Keating by 628,000 votes and won a place in the Senate, though so far back in the chamber because of low seniority that he observed: "I had better seats for *Hello Dolly*." After the election, he solemnly assured members of the Women's National Press Club that he had no Presidential ambitions—"and neither does my wife, Ethel Bird."

Ethel went back to rearing her family, and increasing it at the same time: Matthew Maxwell was born January 12, 1965, and Douglas Harriman on March 24, 1967.

The Senate years were years of rapid growth for Ethel and Bobby. Both became fully acquainted for the first time with the very real problems of minority groups. Both could weep over the plight of rat-bitten children in the tenements and sick and hungry children. Kennedy planned broad new programs to bring new business and industry to Brooklyn slums, establish special tutoring programs for emotionally disturbed children, develop parks and playgrounds.

Both, too, could look now upon the war in Vietnam with different eyes. Once a supporter of the Johnson policies, Bobby became disenchanted, then actively opposed as the killing went on and the Asian quagmire deepened. Foreseeing "only years and decades of further draining conflict," he called for a negotiated settlement and an end to the bombing of North Vietnam. "It is not weakness for this great nation to take a generous step toward ending the war," he said in 1967. "It is not bravery to refuse an act which may save thousands of lives with little risk to ourselves. Can anyone believe this nation, with all its fantastic power and resources, will be endangered by a wise and magnanimous action toward a difficult but small adversary? Not escalation, but an effort to achieve negotiation, now opens the most hopeful prospect to peace."

His stand attracted many able, intelligent people to his side. Young people, especially, regarded him as their champion in a despairing time. As 1968 opened, they would scream for him when he appeared in public to run for President.

And, finally, he did.

◊ ◊ ◊

The day after Bobby jumped in, Ethel was off and running with him.

Had some fashion reporter been alert, she might have

scooped the country on Bobby's intentions, for several days prior to the official announcement, a telephone call had been made on Ethel's behalf to Madame Paul in Georgetown, who had two dressmakers' dummies of her—the newest in size eight—standing at the ready. Could she whip up a travel wardrobe, very fast? She could indeed; with some overtime, she and her seamstresses created a reversible dress and coat combination of non-wrinkle cashmere in two tones of green, and delivered it to Hickory Hill. Ethel had clothes, was ready to travel and did on Saint Patrick's Day.

Bobby had already left for speaking engagements on two university campuses in Republican Kansas as a warm-up for the drive, which was to take him into the Indiana, Nebraska, Oregon and California primaries. To gain national support, he was to criss-cross the country; in the first fifteen days alone, he spoke in sixteen states.

At three in the afternoon on March 17, Ethel was feeding Douglas Harriman at Hickory Hill. With her was Rene Carpenter, one of her several "ladies in waiting," as Washingtonians called the hip young matrons around her. Rene recalls: "Ethel decided at three to go, and we left at five. There was no one to go with her. . . . Her hair wasn't shampooed, so I felt she needed me. I packed in ten minutes and we left for Kansas City."

Ethel and Rene were met by a plane sent by Democratic Governor Robert B. Docking and taken to Topeka, where, with Bobby, they were guests at the Governor's mansion. Ethel spent the next two days at Bobby's side, not doing much more than following him through crowds, smiling and waving. She saw the first of the signs that were to be waved before her face by the hundreds as the weeks went on: "Sock it to 'em, Bobby," "Kiss me, Bobby," "Bobby is Groovy."

On March 18, in the vast fieldhouse at Kansas State, where 14,500 students were packed on the dirt floor, she heard her husband set forth the basic themes of his campaign:

He candidly admitted his share of the responsibility for the Vietnam war but said that past error cannot be offered as an excuse for its own perpetuation. Tragedy must not be a guide by which to live but a tool enabling the living to gain wisdom. He quoted the *Antigone* of Sophocles: "All men make mistakes, but a good man yields when he knows his course is wrong, and repairs the evil. The only sin is pride."

He attacked Johnson's policies as bankrupt. When it all ended, he feared there would only be more Americans slaughtered, more American treasure wasted. He struck hard at what he termed the corruption and lack of commitment of the South Vietnamese, asserting the facts clearly showed that thousands of young men were buying their deferments from military service "while American marines die at Khesanh."

He warned that the United States was in danger, not merely from enemies abroad but from its own misguided policies. A great battle was underway within the country, he said, not for the rule of America but the heart of America. In the months ahead, the decision will have to be made: what will the nation stand for, what kind of men are we?

At the end, he asked for help. "If you will give me your help," he pleaded, "if you will give me your hand, I will work for you and we will have a new America."

The students almost literally exploded. They rose and screamed. They pounded one another. They applauded until their hands hurt, then they hit chairs together for more noise. Many raced toward Bobby and pushed him against a wall, tearing at his sleeves, ruffling his hair, yanking at his cuffs. His staff finally got him outside where he sat on top of an open car. Here the students reached out for him and almost pulled him from his perch.

Ethel saw it all and glowed. Later, the demonstration was repeated by twenty-thousand students at Lawrence.

It had been a tremendous opening for Bobby. As for Ethel, she goofed on the packing, the first of many such incidents. When she left the Governor's house, she forgot to pack Bobby's shirts, her cosmetics, a bathrobe and a pair of ruby-and-diamond bracelets. Mrs. Docking wrapped the items neatly and chased after the Kennedys to hand Ethel the bundle.

As the campaign progressed, Ethel would join it for several days at a time, sometimes traveling along for a week or more, but managing to fly home often to be with the children. Typically, she would visit hospitals, industrial plants and childrens' institutions, make small speeches, sign autographs and stand by Bobby. The strategists often stuck her on the dias when Bobby made speeches on the theory that people would find it hard to believe that a man with such an apple-pie All-American looking wife could possibly be as ruthless as he was pictured.

She gave a few sit-down television interviews and appeared ill at ease with strange reporters. Friends said she was deathly afraid she might say something that would boomerang against Bobby. She was keenly aware that she had been guilty of some memorable gaffes. In 1966, after she and Bobby returned from South America, a New York reporter asked Ethel what lay ahead on her schedule. She replied blithely: "We're going up to New York to campaign for Samuel Silverman—whoever he is." Mr. "Whoever he is" was an important candidate for

Surrogate Court and neither he nor New York Democrats were especially enchanted by Ethel's remark.

Inevitably, there were a few mistakes, though not many. In Fort Wayne, Indiana, she relied on a taxi driver for the information that the city was named for "Mad Anthony" Wayne, the American patriot who had fought the British in the War of 1812. Addressing a group of youngsters later that day, she began by saying how thrilled she was to be in the city bearing the name of the general who had fought in the War of 1812. Later, she learned that by 1812, Wayne had been dead for 16 years; that he was, in fact, a famous Indian fighter.

When she landed in Los Angeles, she announced how happy she was to be in Anaheim, prompting Bobby to tell her: "For Christ's sake, Ethel, if you're going to get the name of the town wrong, at least say it in a whisper." However, campaign advisers were very pleased at her quick thinking and agility in Indianapolis. While visiting the Eli Lilly Pharmaceutical Company, she spotted photographers about to take a shot of her with some employes who were making birth-control pills. She backed away in time.

Once she remained at Hickory Hill to play hostess to some five-hundred wives of members of the American Society of Newspaper Editors. The well-bred, somewhat snooty women clumped in quiet conversational groups on the lawn. Ethel, gracious, subdued and beautifully dressed, walked among them, saying pleasant little things. Joan Kennedy and Eunice Shriver were there, smiling and finishing-school genteel. The food was excellent, the pool, for once, unoccupied, the children on good behavior. Then Brumus blew the whole thing by nipping two of the wives and sending them into near-hysterics. Ethel apologized profusely and took one of the women into the house to lie down from her fright. She worried for days that the incident would hurt Bobby.

She was most at ease while visiting and talking with children at hospitals, homes, Head Start programs and on the street. She would touch them, pat them, smooth their hair, hug them and whisper to them, and they would respond at once, sometimes holding her because they did not want her to leave. Bobby, too, had a rapport with children. Once in Washington, D.C., a car in their motorcade struck a little girl's dog. Both Kennedys sprang into action—he leaped from his automobile, kneeled before the child and spoke softly to her; she rushed for a telephone to call for a veterinarian.

The little speeches she delivered were better than she thought. Saying little of consequence, she was there as the wife of the candidate, to sell him through her own personality. But she did it very well, projecting a wholesomeness, honesty and—her fashionable clothes notwithstanding—simplicity. She giggled and made funny little remarks that endeared her to her audiences: When a baby began wailing, she stopped and said: "That makes me feel right at home." She kidded herself: "This is my first day speaking," she said at Marion, Ohio, "so I confess I'm a little hesitant. In 1960 Bobby sent me to Kentucky, Utah, California, Oregon, Virginia—and we didn't win one of those states." She admitted she was a terrible cook. She talked about families, schools.

Campaigning, at best, is a grueling affair, but Ethel seemed tireless, though she was pregnant again. Her eleventh baby was due in early December. She rode in all the motorcades, which were tests of nerves and endurance, for wherever they went the Kennedys drew enormous throngs whose enthusiasm often approached hysteria. Often people would wait many hours with their children to see them. Then, when the candidate's car approached, they would press dangerously close. They would grab at him as he stood on the rear deck of his convertible, scratch his outstretched hands, yank off his cufflinks (he lost dozens of pairs weekly) and, frequently, refuse to let go of his hand. Several times he was pulled out of the car together with Bill Barry, who would kneel hour after hour on the hard metal, sweat pouring from his face as he held grimly onto Bobby's belt. (Barry was to remember that Ethel, who had noticed his knees beginning to bleed, found some foam rubber to put under them, and once she ran off and returned with elastic bandages that could be pulled over the knees.)

The only thing Ethel actively disliked about campaigning was the need to fly. She had a morbid fear of planes, resulting from a number of personal tragedies we will recount in a later chapter. On take-offs and landings, she would clutch Bobby's hand and stiffen until the aircraft was aloft or on the ground.

Despite this, she was cheerleader-happy practically all the time, pepping up the dispirited, especially Bobby, when things went wrong. When he lost in Oregon, receiving 33.8 per cent of the vote to McCarthy's 44.7 per cent, she figured the best thing to do would be to bomb the state off the map and forget about it. Then she came up with an explanation: "The dog owners of Oregon didn't pull together." At the Benson Hotel that evening, she was Happy Girl all over the place, consoling everyone and offering drinks to ease the pain.

On May 24, Ethel gave a party aboard the "mother ship" as it flew toward Los Angeles from Eugene, Oregon.

It was Bill Barry's birthday. Ethel stocked up with dozens of zany gifts and spent hours making preparations. Somebody kept Barry away from the plane until the last minute. When he finally came aboard, the entire interior was festooned with red, blue and silver crepe paper and balloons and signs reading: "Barry for F.B.I. Director" and "Barry's the One." June Dutton, Fred's wife, had ordered a three-foot-square cake decorated with a caricature, in frosting, of Barry dropping Bobby from a car, with Bobby saying "Whoops!" as he fell.

Barry's habit of dropping off into sound slumber after his day's tiring work was the theme of the gifts. Ethel presented him with a variety of health foods and potions for extra vigor. Sylvia Wright of *Life* magazine found a sleeping mask, with "Goodnight, David" over one eye and "Goodnight Chet" over the other. Someone else gave him a Snoopy nightshirt. Bobby howled with laughter as each present was opened. Ethel and Bobby circulated among the guests filling glasses with champagne. Bobby took a sip from practically every glass he filled

The tensions of the past weeks snapped and soon the newsmen and campaign workers were laughing and singing. Ethel was at the peak of her exuberance. Bobby, thoroughly relaxed, joined in the songs and laughed uproariously at the funny poems some of the newspeople had written.

It was quite possibly the best party Ethel had ever given.

Then, in a few hours, the plane landed at Los Angeles.

FIFTEEN

Two Days in Los Angeles

❧ ❧

Suddenly, very close to her, there was a loud explosion. When it came she was standing alongside Bobby on the rear seat of an open convertible, smiling and waving at the crowds. At the sound, the smile died and her body tensed. She hopped down and sat in the car, squeezing herself small. Five more cracks came in quick succession. Ethel began trembling violently, like the time she was bitten by the coati mundi.

If Bobby Kennedy felt fear up there on the seat of the car, he did not show it. He kept smiling and waving as the automobile moved slowly forward. Looking down, he saw Ethel crumpled in the corner, her fingers twined and her body shaking. He called out to a newsman who was jogging alongside to sit in the car and hold her hand until she could regain her composure.

Shortly before noon on Monday, June 3, 1968, Kennedy was on his way to address a group of Italian-Americans at Joe DiMaggio's seafood place on Fisherman's Wharf in

San Francisco. His route took him through the city's big and gaudy Chinatown, the largest Chinese community outside Asia. He rode down famous Grant Avenue, past the gift shops and restaurants constructed in Oriental architecture, greeting the throngs, shaking hands, doing his best to keep from being yanked out head foremost. At Washington Street, he had stopped to talk about the great contributions the Chinese citizens had made to the city and to the country.

The motorcade started off. A moment later someone set off a string of Chinese firecrackers. Bill Barry's light blue eyes flicked around searchingly. Reporters turned to the sound, some flinching. Faces whitened. Then, in a few seconds, they all saw what caused the pops and the tension subsided.

She would not talk about it publicly or even to close friends, but one cannot escape the conclusion that ever since Dallas—and especially since the beginning of the campaign for the nomination—Ethel had feared someone might try to take her husband's life.

Everyone else around Bobby had the same dread. "It was never far from anyone's mind," Dave Hackett says. "We were always tensed for it." Jimmy Breslin agrees: "From the first day he ran for the Presidency when he went to Kansas by plane to start his first great rush, everybody with him talked only of one thing." John Lindsey, correspondent for *Newsweek,* once said: "He's going to be shot. He's going to be shot as sure as we're here." Edwin O. Guthman, Kennedy's press officer when he was Attorney General, has disclosed that the F.B.I. and local police had received frequent warnings since 1963 that Bobby would be shot. Repeatedly, friends and aides pleaded with him to accept a heavier guard when he traveled but he had refused.

On this trip through the West, Barry had gone to him a number of times asking for more security but Bobby had replied: "That's not the way I want to run a campaign. That's not the United States of America. In some other kind of country a candidate may have to talk through some kind of shield, but not here." Hackett says: "And so he would expose himself freely to crowds. It made us all extremely nervous."

Barry would hide the automobiles at night after the motorcades to prevent anyone from wiring bombs into them and he would ask local police to assign men to guard Bobby's hotel rooms. "But we can use another guy," he said more than once. "I get mixed up with the crowds and I can't see. And I get tired. Maybe I won't be able to react quickly enough. I wish somebody would talk to him."

A journalist did try to talk to him one day, as Ethel looked on, telling him that Barry was getting weary. Ethel wanted to know what he meant. The newsman turned to her. "Do you have anybody looking after your house?" he asked pointedly. "I mean somebody who can handle something." Ethel understood. "Oh, that," she said, and turned away.

All of them—Guthman, Barry, Hackett, Dutton, Mankiewicz—all the good, close friends Ethel and Bobby had gathered over the years were prepared to shield the Kennedys with their bodies if the need arose.

ɷ ɷ ɷ

It was cold for swimming that day at Malibu, the exclusive beach playground northwest of downtown Los Angeles. The temperature had dipped into the fifties and a ten-mile wind, blowing in from the ocean, had whipped up a heavy surf.

Bobby and Ethel had ended the California run and, bone-weary, had come down here to rest at the beach home of movie director John Frankenheimer. Journalist Theodore White was there, with Fred Dutton, speech-writer Richard Goodwin and a few other close friends. The Kennedys had brought their six children, a couple of whom were out there, swimming and playing games under a sunless sky with their father.

The pace of the final day had been punishing, even for the Kennedys. In the last twelve hours of the campaign, they had traveled twelve-hundred miles by air and auto-mobile, touching many population centers, speaking in Watts and Venice at Los Angeles, flying down to San Diego for a motorcade and more speeches. Here they had snaked through the predominantly Negro section of Lo-gan Heights, finally drawing up before the three-story El Cortez Hotel on Ash Street.

For the first time, Bobby Kennedy worried Ethel and his aides. His hands shook as he talked at the hotel, his face was deeply lined and almost gray; his upper lip twitched. He spoke only briefly and somewhat incoher-ently, then stopped and walked to the rear of the platform in the auditorium and sat on the steps, his face in his hands.

Rafer Johnson, the 1964 Olympic decathlon champion who was accompanying the Kennedys, and Barry helped him to his feet and led him to a restroom a few yards away. Johnson stood at the door to insure privacy; Barry talked quietly to Bobby, who leaned against a sink. Fred Dutton came in and Bobby, grinning weakly, said to him: "I just ran out of gas." By now, Ethel was at the door, in-quiring anxiously. Dutton told her Bobby had suffered a dizzy spell and was weak with fatigue. In a few minutes he emerged and returned to the platform to finish his talk.

That night, both had slept heavily at Frankenheimer's home and by morning Bobby felt better. Wearing a gaily colored shirt and bathing trunks, he took David, then twelve, and Max, three, down to the beach where he helped the younger boy build a sand castle. Despite the dismal weather, Bobby and David decided to plunge into the ocean. David, cavorting happily, wasn't aware that a strong undertow was carrying him farther and farther out. The boy began struggling against the powerful pull.

Bobby realized suddenly his son was in danger. He swam after him, grabbed him and pulled him in. In his lunge, Bobby struck his head, either against the sea floor or against David, suffering a small bruise over his right eye.

After that, they returned to the house and spent the rest of the day at the poolside. Ethel watched her husband roughhousing with the children, tossing them into the water, being tossed by them.

At the Ambassador Hotel, a staid six-hundred-room hostelry on broad Wilshire Boulevard where the local Rotary Club meets every month and families with babies are offered free cribs, special rates and a sitter list to choose from, campaign workers were bustling around the Embassy Ballroom on the main floor, hanging up Bobby Kennedy posters, colored streamers and huge banners in anticipation of a big victory. TV crews were setting up their equipment there and upstairs in special rooms where interviews with the candidate were to take place.

In Suite 511, consisting of a large living room, two bedrooms and bath—"Royal Suite," the hotel called it— there were still remnants of a party weary workers and newsmen had thrown for themselves the evening before. There had been dancing, drinking and singing until nearly dawn. Some reporters and aides, having filed their stories and handled their last detail, and now with nothing to do but await the primary results, went shopping. Adam Walinsky and Jeff Greenfield bought themselves brightly colored hippie outfits to wear at the big victory bash planned for that night at a place called The Factory, an in discothèque in West Hollywood.

It had been a restful day at the beach for the Kennedys. They talked quietly with friends, lunched on the terrace, swam. By midafternoon, some results trickled in from precincts that had recorded all their eligible voters: Kennedy was winning 49 per cent of the vote to McCarthy's 41 per cent. Bobby, encouraged, took a brief nap, and by six he was dressed and calling to Ethel to hurry. The polls would close in two hours, and he wanted to get to the Ambassador. Ethel chose a sleeveless orange and white Courrèges minidress, horizontal stripes above the midriff, large circles below, pulled on white stockings, and announced she was ready.

John Frankenheimer drove the Kennedys and the children to town in his big car over back roads at speeds that made Ethel gasp and Bobby, no slowpoke in an automobile, urge caution. The light smog that had blanketed Los Angeles had lifted and a hazy sun still shone as the drove. At 7:15, they drew up before the Ambassador.

A bar in the living room was open for business and business was good. More than a hundred workers, politicians, newsmen and assorted others were milling about in the room and corridor. Ethel and Bobby pressed through the throng and entered one of the bedrooms. Bobby huddled with Ted Sorensen and Dutton. The children—Michael, Mary Kerry, Courtney and David—squatted in front of the big television set in the living room, sipping soft drinks. Chris and Matthew had been taken to the Beverly Hills Hotel, where all the youngsters were staying in care of a governess. Kerry, asked how she liked the show, replied: "It's fun and we can stay up late."

The long night began.

Ethel, her excitement growing, went from room to room, urging drinks on people who needed little urging, squeezing the necks of her children when she passed, asking hundreds of questions, exuding confidence. She grinned broadly when, almost as soon as the polls closed, the Columbia Broadcasting System's computer forecast a Kennedy victory.

At 9:00, Bobby walked into the corridor to chat with reporters. "I like politicians," he said. "I like politics. It's an honorable adventure." Somebody noted that was a good phrase and Bobby asked: "Do you know who made it up? That was Lord Tweedsmuir. Do you know who he was?" None of the two dozen news people around him did. Kennedy explained he was John Buchan, British author, statesman and novelist, once Governor-General of Canada, author of *The Thirty-Nine Steps,* who died in 1940. "It looks like a big Kennedy victory," a reporter told him. "What's next?" Bobby said he was leaving for New York with his family on Thursday. He returned to his suite.

In the living room, astronaut John Glenn made room for Ethel on a large couch. She sat there watching the television report Bobby's increasing lead. Inside the bedroom, Bobby sat on the floor in a corner, knees pulled up under him, smoking a long thin cigar. The phone would ring and he'd move to the chair to answer it, his feet on the bed. From time to time, he would confer with members of his inner circle—Steve Smith, Sorensen, Goodwin, Dutton. Jimmy Breslin knocked and was let in. Soon the little bedroom became crowded and someone locked the door. Outside, Ethel rose from the couch and tried to enter the bedroom. She rattled the knob and was admitted. "Can't even get into my own room," she laughed.

At 10:00, it was becoming increasingly clear that Bobby

was winning. Shortly after 10:30, he went down to the fourth floor where he sat with Sandor Vanocur of NBC for a television interview. Immediately afterward, he returned to the fifth floor for another television session with Roger Mudd of CBS.

Downstairs in the Embassy Ballroom, Pierre Salinger was trying to calm the impatient crowd, now swollen to two-thousand noisy adherents, waiting to greet Bobby. Ethel and Bobby, watching the television, heard him tell the throng the candidate would be there soon. "Is it going better than you hoped," somebody asked Ethel and she replied: "We never thought it was going badly." Soon after 11:00, everyone was sure it was Kennedy.

Frank Mankiewicz: I came up from the ballroom a half-hour before midnight, went into the bedroom and told Bobby: "It's time to go. We've got both networks now. It's almost three o'clock in the east. Let's come on down and make a speech to the crowd, then go over to see the writing press." We had a press room down there, to the right of the stage. Bobby said OK, then Fred Dutton, Bobby and I went over some ideas of what he might say. I had a page of notes and Bobby began scratching out some notes of his own. He put the paper in his pocket.

Ethel suddenly became very tired. She lay back on the bed, legs crossed at the ankles. Bobby whispered to her: "Ready?" Ethel smiled and rose. Bobby called to nobody in particular: "Do you think we should take Freckles down? You know they say I used an astronaut and a dog to win." He moved to the door and paused before a long, narrow mirror. He straightened his necktie and smoothed back his hair.

Followed by about twenty persons, Bobby left his suite,

turned right and was crushed into an elevator to emerge on the ballroom floor. Ethel followed in another car.

❂   ❂   ❂

She was at his right, up there on the platform, a half step behind him, listening and smiling as he joked with the jubilant supporters. She waved at friends, grinned at the screaming girls in the funny Kennedy skimmers with the likeness of her husband on the hatbands, watched the flashbulbs pop, looked up at the gaily colored balloons above their heads.

Bobby was playing with his audience like a skilled actor, drawing laughter with mocking allusions to his "ruthlessness" and his jibes at his opponents. He thanked Steve Smith who, he said, was "ruthless but effective" in the way he conducted the campaign; he thanked hulking Rosie Grier who said "he'd take care of anyone who didn't vote for me"; he thanked his dog Freckles. "I'm not doing this in the order of importance," he said quickly, "but I also want to thank my wife, Ethel." The audience guffawed.

His final words to the crowd were a sharp needle for Mayor Samuel W. Yorty of Los Angeles, an old enemy. "Mayor Yorty," he said, "has just sent me a message that we've been here too long already. So my thanks to all of you, and on to Chicago, and let's win there." He lifted his fingers in the peace sign. The crowds roared, the flashbulbs popped, the newscasters spoke urgently into their microphones. And Kennedy turned to leave.

The cheers came in a solid wave of sound. Bobby leaned over the front of the platform and grabbed hands flung upward. Ethel, separated from him now by a few feet, beamed.

Originally, Bobby had been scheduled to address an overflow gathering on a lower level of the hotel, then hold a press conference for the writing journalists. But while he was speaking, Mankiewicz and Dutton held a whispered conference. It was getting late and the news-men were close to filing time. They had been kept waiting in South Dakota and Oregon and had complained; this time, it would be better if Bobby talked to them first.

Press headquarters was in the Colonial Room, just off the ballroom. Bobby finished talking at 12:13 A.M., was told of the change in plans and started to leave the stage from the left side in front. He was preceded by Barry and Dutton, who were trying to make a path for him through the throng.

But there was a better way to the press room. If one went to the rear of the stage and turned right, there was a long and narrow serving kitchen and pantry. One could walk through and reach the Colonial Room without having to wade through the crowds on the ballroom floor.

Karl Uecker, a maitre d'hotel, seeing the crush in front of the platform, took Bobby's arm and led him to the rear of the podium.

Mankiewicz: I was standing stage right, five feet from Ethel. The stage was still jammed with people. Bill Barry said to me as he passed: "We're going out through the right and through the crowd to the writing pressroom." I leaned over three or four people and tapped Ethel on the shoulder and said we were going out that way and pointed.

She nodded. The Senator, the guy from the hotel, Bill Barry and me went through the heavy gold curtain at the rear of the platform and jumped down four feet to the floor. Bobby started to move off with the hotel fellow through some swinging doors.

I looked back. Ethel, following us, had gotten to the edge of the platform but she still hadn't jumped down, so naturally Bill and I turned back and helped her down. She said: "Now you guys go on, I'm all right." Rosie Grier was with her. Barry and I started off after the Senator and the guy from the hotel.

Accompanied by Grier, Ethel walked through a small anteroom in back of the stage, as Bobby had done, turned right and approached the serving pantry. Bobby was some fifteen feet ahead of her, trying to maneuver through a four-foot corridor between a long stainless-steel warming counter on his left and an ice-making machine on his right. Kitchen workers and excited supporters were jammed in there, and all wanted to touch him and shake his hand.

⊘ ⊘ ⊘

Then she heard them. Pop! Pop! Then six more little pops, like the ones in San Francisco's Chinatown that Monday noon, though not so loud. To Grier they sounded like firecrackers, "not heavy, light." To Dick Tuck, a member of Kennedy's traveling staff who was near Ethel, it was like dry sticks snapping. To Barry, they were balloons bursting.

A scream came from inside the serving pantry. Then another scream, and then more cries. People started running. Irwin Stroll, a 17-year-old boy from Los Angeles, rushed in front of Ethel and stumbled against her. There were more shouts and screams. Rosie Grier shoved Ethel to the ground and shielded her slight body with his huge, 290-pound frame, against what he did not know. Stroll kept on going, shouting, "God, I'm shot!" There was blood on his right shin.

Bedlam exploded in the narrow corridor. A strange man lay on the floor directly in front of Ethel. There was blood on his scalp.

To Ethel's left, at the food-warming counter, a struggle was going on. Grier rose and charged through, joining the battle. Ethel heard shouts: "Oh my God, no! Get his gun! Get his gun!"

A swarthy little man in blue shirt and pants had a small pistol in his right hand. Rafer Johnson, author George Plimpton, Bill Barry burst through the crowd and went for him. Uecker, the maitre d', a heavy man, was holding the pistol hand and squeezing the man's neck. Barry struck the man with the side of his hand and the weapon fell on the steam table. But he grabbed it once again. Incredibly, he held onto it through all the blows and despite the frantic efforts to twist it from his fingers.

To Kristi Witker, an attractive blonde journalist-author walking five or six feet behind Bobby, the scene was a nightmare of confusion.

Miss Witker: I thought there were a whole flock of people shooting at us. I felt if I had to get shot, it was just as well to get shot right there, so I didn't move. Why get shot hiding under a table somewhere? It never occurred to me there was only one man. There seemed to be so many shots I was sure there was a whole band of people. The guy next to me was shot in the head. He fell down and was bleeding on my foot. [Paul Schrade, regional director of the United Automobile Workers, who suffered a scalp wound.] Another man on the other side was shot in the stomach. [William Weisel, of the ABC News Washington Bureau, hit in the left side.]

There was a great fight over the gun. I watched it go on. Nineteen people seemed to be trying to get the gun away from the little man. It all seemed to be happening in slow motion in front of my eyes. Finally they got it away from him but they had to break his thumb to get it.

Ethel rose from the floor and pushed through the crowd, helped by Dick Tuck. They passed Ira Goldstein, a nineteen-year-old youth who was covering the campaign for the Continental News Service. He was seated in a chair and looked dazed. Ethel heard him say: "How is Senator Kennedy? What happened to that so-and-so?" Ethel heard and slapped him across the face. "How dare you talk about my husband that way?" she said. Goldstein said: "I'm sorry, lady, but I was shot too. I'd like to know how the Senator is." Ethel bent and kissed him. "Oh," she said. "I'm sorry, honey."

Still she was unaware of what had happened inside the serving pantry. They rushed through, she and Dick Tuck, and then she was almost upon him before she saw him.

She saw him lying on his back, close to the ice-making machine. His eyes were open and staring outward, lips slighlty apart, legs twisted under him. Blood was oozing from the right side of his head, pooling on the concrete floor. His shirt was open to the waist, his right hand was bloody. A rosary was already in his hand, placed there by Juan Romero, a young busboy.

"Oh, my God!" she said as she kneeled at his head. "Oh, my God!"

Pete Hamill: He was lying with his head at the ballroom end of the kitchen when Ethel came over. She was behind him to his left, and she cradled his head in her lap and began talking softly to him. She began rubbing his chest and opening his shirt, all the while talking to him.

She knew it was bad but she wasn't breaking down. Somebody wrote later that she acted like a tiger protecting her young, and there's a photograph that might prove this. But that was just a momentary reaction to flashbulbs popping close to Bobby. She called out to people to move back, give him room. But there was nothing fierce or panicky about her. She was in control.

Dr. Stanley Abo, a diagnostic radiologist who had been in the ballroom, responding to frantic calls for a physician, found Kennedy's pulse slow and strong, though his right eye was staring aimlessly and his left eye was closed. In his hands, the doctor saw, was a "cross and some beads."

Bobby's open eye now focused on his wife, and he recognized her. "Ethel, Ethel," he said, and she leaned closer, whispering, "It's O.K." He lifted his right hand toward her and she took it, and they held hands there as he lay on the concrete floor—all four hands clasped around the crucifix.

After twenty minutes, police arrived and took away the dark little man, Sirhan Bishara Sirhan, five feet, three inches tall, twenty-four years old, an immigrant from Jordan, who had fired eight shots from a small revolver, a .22 calibre Iver-Johnson. Three bullets had struck Robert Kennedy: one behind the ear, piercing the brain; one below the right armpit, which passed through soft tissue and went out; the third lodging in his neck, narrowly missing his spine. Five other persons had been wounded. Later, a Los Angeles police ballistics expert, DeWayne Wolfer, told the jury at Sirhan's trial that the bullet that entered Kennedy's brain was fired "approximately one inch" from his head, and that the others had come from one to six inches away.

While two policemen, Travis White and Arthur Placencia, were taking Sirhan down the stairs to their patrol car, a tan ambulance arrived from Central Receiving Hospital. The time was now 12:40 A.M.

The ambulance driver and an attendant, brusque and businesslike, wrapped a blanket around Kennedy where he lay. Bobby moaned: "Don't lift me," he said, "please don't lift me." The men raised the Senator and placed him on the stretcher, jouncing him. Ethel, agitated, called out: "Gently, gently!" The men quickly wheeled the stretcher to the elevator. It rocked and jounced. Ethel was horrified and again called out to the men to handle her husband gently. Bill Barry was furious. "That attendant handled the stretcher like a madman," he said, "bouncing it around, pushing it hard, with a wounded man in it."

Downstairs, the stretcher was pushed down a ramp toward the ambulance. Ethel climbed in the back with Bobby; Fred Dutton climbed in too, over the attendant's protests that "only Mrs. Kennedy rides with him." Barry and Warren Rogers, correspondent for *Look* magazine, got in front with the driver.

In less than two minutes they were at the hospital, a little more than two miles away.

◑ ◑ ◑

At Central Receiving Hospital, Dr. Victor F. Bazilauskas, fifty-three years old, was on duty at the emergency center. In the long corridor between treatment rooms, he passed Betty Eby, the nursing supervisor, who told him Robert Kennedy had just been shot.

"You're kidding!" the doctor exclaimed.

"No," Miss Eby replied. "I just heard it on the radio."

The doctor and nurse began walking down toward the ambulance platform. "We were half-expecting him but also half-disbelieving," the doctor says. "After all, people do make grisly jokes. But I told myself, he *is* in town." As they neared the door, a young man hobbled around the corner. His clothes were decorated with many little badges identifying him as a Kennedy campaign worker.

"What's with you?" the doctor asked.

"I've just been shot," the boy answered.

"Shot? Where!" The boy lifted his right leg and showed the doctor a bullet wound in the foreleg. "And they shot Kennedy too," he said. "You're kidding!" the doctor burst out again. The boy said no, it was true. The youth, Irwin Stroll, who had been placed in a taxicab and taken to the hospital, was ordered onto a treatment table.

Dr. Bazilauskas: We stepped out onto the platform. It was a gorgeous, still night. We were standing out there and you could hear the wailing of sirens that seemed to come from all over the city, echoing everywhere. But as we listened a mainstream of sound kept going from the right, which was the west, to the left. To the west was the Hotel Ambassador.

As the sounds grew louder, I said to myself, oh, please, proceed on. I didn't want to go through what Parkland went through with John. [John F. Kennedy was taken to Parkland Memorial Hospital in Dallas after he was shot.] As the sound approached Valencia Street, which is right in front of our hospital, I saw the lights streaming by. It suddenly got louder because the sound out there must have canyoned up that little street.

And all of a sudden I saw them turning in, and I said: "Oh, no!" And they pulled in. The ambulance made a turn, then backed in to the platform. Somebody ripped the back door open and I looked and there was Ethel, and I knew I had a date with history.

She looked frightened and her eyes were very wide. She said to me: "Please help him! Please help him!" Then hands reached in to pull out the stretcher and Ethel had a peculiar reaction to this. Somehow, she didn't want hands reaching out to handle him. Maybe it was because one of those clawing hands that she had seen the past few months of the campaign had shot her husband. "Please don't hurt him, please don't hurt him!" she kept saying over and over as the attendants pulled him out on the wheel stretcher.

When he was on the platform I could see that he was like a blob of Jell-O that you took out of the refrigerator. I immediately realized that he was probably gone, but of course I couldn't be sure of it. There was an oxygen mask on his face, put there in the ambulance. I put my hand in underneath his shirt, which had been partially opened, to feel his chest for warmth and it was halfway to the coldness of death. Cold, clammy. As I felt this, I realized that we were fooling around with something inert, so I had to do something quickly.

I began applying cardiac massage. While we wheeled him to Treatment Room Two, which was about eighty feet away, I kept massaging his heart.

About twenty or thirty people crowded the treatment room, which was only about sixteen feet square. It began to look like Grand Central Station. We wheeled him over to the aluminum table in the middle and, after some trouble, transferred him from the stretcher. An ambulance attendant, trying to help lift him, dropped the portable tank that was feeding oxygen to the Senator through the mask. And all the while, I kept massaging his heart.

At the same time, I slapped his face to get a response. "Bob, Bob!" I called to him. "Wake up!" Ethel, I saw, had recoiled and asked me not to be so rough, but I ignored her. In circumstances such as this, you want to know if a patient will respond to any pain stimulus.

By now there were four or five nurses around. One saw to it that he had good airway suction. Another took his blood pressure, and it was nothing. There were no heart sounds. I called for intercardiac adrenalin [a special hypodermic syringe to inject the potent stimulant directly into the heart]. Someone handed me the needle and I was about to inject when I saw Ethel's face just about thirty inches from my hand. I knew that with the hysteria and everything, this would be a very foolish move. We ordinarily do it under certain conditions. But she would probably have thought we killed him. She was even reluctant to have me do the cardiac massage, thinking I was hurting him. But I had explained quickly in a few words what I was doing and why, and she was very co-operative. I handed back the needle.

But now his body started warming up a little. The nurses were trying to get everybody out of the room, but not succeeding very well. By now, too, we had seen the wound in his right mastoid. Slowly, carefully, we began removing his jacket, ripping it open because we didn't want to hurt his spine in case he had injured that. I felt a pellet right in back of his neck, at the midline point, and I knew there was a bullet wound in his neck somewhere. As it turned out, it hadn't entered in the neck, but I could not know that.

Here, finally, I stopped the massage, which had gone on for ten or twelve minutes. I injected adrenalin into an arm muscle. The heart started slowly, and as it started I relaxed a little. Ethel was immediately

concerned. Why had I stopped? I explained: "His
heart is going and now we do have some hope."

"I don't believe you," she told me. "He's not moving. He's dead. I know he's dead."

It wasn't said hysterically, just quietly and definitely in a "don't try to kid me" tone. I told her
again he was alive, but still she didn't believe me.

So then I handed her the ear portion of the steth-
oscope and placed the diaphragm over Bobby's heart.
She leaned forward, listening, and then her face lit
up. She looked like a mother who had just heard the
heart of a child she thought was gone.

After we had gotten a heartbeat, we set up a portable heart-lung machine, which is nothing but a piston
operated by air pressure that does externally the cardiac massage I had been doing by hand. It helps keep
the heart going.

By now, Dr. Albert Holt had come in. We always
have two men on duty in emergency, and one tries
to catch catnaps while the other one is working.
Somebody woke him and he had come running out.
He tested the Senator's reflexes as I had done, and
agreed there had to be brain damage. We agreed that
we should get a neurosurgeon and a chest man lined
up right away at Good Sam.

The Hospital of the Good Samaritan, three blocks
away at 1401 West Sixth Street, was better equipped for
delicate brain surgery. Dr. Holt put in a call for Dr.
Henry Cuneo, a top neurosurgeon. His answering service
would call back. In moments, Dr. Cuneo was on the
phone, awakened from sleep. Told that Kennedy had
been shot and surgery was essential, Dr. Cuneo said he
would leave at once for Good Samaritan. Before dressing,

he called the hospital and alerted the operating-room personnel. He also called Dr. Nat Downs Reid, an associate, and asked him to come down.

Meanwhile, Father James Mundell, a friend of the Kennedys, had reached the emergency entrance and was trying to convince the policeman guarding the door that he was a priest and that Ethel, just as she entered the ambulance, had waved for him to follow. But since he wasn't in clerical garb, the policeman refused to admit him. Ethel heard the commotion, ran outside and identified herself to the officer.

Still he wouldn't admit Father Mundell. In her anguish and frustration, Ethel raised both hands and pushed the policeman aside. Surprised and angry, he lashed out with his forearm and caught Ethel in the chest, sending her reeling. Others crowding around the entrance surrounded him and pushed him away. Ethel led Father Mundell inside. Standing at Bobby's side, with Ethel watching, he made the Sign of the Cross and granted him Absolution.

Minutes later, the Rev. Thomas Peacha, thirty-six years old, assistant pastor of St. Basil's Church in Beverly Hills, entered the treatment room. A stranger to the Kennedys, he had heard what had happened on his car radio and raced to the hospital. Making the Sign of the Cross on Bobby's forehead with holy oil, he prayed for him and asked for mercy for his soul. Ethel quietly watched this administration of Extreme Unction, the final rites of the Roman Catholic Church.

Dr. Bazilauskas: Ethel was reacting well. Ordinarily, I would have pushed a wife out of there if she had become hysterical, but she was fine, very co-operative. I told her we were going to get him over to the other hospital. She pleaded with me to go with him, but I told her: 'I can't. There are five other people here I have to take care of.' Dr. Holt volunteered to go with the Senator. We don't do that generally; a doctor isn't allowed to leave the hospital.

By now, a mob of people had gathered in front of the place, maybe a thousand or more. We sneaked the Senator out through a side door. As he left, Ethel asked me:

"Will he live, doctor? Is he all right?"

I said: "Right now he's doing all right. Let's hope, let's hope."

But I had seen the Senator's legs go into convulsions, which meant that the damage to the "switchboard" was just too much. He could not survive. But of course I didn't want to tell her that, and there was always hope. . . .

Bobby's wounds were dressed, bandages covering his entire scalp and neck. An oxygen mask was placed over his face. A sheet and blanket covering his body, he was transferred once again to the stretcher, strapped in and wheeled outside to the waiting ambulance. Ethel, still in her orange-and-white minidress, walked at Bobby's head.

The ambulance raced up Wilshire at seventy-five miles an hour to the huge, gray ten-story Good Samaritan Hospital on Shatto Street, near Witmer Street. Bobby Kennedy was placed in an intensive-care unit on the fifth floor where a team of eight medical specialists was assembling for a series of tests. The doctors worked on the Senator, performing a tracheotomy so that a tube could be inserted into his windpipe for easier breathing, X-raying his skull and spine, checking his heart. Ethel was beside him all the time, sometimes standing in the room, sometimes rest-ing on a cot beside him, holding his hand, talking softly to him.

Teddy Kennedy, who had been watching the happenings on television at the Fairmount Hotel in San Francisco, was in the room. "We better get down there," he said to David Burke, his administrative assistant who had come to San Francisco with him to man the northern California headquarters. At Hamilton Air Force Base, twenty miles to the north, a jet fighter was brought out. Teddy, John Seigenthaler and Robert Fitzgerald, a cousin, raced out to the field, flew to Los Angeles and were taken by helicopter to Good Samaritan.

Attendants wheeled Bobby into an elevator and took him to the ninth floor. At 2:45 A.M., surgery was begun.

Jimmy Breslin: They knew from the start it was just a question of time. Everybody knew it was the end. Nobody was fooled. Ethel—she had to know it too. A black nurse there at the first hospital, she told me it was a no-go. She knew. She came out of the emergency room to call the other hospital to tell them they were shipping him over. I asked her: "How is he?" She told me: "Well, he's alive." But it was all over then.

Kathleen Kennedy, a month short of her seventeenth birthday, was asleep at Hinton House, a small dormitory for about a dozen girls, at the Putney Preparatory School in southeastern Vermont. Kathleen was in her junior year at the exclusive coed boarding school atop the Connecticut River valley, three miles from the tiny village of Putney.

There were 189 students at Putney that year, about the average enrollment since the school was founded in

1935. The Kennedys paid $3,600 for tuition and board, with extras bringing the annual total to about $5,000. There were reasons why they chose Putney for Kathleen, best summed up in the words spoken by its founder, Mrs. Carmelita Hinton, when she opened the school. Her aim, she said, was "to make school life a more real, less sheltered, less self-centered venture; to educate the individual in the light of what he can do toward solving the problems of society."

Putney was no fancy finishing school for girls or rest stop for young gentlemen. Kathleen had to care for her own room, and no nonsense about it; besides carrying a tough academic program, she was assigned to work three-and-a-half hours weekly on house jobs. All students were members of outdoor work crews, with student foremen. Supervised by adults, they would work on construction and maintenance of the buildings, grounds, farm, dairy barn, horse barn and surrounding woodlands.

Henry B. Rockwell, the school director, had invited some faculty friends to his home on the campus to watch the California returns on television. With horror, they had seen what happened. Rockwell watched, hour after hour; then, in the early morning, after Robert had gone into surgery, he drove out to Hinton House and woke up Kathleen. As gently as he could, he told her what had happened. He drove her back to his home, where she could remain in seclusion.

Meanwhile, K. LeMoyne Billings, John Kennedy's roommate at Choate in their final year and a lifelong friend of Bobby and Ethel, had heard the news at a friend's home in Washington. He rushed at once to Hickory Hill, knowing calls would be coming soon from California and probably about the children. Kathleen, Joe, Jr., and Bobby, Jr., were at boarding schools in the East. David, Mary Courtney, Michael, Mary Kerry, Chris and Matthew were in California. Only Douglas Harriman, fourteen months old, was at home.

Soon the call came from Los Angeles—have the three other children brought to Hickory Hill.

Billings telephoned Thomas A. Corcoran, a friend of the family and an Olympic ski champion who lived near Putney and knew Kathleen well. He asked Corcoran to go to Putney and bring her home. Corcoran, a nephew of Thomas G. Corcoran, the "Tommy the Cork" of Franklin D. Roosevelt's brain trust, left at once.

Now Billings telephoned Milton Academy, ten miles from Boston, where Joe Kennedy, Jr., then fifteen, was a student. Another friend, academy officials were told, would soon be on his way to take Joe home.

At 6:00 A.M. Washington time, while Bobby was in surgery, Billings went himself to Georgetown Prep, a short drive from McLean, to get Bobby, Jr. When he arrived, he found a priest had already awakened the boy and told him. "He was a very unhappy boy," Billings recalls, "though self-contained. None of us knew yet how badly Bobby had been hurt."

Kathleen, lugging a big suitcase, reached Hickory Hill shortly after 2:00 P.M. Wednesday. Joe arrived minutes later. Both looked pale and shaken. Bobby, Jr., his shirt-tail hanging out of his trousers, greeted them with a brief hello. Earlier that day, he had walked for an hour on the sloping lawns with the Reverend Richard McSorley, professor of theology at Georgetown University.

Friends and relatives flocked to Hickory Hill from all over Washington and New York. The weather was perfect—eighty degrees warm and the sun shining. The estate looked no different than it ever did: Dogs scampered around and underfoot, horses loped around the grounds, a crew of men came to clean the swimming pool, a yard man was cutting grass with a power mower.

"We still didn't know how serious it was," Lem Billings says. "We were waiting to hear. Meanwhile, we hoped and we prayed."

♩ ♩ ♩

A bullet had torn through the right mastoid, the spongy bone protuberance behind the ear, which shattered on impact. Pieces of lead and tiny fragments of bone were scattered throughout the brain stem. This vital area consists of the midbrain, the pons varolii and the medulla oblongata; they control nerve impulses passing between various parts of the brain and body processess such as heartbeat, breathing, blood circulation and food digestion, but not thinking. Doctors could not tell from their tests how much of the brain stem had been injured, but they knew that tissues had been lacerated and that probably important blood vessels had been torn. Their object: to open the skull, remove as much of the debris as they could and repair as much of the damage as possible.

Originally, the doctors estimated that the operation would last forty-five minutes, perhaps an hour. But when they opened the skull, they discovered that the flying bone and bullet fragments had done more extensive damage than they thought. The pieces had to be removed slowly and carefully; the destroyed brain tissue taken out; the lacerated blood vessels repaired. They worked through the morning hours and when dawn rose they were still operating.

In a small room nearby, Ethel paced the floor, wrung her hands, bit her lower lip. A nurse came in and offered her a sedative but she refused. Jean Smith and Pat Lawford persuaded her to remove her shoes and lie down. She did, a hand flung over her eyes, her face to the wall.

At 6:20, after an operation lasting three hours and forty minutes, Bobby was taken to the recovery room on the fifth floor, Ethel descending with him on the same elevator. Here electrodes were taped to his head and chest so that nurses and doctors could get instantaneous readings on his brain waves, blood pressure, respiration rate and heart function. He lay on an ice mattress so that the temperature of his body would be reduced and the flow of blood to his brain diminished, lessening the strain on the damaged areas.

Shortly after 7:00 A.M., Frank Mankiewicz, his eyes glazing with weariness, deep lines now in his face, gave this report to the newsmen waiting outside:

"Mrs. Kennedy is with him. Senator Ted Kennedy has arrived at the hospital. His condition is described as extremely critical. The vital signs are about the same; his heart is good.

"All but one fragment of the bullet was removed from the brain. Apparently one bullet remains somewhere in the back of his neck although this is not regarded as a major problem.

"Some fragments of the bullet and the bone penetrated the brain. Also, there may have been impairment of the blood supply to the midbrain. This section affects the pulse and the heartbeat, and consciousness. It does not have a direct responsibility to the thinking processes. The next twelve to thirty-six hours are critical. His condition is very critical.

"He's living. He's not conscious. He's breathing on his own."

But even as he spoke, Mankiewicz knew there was no hope. Immediately after the surgery, Dr. Cuneo had told him it was only a question of time.

Soon afterward, Dr. Cuneo talked by telephone to a colleague, Dr. J. Lawrence Pool of the Columbia Presbyterian Medical Center in New York who, quoting Dr. Cuneo, said that even if Kennedy survived, the outcome might be "extremely tragic because of the brain damage." He would not have been the same Bobby. His mind would not have been affected but the right side of his face would have been paralyzed; he would have been totally deaf in the right ear; his vision would have been impaired; his arms and legs would probably have jerked spasmodically and uncontrollably.

In midmorning, Dr. James Poppen, chief of neurosurgery at the Lahey Clinic in Boston, well-known to the Kennedys, arrived and examined Bobby. He had treated Ted when he broke his back in a plane crash four years earlier, helped care for Joseph Kennedy after he suffered a stroke and attended John Kennedy for his back problems. Teddy telephoned him and asked him to fly in; Vice-President Hubert Humphrey supplied an Air Force jet. Dr. Poppen told the family that everything possible had been done for the Senator, and now they must wait.

◊ ◊ ◊

Jackie Kennedy paid a brief visit Tuesday evening to Bobby's campaign headquarters in New York City. She remained long enough to be convinced that he was ahead in the balloting, then left at 11:30 P.M. for her ten-room apartment at Fifth Avenue and Eighty-fifth Street, overlooking Central Park. "I feel wonderful," she said to reporters. "I'm delighted."

At 4:30 A.M., New York time, she was awakened by a call from London. Prince Stanislaus Radziwill, husband of her sister Lee, was asking: "How is Bobby?" Jackie replied sleepily: "You heard that he won in California."

"But how is he?" Radziwill insisted.

"I just told you," Jackie answered. "He won in California."

The prince realized àt once that Jackie did not know. He told her of the shooting. She cried out: "Oh, no! It can't be!" Shocked and anguished, Jackie said she would call Los Angeles at once for more information. Radziwill replied that he would leave London at once for New York.

Jackie called Steve Smith at the hospital, was told the facts as they were known at that time. She remained secluded in her apartment all Wednesday morning, receiving information by phone and from news sources. At 2:30 in the afternoon, she emerged from the building, escorted by Roswell L. Gilpatrick, an old friend and former Deputy Secretary of Defense. She entered a blue limousine, which took off. immediately for Kennedy International Airport, where she boarded a private twin-engine jet owned by the International Business Corporation. With her were Thomas J. Watson, board chairman, and Burke Marshall, general counsel for IBM, who had been Assistant Attorney General in charge of the civil-rights division. At 3:45, the jet lifted off the runway.

Jackie reached the hospital at 7:34 in the evening. About an hour-and-a-half earlier, Coretta King, widow of Martin Luther King, Jr., had come in and remained until nearly nine. Andy Williams, the singer, and his wife, Claudine, were there. Jess Unruh, David Hackett, John Glenn, Rafer Johnson, all the people who were close to Kennedy crowded into the elevators and walked silently through the fifth-floor halls. Senator Eugene McCarthy spoke to Ethel quietly for a moment.

Only close members of the family were permitted in the intensive-care unit where Bobby lay; other friends remained down the hall. Newsmen were kept downstairs, below the main floor, then shifted to an improvised press room in the hospital gymnasium in an annex diagonally across the street.

◎ ◎ ◎

At Hickory Hill, Lem Billings finally got the call he knew would come. Ethel had decided that Kathleen, Joe and Bobby, Jr., should fly out at once to Los Angeles. Billings and Kay Evans, wife of the columnist Rowland Evans, accompanied them in a small private jet.

Most of the trip was spent in silence. The children had been somewhat encouraged by news reports that the operation had been completed. "None of them, none of us, knew how serious it was," Billings says.

The children reached the hospital at 10:30 Wednesday evening and were taken upstairs at once to see their father. They stayed only a few minutes, then were taken to join their brothers and sisters at the Beverly Hills Hotel.

At Hyannis Port, Mrs. Rose Kennedy and her paralyzed, speechless husband, Joseph, prayed for their son. Teddy Kennedy had telephoned them the news. In Washington, President Lyndon Johnson sent Ethel a personal message, spoke to Ted at the hospital by phone and issued a statement saying all America prayed for the Senator's recovery. At the Vatican, Pope Paul VI announced that he was praying for Bobby.

◎ ◎ ◎

The vigil went on.

Ethel rarely left Bobby's side. Her face was drawn with fatigue, her fingers trembled, but she was under control and she did not weep. The hospital chaplain, the Reverend Lawrence Joy, walked into the room to intone the Last Rites of the Church once again. Told afterward that they had been said earlier at Central Receiving Hospital, he replied: "That doesn't matter. The more prayers the better." He saw the grief in Ethel's face but he also saw the strength. "She showed no sign of weakening," he said.

All throughout the day and into the evening, she sat close to Bobby as he lay unconscious, holding his hand, whispering to him, bowing her head over him and praying. When weariness overtook her, she lay on a cot next to him and reached out to hold his hand.

At 5:30, Mankiewicz reported that, as of 5:00, Kennedy's condition was "still critical as to life." There would be no more bulletins, he said, until early morning.

Night fell. Clusters of people, whites, blacks, Chinese-Americans, Mexican-Americans, gathered outside to watch and wait. Many carried "Pray for Bobby" bumper stickers, quickly printed during the night.

Reporters cornered every person who emerged from the intensive-care unit. "It's bad in there, very bad," Bill Barry told them. From others they heard the same thing. Hope, if it existed at all, was no longer in anyone's heart in the press room. "We knew, absolutely, that it was coming," Kristi Witker says.

It came at 1:44 A.M. Jackie Kennedy, Ted Kennedy, Pat Lawford and Jean and Steve Smith watched silently as Ethel prayed and Robert Kennedy died.

SIXTEEN

"Is There Some Awful Curse?"

On July 25, 1969, Senator Edward Moore Kennedy strode into the booklined study of his father's Hyannis Port home and faced the television cameras to give his version of a car accident on Martha's Vineyard the week before. Mary Jo Kopechne, a slim, attractive blonde, drowned in his automobile when the young Senator drove off an unrailed bridge in the dark into Poucha Pond on Chappaquiddick Island. There had been a cookout reunion on the remote island that fateful night, attended by six young women, all former campaign workers in Robert Kennedy's office during his race for the Presidency, and six men, including Ted. About 11:00 P.M., Kennedy and Miss Kopechne left the party and headed for the ferry that plied between the island and the mainland. In the dark, he turned down a dirt road away from the ferry and came suddenly upon the twenty-year-old, eighty-one-foot wooden span. After traveling eighteen feet, the right front wheel of Kennedy's black Oldsmobile slipped over the edge and the car plunged into the black water. Kennedy managed to struggle free but the pretty young secretary drowned.

Kennedy told how he dived repeatedly into the water in a futile attempt to rescue Miss Kopechne and how, exhausted and confused, he left the accident scene to return to his hotel, reporting to police the following morning. The young Senator's square, handsome face was unchangingly grim as he told the watching millions, answering the whispers that were sweeping across the country: "There is no truth, no truth whatever, to the widely circulated suspicions of immoral conduct that have been leveled at my behavior during that evening. There has never been a private relationship between us of any kind."

Halfway through his account, Kennedy leaned forward almost imperceptibly and a look, half of perplexity and half of resignation, passed over his features as he told of the "scrambled thoughts" that raced through his mind during those moments following the accident. Among these was the question "whether some awful curse did actually hang over all the Kennedys." *

---

*The strange and terrible tragedies that have struck the Kennedys:

Joseph, Jr., first-born son, killed in August, 1944, when his bombing plane exploded over England during World War II.

Rosemary, eldest daughter, born retarded and now living in an institution.

Kathleen, widow of the Marquess of Huntington, killed when her small plane crashed in France in 1948.

Kathleen's husband, killed in an infantry attack in Normandy four years before.

Patrick Bouvier Kennedy, dead of hyaline membrane disease in 1963 before he was two days old.

John Fitzgerald, killed by an assassin in 1963.

Robert Francis, killed by an assassin in 1968.

Edward Moore, almost killed in 1964 in a plane crash near Springfield, Massachusetts, which hospitalized him for months, and involved in the death of a young girl in the summer of 1969.

There are many who have asked the same frightening question about the Skakels. Tragedy has shadowed them too, striking with a brutal, terrifying suddenness that allowed no time for preparation and left only sadness and wonderment.

ᘘ ᘘ ᘘ

In the closing days of September 1955, the Father Abbot of the Abbey of Gethsemani, a Trappist monastery in Kentucky, returned from a worldwide meeting the order had help in Citeaux near Dijon, France. A close friend of the Skakels for many years, the Father Abbot had made it a practice to visit the home whenever monastery affairs took him to New York. On these occasions George Skakel, Sr., would often walk with him around his spacious grounds, speaking of his business projects, his personal problems, his other experiences.

On this afternoon, the Father Abbot was sitting alone in the library when Mr. Skakel entered and sat down next to him. The Father Abbot, looking searchingly at his face, saw he was more serious than usual. Intuitively the clergyman knew something was profoundly troubling his old friend. Finally Mr. Skakel spoke.

"Father Abbot," he said, "you have known me now for a number of years. Now, in the next world, I do not want to be left on the outside. I love my family. I want to be where they are—all of us, all together."

It was the climactic moment in the spiritual life of George Skakel.

(Later, the Father Abbot, recounting the story, was to say: "I realized at once, even though he expressed himself in this simple way, that grace was working in his soul.")

The Father Abbot thought rapidly. At last Ann Skakel's years of prayer were being answered: Her husband was prepared to join her faith. But urgent business required him to leave for the monastery next morning.

("I remembered the axiom—'Strike while the iron is hot'!)

"George," the Father Abbot said, "I have a proposition for you. Come to Gethsemani. There we can talk together more freely, and for as long a time as is necessary. How about it?"

George smiled and said: "Father Abbot, I'll do it."

His friend smiled back. "Wonderful. Let's fix a date."

At that moment, John McCooey, husband of Ann Skakel, youngest of the seven children, entered, saw the two in earnest conversation and started to leave. His appearance seemed providential to the Father Abbot who, knowing Mr. Skakel and fearing a change of heart, wanted a witness. He called to John and explained what his father-in-law had decided. John, aware of how long the family had wished for this moment, was delighted.

"I have to make one trip with Mother to the West Coast," George Skakel said, "but only for a few days. On my return, I'll fly to Gethsemani."

"John," said the Father Abbot, "you heard that? I myself must return tomorrow, but can I rely on you to fix a date and the trip for George?"

"You sure can, Father Abbot," said John warmly. "Just leave that to me. This is wonderful. Look—to make sure, I myself will go with Dad." The Father Abbot smiled and said: "George, that's a firm contract, bilateral."

Before the day had ended, the entire family knew and was rejoicing. Ann Skakel, weeping with joy, hurried to church to pray her thanks. In Washington, Ethel Kennedy, now the wife of the chief counsel of the Senate Rackets Committee, talked to her parents by telephone and said her father's decision was "terrific."

Sunday, October 3, was an almost perfect day. By noon

the mercury had moved into the pleasant sixties and a soft breeze came in from the Sound. After an early lunch, Skakel and his wife drove up to Bridgeport thirty miles away and headed for the airport on the edge of the city, where the Great Lakes Carbon Corporation kept its company plane, a converted Air Force B-26 bomber.

The pilot, Joseph W. Whitney of Lordship, Connecticut, had arrived several hours earlier and, with co-pilot John E. McBride of Stratford, had completed the check-out of the craft. They were waiting at the airport rim, chatting with some mechanics, as the Skakels drove up. The men shook hands and then George Skakel said they'd better get moving. "I'd like to get to Tulsa before dark," he said. "Can't miss," grinned Joe Whitney, and the four boarded the gleaming two-engine plane.

Whitney started the motors and soon the big plane trundled out to the head of the runway. Within minutes he got his clearance and, with a roar, the big craft roared down the strip and soared effortlessly into the skies. The flight was uneventful; hours later, the B-26 landed at Tulsa.

At 9:45 the next evening, after a busy round of conferences in the beautiful city, the Skakels boarded their plane for the flight to Los Angeles.

Thirty minutes later, the B-26 exploded in midair and fell like a burning meteor near Union City, twenty miles northwest of Oklahoma City. The four aboard were burned beyond recognition; rescue workers had to wear asbestos suits to recover the bodies from the wreckage.

Officers of the Oklahoma State Highway Patrol identified George Skakel from charred but decipherable credit cards in his wallet. When Ann Skakel's body was discovered, her rosary was entwined around her arm.

Although George Skakel had not yet undergone formal

instruction for conversion to the Catholic faith, he had, the Father Abbot explains, received the Baptism of Desire. "God had answered Mrs. Skakel's and the family's lifelong prayers," he says. "Mother had actually, in the kind providence of God, pulled George into Heaven with her."

Ethel knew this. That is why, when her sister Ann called to tell her the dreadful news, she whispered only: "It's all right." And then, after a brief silence, once more: "It's all right."

Ethel Kennedy sat dry-eyed, her features composed, in a front row at St. Mary's Church as the bodies of her mother and father, each in their sixty-third year, lay in twin coffins a few feet away. The church was overflowing with friends and dignitaries, among them Francis Cardinal Spellman. Robert Kennedy, at his wife's side, held her hand throughout the brief service. Together they went to St. Mary's Cemetery on North Street and watched as George and Ann Skakel, so suddenly gone, were lowered into the ground.

ᵩ ᵩ ᵩ

In the fall of 1966, George Skakel, Jr., square-jawed, rugged but still boyish looking despite his forty-four years, invited a number of special friends to hunt elk with him in the Idaho mountains. He knew just the place —the Shepp ranch near the fast-flowing Salmon River —"river of no return" the natives call it—in western Idaho. Skakel knew the terrain well; he owned a cattle ranch in Bruneau in the southern plains and had spent many exhilarating days tracking the elk, moose and grizzlies that roamed free in the highlands. He called Keith McCormack, who managed his ranch, to make arrangements at Shepp for a party of twenty, which would arrive on Saturday, September 24. They would stay ten days. McCormack assured Skakel everything would be ready for their arrival.

Skakel began inviting people, including his son Mark, then twelve. The entire party boarded a plane at La-Guardia Field and flew to Boise, where they divided up into four smaller aircraft for the half-hour hop north to McCall. There they changed planes again for the final lap, the short flight to the airstrip directly on the Shepp ranch.

By late afternoon, three of the five small planes carrying the guests had landed safely. Soon a single-engine Cessna 185 appeared. Aboard were Lewis Werner II of St. Louis, socially prominent and director of the Civil Intelligence Agency's St. Louis regional office; Dean P. Markham, who had served for a while as a White House aide to President Kennedy; and Earl F. Ranft, a Jersey City businessman. Aboard, too, was George Skakel, who owned the plane, which was piloted by Master Sergeant Donald W. Adams, a native of Oklahoma who was attached to the Mountain Home Air Force Base and worked in his off-duty hours at the Skakel ranch.

The Cessna dipped for a landing but came in too high for the short runway and zoomed up again. Directly ahead were the sheer cliffs of Crooked Creek Canyon, which reared upward from a valley. The pilot applied full power in an attempt to clear the mountains but was unable to gain enough altitude and found himself trapped between the nearly vertical canyon walls. Ahead were still higher cliffs. There was just one chance—a 180-degree climbing turn out of the trap and back into the valley.

But the little Cessna couldn't make it. The plane's engine stalled. It faltered, then nosed down and plunged. It crashed propeller first on the desolate banks of Crooked Creek, disintegrating upon impact.

All aboard perished. At the Shepp ranch, Louise Werner, now a widow and the only woman in the party, went to young Mark Skakel and held him. Together they comforted one another.

Nearly three-thousand miles away, Robert F. Kennedy, by then the Junior United States Senator from New York, arrived at the Manchester, New Hampshire, airport for a two-day swing in his campaign for re-election. That afternoon, he was scheduled to make the keynote speech at the New Hampshire State Democratic convention and later to address a fund-raising dinner in Burlington, Vermont.

Aides were waiting at the airport. As soon as they glimpsed the hatless Senator at the top of the gangway, they rushed over and hustled him into a small office at the terminal. There they told him the news: George Skakel was dead. Kennedy shut his eyes for a long moment, then reached for a telephone. He asked the operator to connect him with his home.

At Hickory Hill, Ethel Kennedy answered gaily, then her voice froze as she listened. For nearly a half hour, Robert and Ethel talked and when they hung up, Ethel sat motionless for a long time and Robert announced that he was returning at once to Washington.

He did, but first he made an intermediate stop at Bradley Field, an airport near Hartford, Connecticut. There he picked up the two children of his close friend, Dean Markham, and took them to Washington where they could be with their mother and mourn the death of their father.

In Colorado, Senator Edward Kennedy cancelled the remainder of a speaking tour during which he planned to cover Utah and Wyoming, and flew to the funeral.

Ethel, dry-eyed, head up, once again sat in the front row of St. Mary's church.

ᵹ ᵹ ᵹ

On Thanksgiving Day two months later, George's daughter Cathleen, an attractive young girl of seventeen, was driving a convertible automobile along winding Fox Run Road in Greenwich. The leaves of the trees that lined the road had long since turned to gold and russet but the day was bright and sunny, and so Cathleen had lowered the top. In the back seat was seven-year-old Hope O'Brien, the daughter of Royall O'Brien, an architect.

Suddenly the car hit a bump in the road. The car bounced and Hope was flung onto the pavement. She was rushed to Greenwich Hospital where she died two days later.

ᵹ ᵹ ᵹ

On a Thursday evening in mid-May 1967, Joan Patricia Skakel, a widow of less than eight months after eighteen years of marriage to George, invited Captain Hilbert Heberling of the Greenwich Police Department and his wife for an informal dinner. The Heberlings were long-time friends. This evening there was to be shishkebab, prepared by Mrs. Skakel herself and served in the spacious kitchen of her home on Vineyard Lane.

It was a gay little party. Cathleen was there, recovered now from the shock of the accident; George Skakel III and Susan completed the small group. Mark, unfortunately, could not be present; he was in the hospital, injured the week before. He and a friend had been experimenting with gunpowder in a glass bottle when it blew up in his face.

Pat Skakel served the shishkebab, and began to eat. Suddenly she excused herself and left the table. Minutes passed and she did not return. Captain Heberling and his wife looked anxiously at each other. Ten minutes and Pat still had not come back.

The police captain pushed back his chair and went to look for Pat. He found her unconscious on the floor of a bathroom. She had suffocated when a piece of meat lodged in her windpipe. An ambulance was summoned and Pat was rushed to Greenwich Hospital but she was dead.

Ethel Kennedy heard the news in Washington and once again she and her husband made a sad visit to her girlhood town.

෧ ෧ ෧

A little more than one year later, tragedy was to strike at Ethel once more, this time in a California hotel, and it would occur within her hearing and almost her sight.

Few today believe in "curses" that can afflict whole families. Yet, faced by bizarre repetitions of terrible happenings, even Edward Kennedy can be led to wonder if there was indeed "some awful curse" on his family.

Ethel's family can wonder too.

SEVENTEEN

Long Journey Home

❧ ❧

Following a six-hour autopsy, the body of Robert Kennedy was taken in early afternoon to Los Angeles International Airport where an Air Force 707, sent by President Johnson, was waiting. Ethel, who had spent the night and morning at Good Sam, was composed as she entered the front seat of the blue hearse with Ted Kennedy for the ride to the West Imperial Terminal.

The body, in a maroon-draped casket of African mahogany chosen by Ted, was wedged into the narrow area between the forward compartment and the cockpit. The passengers, seventy of Bobby and Ethel's family, closest friends and co-workers, began embarking from the rear.

Almost at the start, a small drama was enacted at planeside. Jackie Kennedy, among the first in line waiting to board, stopped and looked down the length of the plane. The big jet, she realized suddenly, looked like the one that bore her husband's body from Dallas' Love Field to Andrews Air Force Base in 1963. She demanded to know:

Was it the same plane? If it were, she could not enter. Crewmen assured her it was not. Both were blue and silvery-white 707s but this was Number 86972,* the other 26000. Actually, there were a half-dozen identical planes assigned to the President, but only one served as the President's flagship. Reassured, she went aboard.

The cortege was followed to the airport by a ragtag-and-bobtail group of motorcyclists who had volunteered to act as escort to Bobby's motorcade during his stay in Los Angeles. It was a completely unofficial group, consisting of off-duty policemen and private citizens who wanted to help. They were always with him, sometimes only a few, sometimes dozens of them.

After Bobby died, one of their number asked the Secret Service if they could lead the cortege to the airport. The request was denied; Los Angeles city police should take over the function. Members of the volunteer guard, hurt by the refusal, followed the procession instead of going before.

At 1:28, Number 86972 took off. Behind the plane, lined up in formation, was the volunteer guard astride cycles of all makes and sizes. As the Presidential craft hurtled down the runway, the men started their motors and roared off after it in formation. Ray O'Connell, looking back at them from the plane, says: "It was the goddamnedest sight you ever saw. In unison, coming down the

---

* Number 86972 did have a history, though. It was the one in which Secretary of State Dean Rusk, accompanied by Pierre Salinger, President Kennedy's press aide, and five other Cabinet members, were on en route to Honolulu and Japan for conferences on Vietnam and other Far Eastern matters when word reached them that the President had been shot. The plane was turned in mid-ocean and returned to Andrews.

runway after him. Just guys on motorcycles, in one final salute to the Senator."

All those whose names were closely linked to the Kennedys were there: Rosie Grier, Lem Billings, Dick Goodwin, Rafer Johnson, George Plimpton, Frank Mankiewicz, Pierre Salinger, Dick Tuck, Ed Guthman, Jesse Unruh, Andy Williams. There were no working journalists aboard, just a few newsmen like Sander Vanocur of the National Broadcasting Company, and columnists Joseph Kraft and Rowland Evans, who had come as friends.

Ethel, with Ted, Jean and Steve Smith, Pat Lawford, Bill Barry and John Seigenthaler, had gone aboard on the hydraulically operated cargo lift with the casket and sat in the front section. In the rear were three close kin of other martyrs: Mrs. Kennedy, sitting with Lee and Stanislaus Radziwill; Mrs. Martin Luther King, Jr., and Charles Evers, brother of Medgar Evers, the director of the Mississippi N.A.A.C.P. who was murdered in front of his house in Jackson in 1963. From time to time, Ted Kennedy would call friends from the cabin to keep a vigil around the coffin. They came and sat on the floor beside it.

Ethel talked quietly with Ted as the plane headed eastward, then went to lie against the coffin where she fell asleep. Jim Whittaker, seeing her asleep, placed a pillow beneath her head and held out her rosary, hesitating because he wasn't certain where to place it. Joe suggested he put the beads next to her and he did.

In back, the prevailing moods were quiet rage, horror at what one called "this gruesome repeat of 1963" and, most pronounced, a deep hurt. For among these men and women who had been attached to Bobby and his crusade for the nomination there had grown a strong affection for the man rising at times to adoration. Most of these people were canny and hard-headed realists but they had been caught by a fire. They had come to believe that Robert Kennedy could lead the country into a new day. "We are a nation which has reached the height of its power and influence at a time when the old order of things is crumbling and the new world is painfully struggling to take shape," he had said two years before in New York at a Columbus Day Dinner. "It is a moment as fully charged with opportunity as that granted to Columbus or the heroes of the Italian Renaissance. It offers to this nation the chance for great achievement—or perhaps the greatest and most destructive of failures." The brutal destruction of the man and with him the hope for the future caused a profound anguish.

There was admiration, too, for the way Ethel had taken the blow. During the flight, she walked through the cabin, stopping to talk to each of the passengers as she was to do later on a large scale on the funeral train. She had asked them if they needed anything, a drink, a sandwich. In the front, when Bill Barry dozed off, she carefully draped a blanket around him.

The big plane touched down at 9:00 P.M. at La-Guardia Airport in sticky midsummer heat. Ethel, Jackie, Ted and others of the family descended with the coffin on the hydraulic lift. Bobby, Jr., his brother Joe and Teddy helped to place the casket on the boxlike elevator. Hundreds of political and civic notables watched the solemn scene—Governor and Mrs. Nelson A. Rockefeller of New York, Mayor John V. Lindsay and his wife, U.N. Ambassador Arthur J. Goldberg, Senator Jacob A. Javits of New York and his wife, former Defense Secretary Robert S. McNamara among them. Archbishop Terence J. Cooke of New York moved to the coffin and recited a brief prayer.

In the throng, unrecognized by newsmen, was Ethel's brother Rushton, head of the family business. He and his wife had faced their own special agony. Their youngest child, a two-year-old boy, had undergone surgery the day Bobby was shot. They had remained at the hospital. As soon as they received word that the child would be all right, they raced in the middle of the night from Greenwich to Kennedy Airport to fly to Los Angeles. En route, they heard the announcement that Bobby had died. They returned home, and were at LaGuardia when Ethel arrived.

Rushton embraced his sister at the field, but said almost nothing. "How can you speak?" he said afterward. "What words do you use? She was unbelievably strong. If it were me, I know that I just, just . . ." His voice trailed off.

Bobby's body was placed in a gray hearse. Teddy took Ethel's arm and led her to the front seat; he climbed in and she followed. A motorcycle escort guided the cortege out of the airport toward New York City. As millions watched on television and hundreds of thousands jammed rooftops, overpasses, streets and highways, the procession moved rapidly down the Grand Central Parkway, across the Triborough Bridge, down the East River Drive to St. Patrick's Cathedral, the twin-spired Mother Church of the New York Archdiocese at Fifth Avenue and Fiftieth Street. Thousands massed across the street looked on in silence as the hearse stopped at the Fifth Avenue entrance and the casket was borne up the broad steps through the high bronze doors into the cathedral. There, watching the casket placed in the nave of the church, in the center aisle just beyond the apse, was Rose Kennedy, who had come down from Hyannis Port and slipped unnoticed into the cathedral.

A short service was conducted and it was here that Jackie, who had borne her own sorrow with such astonishing composure five years earlier, broke down. She wept as she knelt beside the coffin and had to be helped to her feet. Once outside, however, she stood on the steps waiting for her car, staring out over the heads of the crowd with bright dry eyes.

In a spontaneous show of grief and affection, friends formed an honor guard around Bobby's bier, six at a time, each to stand a quarter of an hour. It began that night and was to continue until the body was taken away. All the great names linked to the New Frontier, literary and theatrical celebrities, civil-rights and labor leaders, were to stand there for Kennedy, six hundred in all. Teddy Kennedy, who had left the cathedral with the family, changed his mind as he was about to enter a limousine and returned. He remained all night with his brother's body, praying at the casket, walking, sitting in a pew.

Outside, the crowd thinned when an announcement was made through a police bullhorn that the cathedral would not be opened to the public until 5:30 the next morning. Toward midnight, New Yorkers began lining up behind the police barricades. By first light, more than a hundred thousand were standing quietly in the fading darkness.

Ethel had gone to her apartment at United Nations Plaza and was up by 7:00. Joe dressed in a blue jacket and gray trousers and went to the cathedral where, at 8:00, he stood for half an hour as a member of the honor guard. His slender fingers touched the coffin as he stood facing it and occasionally he would lean against it. When his relief came, he walked down the center aisle toward

the communion rail, facing the altar. Then he went along
the apse to the deserted circular ambulatory behind the
altar, where he put his face in his hands and cried.

At 9:00, friends began arriving at the apartment and
at 11:00, dressed all in black even to her handbag, Ethel
walked to Holy Family Church on East Forty-seventh
Street for a low requiem mass. Afterward she drove to St.
Patrick's where mourners by the thousands were shuffling
slowly past the closed coffin. She sat in a pew directly behind the shiny casket and looked at it steadily, her eyes
fixed upon it even when a priest came to whisper to her.
Still gazing at the casket, she rose after a few moments
and stood behind it. She reached out a hand to caress the
wood, and then left.

Jackie Kennedy came to the cathedral twice that day,
the first time at 12:30, shortly after Ethel left. On one
of her visits, a child in the line popped a paper bag.
Startled, she reacted, according to one observer, "with
frenzy like a rearing horse." She returned at 4:30 with
her mother, Mrs. Hugh D. Auchincloss, her children,
Caroline and John, and blonde Mary Nelson, Caroline's
best friend and classmate. Caroline, in a blue short-sleeved
dress and a ribbon in her hair, held her mother's hand.
The group entered a pew near the casket, genuflected
and prayed for a moment. Mrs. Kennedy rose and walked
to the coffin, which had been covered with a flag during
the early afternoon. She touched it softly, and the children
did the same. Then she left, walking up the main aisle to
the Fifth Avenue entrance.

As the afternoon wore on, mountains of floral offerings
were gathering at the cathedral, many of them symbolic.
There was a small plastic football surrounded by circles
of white carnations. The Kennedy for President Club in
California sent a flag made of alternating red and white

mums, with stars of blue mums. All the cards were removed and sent to the family.

Bobby, Jr., came three times, twice standing a thirty-minute vigil with tear-filled eyes. Rose was there twice. At 8:30 in the evening, after staying for a while at the home of Mr. and Mrs. C. Douglas Dillon, President Kennedy's Secretary of the Treasury, Ethel returned once again, remaining nine minutes.

Later in the evening there was open house at the United Nations Plaza apartment for friends. Ethel bustled about, greeting everyone. About 10:00, Jimmy Breslin came in with Fred and Jane Rosen, who lived in the same building but had never met the Kennedys. Ethel met them at the door. "Come in, come in," she said. "I'll get you a drink. What will it be?" The Rosens, in solicitude for Ethel, hastily told her not to bother. Ethel insisted and Breslin told them: "Don't be so upset, this isn't a Jewish affair, it's an Irish one."

Joe, limping slightly, passed. "What's the matter with him?" Breslin asked.

"Nothing much," Ethel replied. "He hurt it in the pool the other day. He's got a couple of friends from school staying with him." That was good; friends would help Joe over the bad time. In a little while, Jimmy said goodbye to Ethel, saying he and Bill Barry were going out to have a couple of drinks. Ethel grinned at Breslin. "Look out for that fellow," she told Barry, "he'll get you in trouble." She returned to her guests.

After a few hours sleep, Ethel rose before dawn and went to see Bobby's coffin one more time, arriving at the cathedral at 4:45 as the police were closing the doors to the still-flowing lines of mourners. She sat in a front pew for fifteen minutes, then knelt by the casket. A friend brought her a chair. The cathedral was in total darkness but still she sat there, and finally she went home.

ᵟ ᵟ ᵟ

The great Gothic cathedral was filling up with 2,300 special guests, invited by telegram from lists compiled during the previous day and night by Kennedy staff people. They had worked throughout the night at Steve Smith's Park Avenue office, from a card file containing the names of 100,000 national and international dignitaries, and Kennedy friends. Jackie Kennedy and Ted Kennedy contributed suggestions. Ethel sent over names of people she wished to invite. She remembered all her friends from Washington, Hyannis Port, Greenwich, wherever she had lived. Though she hadn't seen her in years, Ethel sent an invitation to Mrs. Arthur Pethick, the spunky little athletic coach and tap teacher at Greenwich Academy who, white-haired and frail now, came down for the service.

Limousines came and went, depositing some of the world's most famous people at the doors of the church. There were four Presidential candidates: Vice-President Hubert Humphrey, Senator McCarthy, Governor Rockefeller and Richard M. Nixon. There were three Prime Ministers (of Ireland, Jamaica and Guyana), United Nations officials headed by U Thant, the Secretary General; Chief Justice Earl Warren, Cabinet members, members of Congress, Governors, admirals and generals, Ambassadors, high administration officials. There were movie stars and show-business personalities, such as Cary Grant, Harry Belafonte, Sidney Poitier, Jack Paar, Tom Smothers. There were labor leaders and civil-rights workers: Walter Reuther, Charles Evers, Cesar Chavez. As they entered, each received a card bearing a smiling portrait of Robert Kennedy and, on the reverse, a short prayer, a quotation from Tennyson and an excerpt from remarks Kennedy made in Indianapolis in April 1968, on the death of Martin Luther King, Jr.: "What we need in the United States . . . is love and wisdom and compassion toward one another, and a feeling of justice toward those who still suffer within our own country, whether they be white or they be black. Let us dedicate ourselves to what the Greeks wrote so many years ago: to tame the savageness of man and make gentle the life of the world. Let us dedicate ourselves to that, and say a prayer for our country and our people."

A mourning veil attached to a small black hat covered Ethel's pale, tired face. She had entered the cathedral by a side door on the arm of Ted Kennedy and walked unfalteringly to the front pew to the right of the center aisle. Now she sat between Ted and her eldest daughter Kathleen. Alongside were Rose Kennedy, Jackie Kennedy, Caroline, John and Ethel's older sons, Joe and Bobby.

Across the aisle to the left sat President Lyndon Johnson and his wife, who had flown from Washington that morning to Floyd Bennett Field and landed by helicopter at the Sheep Meadow in Central Park. The President had knelt and prayed at the coffin for a few moments before taking his seat.

Ethel wanted the mood and content of the requiem mass to stress hope and joy rather than sorrow. Five years before, the low mass for the slain President at St. Matthew's Cathedral in Washington had been traditional, with bereavement the theme. Richard Cardinal Cushing, who had celebrated the mass, had worn black and red vestments, the sign of mourning, and had spoken entirely in Latin except for a few sentences at the close. But a new wind had risen in the Church; following the Ecumenical Council summoned by Pope John XXIII, great changes had come about in Catholic liturgy. A participatory theme of Christian joy had been added to the Latin requiems; the belief that death is the beginning of the full life of eternity with God had been underscored.

Ethel insisted that the service be conducted entirely in English so all might understand; that white vestments, symbolizing hope, rather than the black of sorrow be worn by the celebrants; that the female children wear white for the promise of life eternal; and that the music, too, should reflect not only the liberalization of liturgical rules but strength and hope and glory.

The service began a few minutes before 10:00. The nine-thousand-pipe organ, one of the most superb instruments in this country and Europe, pealed and a white-robed choir in the organ gallery sang: "All hail, adored Trinity; All hail eternal unity." Gathered in the vestibule at the head of the center aisle were more than two-hundred clerical figures, some of the highest importance. At the sound of the organ, a crucifer, bearing aloft a tall golden cross, led the solemn procession down the aisle. Behind him, in robes of white, brown, purple, violet and scarlet, walked seminarians, monks, monsignori, Bishops, Archbishops and, finally, six Cardinals. Richard Cardinal Cushing, now seventy-three years old and suffering from asthma and emphysema, who had blessed the body and commended the soul of one Kennedy brother, walked erect to perform the same ritual for another. With him were Angelo Cardinal dell'Acqua, the personal vicar of Pope Paul VI, Patrick Cardinal O'Boyle of Washington, John Cardinal Cody of Chicago and James Francis Cardinal McIntyre of Los Angeles.

The new mood was apparent in the opening eulogy of
Ted Kennedy, which had not been expected. The young
Senator, led to a wooden lectern in the sanctuary by Monsignor Eugene V. Clark, secretary to Archbishop Cooke,
spoke clearly at first, then his voice broke. Finally, fighting
to keep control, he told the mourners that Bobby should
not now be idealized as a larger-than-life figure but remembered for what he was, a "good and decent man"
who had hope in his heart for the world. The last surviving Kennedy brother ended with the words Robert Kennedy had spoken so often in the months just gone by:
"Some men see things as they are and say why? I dream
things that never were and say, why not?"

The congregation, in the opening meditation, spoke
aloud the words:

"Happy are those who die in the Lord! Happy indeed,
the Spirit says: Now they can rest forever after their
work, since their good deeds go with them." From St.
Paul's First Epistle to the Thessalonians, a priest read:
"The Lord himself, when the order is given, at the sound
of the archangel's voice and of God's trumpet, will come
down from Heaven and the dead in Christ will first rise."

Archbishop Cooke, the principal concelebrant, carried
the theme of hope forward: "We mourn Robert Kennedy
and we know that America shall miss him," he said. "But
let us not miss the meaning of his life. We, too, must live
in faith. We must respond to God's call. We must answer
our neighbor's call for true freedom and equality.

"Our response will be made in loving God and loving
our neighbor, in proving our love by service, in serving
by confronting and resolving problems of poverty, race,
violence and war.

"For Senator Kennedy there shall be no more mourning
and no more sorrow, and death shall be no more."

The participation of the Kennedy children in the service also marked a meaningful departure from traditional ritual, which had tended to keep the "performers" and "audience" separate. Eight youngsters, led by two candle bearers, marched up to the white marble sanctuary in the Offertory, bearing the holy vessels and ciboriums containing the Host and the wine for the Communion.

The music, too, was significantly different. Thirty-two members of the New York Philharmonic, directed by Leonard Bernstein, played symphonic music, rarely if ever permitted at a Catholic service. During the Offertory, they played the Adagietto movement from Gustav Mahler's Fifth Symphony, chosen by Bernstein because of its solemnity.

The one hour, forty-minute mass ended when Cardinal Cushing circled the coffin twice, once sprinkling it with holy water for God's mercy, then swinging a thurible, or portable vessel containing burning charcoal and aromatic substances symbolizing the prayers of the faithful. "May the angels take you into paradise," the Cardinal intoned in his gravelly voice. "May the martyrs come to welcome you on your way and lead you into the holy city, Jerusalem. May the choir of angels welcome you and with Lazarus who once was poor, may you have everlasting rest."

As the clerical procession moved back down the center aisle, Andy Williams began to sing without musical accompaniment. In 1861, Julia Ward Howe, the writer and social reformer, visited Army camps near Washington and watched soldiers go off to war singing "John Brown's body lies amouldering in the grave" to an old Southern camp-meeting tune. That evening, she wrote the stirring words of "The Battle Hymn of the Republic," which became the marching song of the Union forces during the

Civil War. Williams, his voice clear in the hushed cathedral, sang in slow measure these words for his friend:

> *Mine eyes have seen the glory of the coming*
>   *of the Lord:*
> *He is trampling out the vintage where the*
>   *grapes of wrath are stored. . . .*

At the chorus, some in the congregation joined in. Ethel, who had been looking at Williams, turned her head slightly, as though surprised. With the second stanza, more voices had come in. By the end of the hymn, most of the persons in the church, accompanied by the mighty organ and the choir, filled the cathedral with triumphant sound:

> *Glory, glory, Hallelujah!*
> *Glory, glory, Hallelujah!*
> *Glory, glory, Hallelujah!*
> *His truth is marching on.*

☙ ☙ ☙

Ethel was seated in the last of the twenty-one coaches in what the railroad called a "business car." There are six of these on the Penn Central, each eighty-five feet long, used as traveling offices by executives. At the front there was a parlor section furnished with sofas and chairs, followed by four bedrooms, a dining room with a table accommodating eight persons, then a kitchen with berths for two crew members.

Robert Kennedy's flag-draped coffin lay on red velvet covered chairs in the dining section, raised so that the throngs lining the tracks could view it as it passed on the journey to Washington and burial in Arlington National

Cemetery. At the rear of the car, draped in black bunting and green foliage, was an observation platform where Ted Kennedy stood for much of the trip.

The coffin had been borne from the cathedral and, as Ethel watched from the top of the steps, placed in a gray hearse. She, Joe and Ted rode in the front seat as the hearse led a thirty-car cortege down Fifth Avenue, then west to Pennsylvania Station.

The special train had pulled out of Pennsylvania Station on Track 12 at 1:02 P.M. for the 226-mile journey to Washington, usually a 4-hour trip by regular service, with no ceremony other than the railroaders' call of "all aboard." Engineer John F. Flanagan had his instructions: Throttle down only at a few key cities along the route. But the train had barely emerged from the tunnel into the New Jersey flatlands when everyone realized this would be no ordinary ride.

"I have never seen anything like it in my life," the engineer said afterward. People were everywhere, all along the route, even in the lonely rural stretches. Soon Ethel sent word to move slowly wherever crowds had gathered. In Newark, seven-thousand persons, sixty-five per cent of them black, crushed into Penn Station, lining six to ten deep along Platforms Two and Five and the main-line tracks. Here an elderly woman suddenly wailed in the hushed crowd. A young girl held a photograph of Bobby close to her breast, another wept softly on her boyfriend's arm. Many carried small flags and waved them at the cars. As the train, moving at five miles an hour, crossed a railroad bridge spanning the Passaic River, the crew of the city's fireboat, the *John F. Kennedy,* was standing on deck, every man at rigid salute.

At Rahway, two black children bore a sign: "Now we are losers, but in time we'll be winners because of RFK,

JFK and Dr. King." At New Brunswick, where four thousand had gathered, a high school band played "Holy God
We Praise Thy Name" and "Battle Hymn of the Republic" over and over until the train passed; then it
played "Taps." In Trenton, an all-service color guard
stood at stiff attention, lowering their flags as the cortege
went by. In open areas, Little Leaguers saluted with their
caps or gloves over their hearts. Even in the rural sec-
tions, groups of people with cars had drawn up to the
trackside, many with flowers in their hands or hand-
lettered signs that said good-bye.

Ethel and Jackie waved often to the crowds from their
seats in the lounge of the business car. At 3:15 in the
afternoon, as the train approached the outskirts of Trenton, Ethel told Bill Barry and Lem Billings she wanted
to thank the people who had come along on the last journey. Her eldest son, Joe, neat in a dark blue suit with a
PT-109 clip holding down his tie, had already walked
the length of the train, sticking out his hand and telling
everyone: "Hi, I'm Joe Kennedy. Thanks for coming."

Followed by Rosie Grier, Barry and Billings, she walked
through every one of the twenty cars and talked to almost
all of the eleven-hundred passengers. Her black chiffon
veil perched over her head, she squeezed shoulders, shook
hands, kissed friends.

Astounded, the men stood awkwardly and murmured
some words. Seeing her approach, they hastily struggled
into their jackets, removed because the air conditioning
was not working. To keep the batteries charged so that
the cooling system could operate, the train had to travel
at a minimum of thirty-five miles per hour, and it rarely
made it.

She took both of Andy Glass' hands in hers and told
him how nice it was that he could be there. Andy murmured condolences and Ethel smiled and said it was all

right. A woman across the aisle burst into tears and then there was an almost complete reversal of roles, to be repeated many times during her walk: The wife who had just lost a husband consoled the mourner who had come to the rites.

She smiled as she greeted the passengers, joking and teasing with her oldest and best-liked friends. "I thought this was for good friends only," she said to Ray O'Connell, an old and good friend. She came to burly, usually irreverent Jimmy Breslin, who tried to smooth his tousled black hair as he stood. "What are you standing for?" she kidded him. "It's embarrassing. After all, you're not a gentleman."

"Okay, lady," Jimmy kidded back, "so I'll sit down." He did, and they chatted a moment.

Pete Hamill was sitting with José Torres, the former light heavyweight champion who was active in the affairs of the New York Puerto Rican community. Torres's leg was in a cast because of a torn Achilles tendon at the back of the ankle. Ethel embraced them both, then, noticing Torres's cast and the crutch beside him, asked: "What happened?" Torres explained he had been injured while working out in a gym but expected to be able to discard the crutch in a short while. Ethel embraced him again and told him to take care of himself. When she left, Torres sat and wept.

After she had gone through every car, she stopped for a brief rest, drank half a paper cupful of Coca-Cola, handed the rest to Bill Barry and closed her eyes for a moment. The train swayed on and nobody said anything. "Have you ever been to Disneyland?" Ethel asked, to keep the conversation going. "Disneyland is green and big and there's a mountain." Yes, a few had been there and they agreed it was a nice place.

They were coming into the North Philadelphia Station,

85.9 miles from New York but hours behind schedule.
The train slowed to a crawl and Ethel waved at the silent
crowd of 2,500. At the main station a few minutes later,
3,000 persons had disregarded a police ban against entering the area. Here men and women were sobbing openly
as they watched the cortege.

Ethel made her way back. As she entered the press
car near the rear, she saw Frank Mankiewicz standing
in front of a throng of newsmen. Catching sight of her,
he stopped talking.

"What's going on?" Ethel asked. Frank replied hastily:
"Just having a little discussion, a little briefing." Ethel
said: "It's too hot to have a briefing about anything."
She went through the car, then left.

Nobody had told her. Five-and-a-half miles below Newark, at the West Grand Street station in Elizabeth, New
Jersey, New York-bound Penn Central train Number
Fifty had come through the same time as the funeral train.
Because of the commotion, the noise of the Kennedy
train and the engines of the low-flying Secret Service and
news-media helicopters, the warning horns of the northbound express could not be heard clearly. The throngs,
unaware that another train was coming, pressed too close
to the track. The Penn Central's Admiral rounded a curve
and sheared the edges of the crowd, killing a man and a
woman and injuring six persons, including a three-year-old
child. Mayor Thomas C. Dunn of Elizabeth cried out
in anguish moments later: "I knew it! I swear to God I
knew this would happen!"

Horrified by the tragedy, fearful another might occur,
Jerry Bruno of the Kennedy staff wired Penn Central
officials: Unless they halted all northbound trains along
the entire route, the funeral train would not proceed.
He received assurance this would be done. Despite all pre-

cautions, there was another incident: A youth, eighteen, climbed atop a freight car in Trenton to get a better view and was severely burned by a high-voltage power line.

The train moved on. At Baltimore, a few persons began singing "The Battle Hymn of the Republic" and soon most of the 5,000 waiting at the station were joining in. Crowds had sung the same hymn 103 years earlier, on April 15, 1865, when the body of Abraham Lincoln was borne by train from Washington en route to burial in Springfield, Illinois.

At 9:47, four hours and forty-five minutes late, the train finally pulled into Union Station. Ethel was led into one of twenty-five waiting limousines and the cortege moved slowly through the city where more thousands, many holding candles, had been waiting patiently through the heat of the afternoon and early evening thunder showers. The rain had stopped now but there were threats of a renewed downpour. President Johnson, who had flown back to Washington after the services at St. Patrick's, had driven with Mrs. Johnson to the station at 9:00 to greet the Kennedy family and join the funeral procession.

The cortege moved up from Union Station to the Senate Office Building, where Ethel had gone so often in happier days to "watch Bobby in action," then turned down Constitution Avenue and drove past the huge square Department of Justice Building, where Bobby had served three years. It passed the ellipse where the lights of the White House could be seen far to the right and paused at the Lincoln Memorial, while a choir sang "The Battle Hymn" once again, then continued across the Arlington Memorial Bridge to the cemetery where John Kennedy lies buried and a new grave had been dug beneath the shade of two Japanese magnolia trees a few yards away.

Joe helped his mother from the front seat of the hearse, and she stood and watched as her two sons, her brother-in-law Teddy and other pallbearers bore the casket from the hearse to the gravesite.

It was nearly 10:30 now, the threat of more rain had passed and a bright moon had come up. Harshly bright floodlights for the television cameras shone on the slope as the mourners gathered for the brief burial service conducted by Patrick Cardinal O'Boyle, officiating in place of Cardinal Cushing, who had buckled under the strain of the long, long day.

Robert Kennedy's body was committed to the grave. The flag covering his coffin was removed, folded into a triangle and handed to John Glenn. He wheeled and gave the flag to Senator Edward Kennedy, who passed it on to young Joe Kennedy.

Joe put the flag in the outstretched hands of his mother, who took it back to Hickory Hill.

EIGHTEEN

First Year Alone

❦ ❧

Four months after the murder of her husband, Ethel had to face the possibility of still another personal tragedy, the loss of Bobby's last baby.

On a Saturday morning in October, she was threatened with premature labor. When the warning signs came, she telephoned her obstetrician, Dr. John W. Walsh, clinical professor of obstetrics and gynecology at Georgetown University, who had delivered John F. Kennedy, Jr., and several of Ethel's children.

Dr. Walsh ordered her to Georgetown University Hospital without delay. Apprehensive, Ethel called Ted, who rushed over and drove her to the hospital, a complex of red-brick buildings at 3800 Reservoir Road in Georgetown. Once there, Ted called Luella Hennessey at Walpole, Massachusetts, the nurse who had assisted at the births of every grandchild of Rose and Joe Kennedy but one, twenty-seven babies in all, and was much loved, respected and depended upon at times such as this.

Ted asked her to come down at once, that very day, because Ethel needed her. "This baby," he said, "means so much to her."

Miss Hennessey packed quickly, went to the airport and by 11:00 that evening, starched and capable looking, entered Ethel's room and took charge. Ethel lay in bed, tense and frightened. There was reason for her fear. "If she delievered it then," Nurse Hennessey explains, "the baby probably would not have lived."

"Thank you for coming," Ethel said, as Miss Hennessey bustled about the room. The arrival of the nurse cheered her enormously. Her anxiety began to subside and soon she drifted into sleep.

She spent a restful night. The symptoms did not recur, and in the morning Dr. Walsh discharged her, but with strict instructions: She must go home and remain in bed until the arrival of the baby. En route to Hickory Hill, Ethel asked Miss Hennessey to remain with her until the delivery, which was to be by Caesarian section.

All through that fall, Ethel remained in her room on that enormous bed. Nurse Hennessey has vivid recollections of scenes in her bedroom those crisp fall days and nights that were almost unbearable in their poignancy:

"The older children—Kathleen, Joseph and Bobby, Jr., had gone back to school," she says, "and only the younger ones were left, the two girls and the five boys. They loved her so, and they showed it every day, every hour. Knowing she wasn't feeling well, they would go out and pick buttercups and daisies in the garden and bring them to her. She would make so much of those little bouquets and the children would be so proud.

"They'd be running up there all the time, telling her things they did and saw. The moment the older ones came back from school, they'd drop their books and run upstairs to her. Some of them would have their dinner on trays in the bedroom with her. And before they went to bed, the younger ones would climb into that tremendous bed with her, and she would lie there with one arm flung out and hugging them and read Bible stories to them."

On December 11, Ethel, accompanied by Ted Kennedy, Fred Dutton, Rafer Johnson and Nurse Hennessey, and loaded down with five suitcases and a three-speed electric fan, drove once more to Georgetown University Hospital. Next morning, she was taken to Delivery Room Five on the third floor, which had recently been converted into an operating room for obstetrical patients.

Ted Kennedy followed the stretcher into the room, watched her placed on the table under the big lights and remained until a light anesthetic was being administered. Then he left. Seconds later the operation was begun and, at 8:40, Dr. Walsh delivered an eight-pound, four-ounce little girl with light brown hair, like her mother.

She awoke in the recovery room on the fourth floor. When her new baby was placed in her arms for the first time, she exclaimed: "Isn't she beautiful!" and she held her closely and kissed her head. It was six months and a week after the assassination of the baby's father. Nurse Hennessey watched Ethel cooing and murmuring to the infant beside her, heard her say: "I love you. I love you so much. You're so beautiful. . . ." There were, she saw, some tears in Ethel's eyes as she cuddled her baby. "Because," Nurse Hennessey says, "Bobby wasn't there."

The baby was named Rory Elizabeth Katherine—Rory for no special reason except that Ethel and the other children liked it, Elizabeth for Elizabeth Stevens, wife of George Stevens, Jr., director of the American Film Institute, and Katherine for Katherine Evans, wife of columnist Rowland Evans.

On December 19, Ethel left the hospital with Rory. She did not go directly home. She took her baby first to Arlington, to Bobby Kennedy's grave, where, with Rory in her arms, she knelt in prayer.

ⓘ ⓘ ⓘ

She appears to be the same Ethel. She whips through life nonstop—racing for the air shuttle to New York from Washington, flying to Colorado for skiing, playing hard at her beloved sports, laughing and joking at parties, chattering, giggling, coming on strong.

And life at Hickory Hill seems almost the way it was. The aura of high importance is no longer there but the same marvelous mix of people comes to lunch and dinner —newsmen and Senators, labor leaders and Governors, sports figures and show people, students, community leaders, civil-rights workers, clergymen. The old friends Bobby liked best are there most often—Rosie Grier, John Glenn, Kenny O'Donnell, Adam Walinsky, Frank Mankiewicz, Jim Whittaker, Rafer Johnson, and author-journalists like Jack Newfield, Art Buchwald, Theodore White, Hays Gorey and Warren Rogers. The horses and ponies roam as before, the children and their friends dart all over the place, and Brumus still gets in everybody's way. Dave Hackett once remarked it was almost as though Bobby himself was expected to walk in.

All this is no accident. From the day she buried Bobby, Ethel determined that her family's way of life must remain as normal as possible under the tragic circumstances. Strong rumors arose that she would sell Hickory Hill to escape the painful memories every room and square foot of lawn would evoke; Greenwich was abuzz with stories that she was planning to purchase an estate in her girlhood home. "There was never any thought of leaving Hickory Hill," Ethel says. "This is where we'll stay."

In fact, the children made the decision themselves. About a week after the funeral, all the young Kennedys gathered around their dining-room table after lunch to discuss the momentous question of moving or staying put and the debate was lively. One objected to pulling up stakes and moving to "that gloomy old apartment" in United Nations Plaza. Another turned thumbs down on setting up permanent residence at the Bobby Kennedy home in the Hyannis Port compound, though admitting its merits as a place to go for vacations.

Kathleen spoke up: "Why," she asked, "can't we stay right here at Hickory Hill?" "Why not?" Joe put in. A buzz swept the table. There were nods of approval, and the suggestion carried the day. However, they agreed they had better consult with Mom.

They did, and she couldn't have been more pleased.

From the beginning, Ethel would not permit any expression of sorrow in her presence. She didn't want people unhappy around her, and if they were, she would just as soon they weren't there. Her personal letters to friends and relatives who sent condolences all reflected her determination to avoid self-pity. Most important, she would never show or voice sorrow, or permit anyone else to do so, when her children were present.

It wasn't that mention of Bobby was forbidden. She would speak of him often, not sadly or tragically but matter-of-factly, to friends and the children. There are innumerable reminders of Bobby all over her house. A thirty-foot wall of the cabaña at the pool is covered with dozens of photographs of him on his last campaign. The top of the piano in the living room has many pictures of the slain brothers.

"If she's downbeat," Art Buchwald said that first year, "she never lets on." Long before the mourning period ended, Ted Kennedy remarked: "Ethel has no idea how much her strength and her own warmth and good will have meant to others, how much these things have meant to her children, how much she has helped me and the Kennedy family."

While things seem to be the same at Hickory Hill, Ethel has had to tighten the financial belt more than a little: She is not as well-fixed as many people suppose. As a friend explains: "Like all widows, she didn't only lose a husband, she inherited money problems."

"Please understand me," continues the friend, who knows what is in her accounts and what she must spend. "Ethel is by no means a poor woman. I wish I had as much money as she has. It's something like this: Suppose you have an income of $75,000, then suddenly it drops to $50,000. You're still comfortably off, aren't you? But you've still got to work out how to get along without that extra $25,000." While Ethel's income, of course, was considerably higher than $50,000 after Bobby's death, she too had to figure out how to get by with less. The scale may be different, but her problem is not unlike that of millions of other households: how to keep the spending less than, or at least even with, the amount coming in.

Most of Bobby's estate, which was divided between his wife and children, is tied up in trust funds. According to his will, as filed in the Manhattan Surrogates Court, Ethel may draw up to ten percent of the principal of her share for living expenses. In addition, she may use up to 20 percent of the principal of the children's trust. Other wills, disposing of property held in Virginia and Massachusetts, have similar provisions. Ethel also owns stock in the Great Lakes Carbon Corporation, bequeathed to her by her father, but shares in family-owned companies do not pay large dividends and, moreover, are not easy to sell. (She sold off some of her shares less than a year after Bobby was killed.)

So while there is money, the supply is not unlimited. Aware of this, Ethel now pays attention to costs. She sold the apartment at United Nations Plaza, including fifteen paintings she had collected. She no longer picks up expensive antiques or lovely little pieces of jewelry that strike her fancy, nor will she order new living-room drapes on a whim as once she might have done.

She has reduced the staff at Hickory Hill to nine, but Ruby Reynolds, the family cook, remains, though unable to work because of illness. Ethel has insisted she stay on. Ruby has her own room and is seen daily by a local visiting nurse. She is able to walk outdoors and, on occasion, Ethel will take her for a stroll on the grounds.

Despite the surface normalcy at Hickory Hill, let nobody doubt for a moment that the tragedy has left its mark. Indomitably, Ethel seeks to hide them, but they emerge:

She is unable to view even a scene of a movie that involves shooting and somebody dropping dead. Films are shown once or twice a week in the thirty- by thirty-foot cabaña near the pool. As Lem Billings explains: "Movies are so rough these days there is hardly one that hasn't got blood and shooting somewhere. And when it comes, Ethel cannot remain there and watch. She rushes out." Another subject Ethel clearly indicated was taboo was the trial of her husband's slayer while it was in progress in early 1969, and any talk of his subsequent conviction.

Lem, the faithful bachelor friend who loves the family as his own, lifts his long frame from a couch, and goes to stare at the photographs strewn around his mid-Manhattan apartment. There are pictures of Bobby and John Kennedy as fresh-faced children, gawky adolescents, young men and, finally, men of importance in public life. Lem knew them both through the happy years, and emotion overtakes him as he looks at the photos: "She's human, for Christ's sake," he bursts out.

She moves *too* much and races *too* fast. Ethel has always had a built-in antidote for worry—her constant activity. We cannot dwell upon our problems if we do not sit still long enough to fix our attention upon them. Her close friends have observed in her a hyperactivity following the death of her husband, as though de-accelerating even for a short time might force her to dwell upon the early morning in Los Angeles. But then, quite suddenly, Ethel will stop, and a change will come into her face, altering it completely. The radiance, the zest-for-life look, will vanish and in its place there will be a sadness, and nobody can doubt that in these fleeting moments there is a remembering.

Always gregarious, hating to be alone, Ethel more than ever must be surrounded by people, and her friends oblige. Rene Carpenter, Kay Evans, Ann Brinkley, wife of television commentator David Brinkley, Polly Kraft, wife of the columnist Joseph Kraft, Elizabeth Stevens, and other members of a group someone has tagged "Ethel's Mafia" are frequently around. Friends who live in the area have been drawn, as by some powerful magnetic force, into Ethel's orbit. They descend upon Hickory Hill to help answer the hundreds of letters that arrive weekly, take care of the children Ethel cannot handle herself, play games, talk and joke and laugh with her. They come, too, from New York, Philadelphia, Chicago. In some curious way, they have all become almost fiercely protective toward her, shielding her privacy. Ethel, a little spoiled, accepts their homage. But, what is more important, she needs the human presence.

However, there are few tears. Her remarkable self-control, so evident to everyone around her, snapped only rarely in the hard months of readjustment.

Two months after the assassination, Teddy Kennedy emerged from seclusion and spoke out on the vital issues of the day in an address at Worcester, Mass. Declaring that he was resuming his public responsibilities, he said he was picking up a "fallen standard" dropped by his brothers. He pledged himself to carry forward their special commitment to "justice, excellence, and courage."

Ethel was listening over the radio at Hickory Hill. As he spoke that moving passage, she collapsed in sobs, her face in her hands. She wept convulsively for many minutes. Subsequently, newspaper accounts reported that many other viewers were saddened to tears as they listened to Ted Kennedy.

There are not many of these incidents, at least where people can see. Lem Billings puts into words what millions must wonder:

"You never know what happens to Ethel when she goes to bed at night and closes the door. You don't know. Nobody knows."

⑨ ⑨ ⑨

And so Ethel, being human, has reacted. Nonetheless, her strength and resilience, as we have seen, have been truly remarkable. ("Unbelievable," Lem Billings says. "Incredible—just incredible!" brother Rushton exclaims.) Of all her qualities, these are the ones most talked about and wondered over by Americans who have watched Ethel buffeted—it seems so often and so mercilessly—by life. It is probable that her courage in the face of recurrent tragedy was mostly responsible for her choice as the world's most admired woman in a 1969 Gallup Poll. (Mrs. Rose Kennedy placed second, Mamie Eisenhower

third, and Lady Bird Johnson fourth. Mrs. Pat Nixon
was sixth and Jackie Onassis seventh.)

Where does she get her strength? How does she en-
dure all the terrible blows?

We can talk about her feeling of self-worth, her conviction that she is a capable human being, able to deal
with the crises of life. We know that her parents neither
pampered nor protected her, permitting her to experience pain and discomfort and to learn she could surmount
them.

We can talk about the powerful Kennedy family soli-
darity which enables one member to draw strength from
the other. Or Ethel's unquenchable thirst for life, which
give her an essentially forward-looking spirit. Or about
her desire to "do for others"; persons who give of themselves have less time left for grief or self-pity.

We can talk about her total commitment to Robert
Kennedy, and speculate that she feels she must remain
strong in order to keep alive his memory.

We can say that she has to remain strong for the sake
of her children. Or we can cop out by asserting that some
people take adversity better than others.

Lacking a full-scale psychological workup of Ethel,
we cannot say with any authority to what extent any of
these factors has contributed to Ethel's strength.

But we do know about her powerful religious faith,
and it is here that we approach the heart of the matter. A
friend once said: "If she will only write down her phi-
losophy in the face of so much grief as she has known,
it will make a living document on the true meaning of
courage." She never has, but such a document discussing
in precise detail how her faith gives her strength has come
from a hut deep in the forests of Nelson County, Kentucky.

The Father Abbot of Gethsemani, no longer the active abbot of the monastery, has retired to a hermitage on property owned by the Trappist Fathers to be "alone with the alone." He was sought out to answer the question: "How does Ethel stand up as she has under all the blows she has received?"

From his hermitage came the Father Abbot's reply:

Ethel has what such a large portion of the human family seems to lack today, a living and vivid awareness of the reality of God.

Her faith is not a mere intellectual assent to a certain body of propositions and formulae. Rather, it is a faith which penetrates her entire being—and which motivates her everyday's round of duties, of sorrows and of joys.

This faith is due, in a very large part, to the wonderful atmosphere of her family. In its turn, the family atmosphere was due to her mother, who was the dominant factor in all the domestic relations.

Mrs. Skakel created this milieu of deep faith, not only by her instructions and counsels but especially by her sincere and positive example. Her faith was generous, warm and joyful; yet it was also a serious, no-nonsense, down-to-earth type.

Ethel grew up in this wonderful environment; her faith, consequently, is not a mere go-to-church-on-Sunday type which is forgotten for the next six days of the week. No, her faith, *i.e.*, her awareness of the great reality of God and of all that He has done for the human family, is living and pulsating in her, every hour of the day, every day of the week.

For Ethel, God is not a Being off somewhere in interstellar space who is so concerned with Himself that He has no "time" to bother about what we think, do or say.

For Ethel, God is indeed a transcendant Being, outside of all time, space and matter, and He is also a Being very immanent and so close to her that He is giving her her own being and existence with every breath she breathes and with every beat her heart beats.

Thus, for Ethel, God is her heavenly Father who created her, redeemed her, who loves her as His child, and who loves every one whom she loves.

For this realization, she has two dominant and guiding principles:

1. Nothing happens in her life tha God does not will directly, or at least permits indirectly.

2. And that whatever happens is for best eternal interest even though she, in her limited finite vision, does not see the connection. Yet the connection is there in God's plan.

And therefore she knows that it is up to her to try to correspond, no matter what, where, when, how or by whom an event has occurred.

This is not a negative thing, a mere resignation to blind fate. It is rather a positive going out to embrace tragedies, catastrophes and accidents, as so many mysteries of God's Providence in her regard.

She may experience, indeed, piercing pain and poignant anguish of mind and of heart. Yet there is a tremendous calm, stability and peace in the depths of her soul. She has that utter and absolute trust and childlike confidence in the doings of her Father, who is in Heaven and who is also within her.

She knows that God loves her, and she knows that one never hurts one whom he loves.

The only real harm is not that which obtains in the earthly, temporal order of things, but that which would be eternal. This is a most important distinction.

She knows that if she is faithful, on her part, to the various duties of wife and of mother and of friend, and corresponds to the many sacrifices God may ask of her, that He, on His part, will be ever true to her.

Thus Ethel has profound convictions of the power of prayer to God. Many times, on the occasion of some great trial or tragedy, she would phone the Abbey to ask for the prayers and sacrifices of the monks for her intentions.

Ethel has a vivid realization that all of the human family, herself included, are not made for time but for eternity. She knows that, although we may be separated from one another when death occurs here on earth, some- day her family will be together again, never to be sep- arated any more, for all eternity.

NINETEEN

New Life Plan

How is Ethel remaking her life?

She has set two major goals for herself. Her closest friends foresee nothing that can change them, not even remarriage.

Bobby Kennedy would have wanted Ethel to marry again. Dave Hackett, one of his closest and oldest friends, discloses this. And Ethel? "She jokes about it occasionally," Hackett says. "But it would take an extraordinary fellow. It would have to be someone very strong, enlightened and flexible."

Above all, flexible. For the man Ethel marries, if she does at all, must know, and accept unquestioningly, that she won't swerve from her new life plan.

By mid-1970, she had been linked to two men, and rumors flew about several others. In July of 1970, the Toronto *Star* was busily tracking down a report that she was having a romance with a Canadian lawyer. William J. vanden Heuvel, a friend and former aide to Robert Kennedy, has denied published reports that he and Ethel might marry. There were recurring stories, too, stronger throughout Europe than in the United States, about a romantic involvement with Warren Rogers, a widower, the bureau chief of *Look* magazine. Rogers has stated there wasn't a "whisper of truth" to them.

Let us see, in closeup, how Ethel Kennedy is living in her widowhood and how, in her day-to-day activities, she is trying to achieve aims she has charted.

🙰 🙰 🙰

Her first concern is her children. She will devote as much of her time and strength to them as she can, raising them in as close and loving a family atmosphere as possible, subordinating almost everything else to their welfare.

On a warm May morning, Ethel charged through several games of tennis at Ted and Joan's home two-and-a-half miles away. Then, still in her white tennis dress but changed from sneakers to white patent pumps, she waded into a crowd of two-thousand grownups and children gathered at Hickory Hill for the Big Pet Show.

The annual event, for the benefit of the Northwest Settlement House, was begun six years before by Bobby and Ethel. Guests, most of them strangers, come and watch the fun. They bring their children, who drag or carry a weird assortment of pets. The lawns, tennis court and flower beds would always take such a beating, it took weeks to get them back in shape.

This year's show came less than three weeks before the first anniversary of her husband's assassination. Ethel had spent the year in mourning, making no public appearances, remaining close to Hickory Hill. She had, as usual, gone to mass every day, helped with the car pool, cared for her family. None would have blamed her had this year's event been canceled.

But Ethel wouldn't think of it. A cancellation would have signified a break in the familiar for her children. They loved the excitement and gaiety of the pet show; they looked forward to it every year. To have it taken away abruptly would have meant another break in the continuity of life.

Her initial plunge into a public function was hard. Ethel, a Mickey Mouse watch strapped to her wrist, paused at the red front door and swept her eyes over the throng swarming over the grounds. She stood there, quivering slightly. Then, as though diving into icy water, she gulped in a deep breath and went out into the crowd of pets and people.

It was a grand show. There were puppets going through their hilarious paces, a jungle gym, a wild fortune teller, games everywhere. The French Embassy, which had donated a carload of food, also supervised a wine-tasting booth for grownups. Humorist Art Buchwald, in ringmaster's scarlet coat and white breeches, was master of ceremonies, assisted by Matthew Kennedy, four years old, dressed identically.

On the terrace, Chris Kennedy, not quite six, was operating a Kool-Aid stand. His Uncle Ted, red with the heat, was a grateful customer. Near by, Rory Elizabeth, in a short pink dress and ruffled pink pants, was asleep in a playpen. Twelve-year-old Courtney paid for a pony ride on the tennis court and found after she left that she hadn't been given the right change. She returned and got the rest.

Then there was the judging—for the most unusual pet, for the dog with the longest hair, for the longest fish, the slowest animal, the wildest costume. In the judging ring, a brother and sister, seven and eight years old, picketed with a sign reading: "Why do the Kennedys win all the prizes?" It was a put-on, and it won a prize for originality.

The most exciting game of all was the obstacle course, built by members of the Washington Redskins football team. It had taken the players two weeks to rig up the high barriers, cut the waterholes, hang the rubber tires, set up the hurdles. Racing over the course in competition with the other kids was fun for the Kennedy youngsters. But more important—and Ethel knew this—were the two weeks of busy activity helping to set it up.

One friend has remarked that Ethel is probably a fiercer mother because she is aware of the tremendous task she faces. She still bathes and feeds the youngest, breakfasts with the older ones, car-pools, sits with them at lunch and dinner, reads to them, teaches them their faith and puts them to bed. She flies off to see the older ones at school and at their vacation jobs. When Joe Kennedy III spent the summer of 1970 learning to be a guide for mountain climbers on Mount Rainier in Seattle, Ethel flew up and climbed halfway up the slope with him.

Ted Kennedy drops by frequently to play with the children. Dave Hackett has attended every Father's Day event at their schools. John Glenn, Andy Williams and Art Buchwald come to take the youngsters on outings. All of these men know it is important for the children's development to be close to a man and maleness.

In August, two months after the assassination, the children gave a party at Hickory Hill. Ethel was nearby but not at home. About twenty-five youngsters were there, friends from Washington and school. One of the guests, a perceptive eighteen-year-old, gave this account of the party:

"It was a wild kind of night. We were all down by the swimming pool. The Kennedy kids were there, all but the very little ones. I remember very distinctly getting the feeling from the way they were acting that a kind of recklessness had taken hold.

"They began throwing pool furniture in the swimming pool, tossing in tables and chairs, breaking soda bottles and tossing the ash trays around. It was a raucous scene of kids getting up on tables and yelling and lots of noise, with the jukebox playing. A few of the other kids were doing it too, but it was mostly the Kennedy kids, all but Kathleen.

"I got the feeling very definitely that it was a kind of reaction on the part of the older Kennedy kids, a kind of letting loose."

They felt the impact of the sudden, brutal tearing away of a father who had been so central to their lives. How could they not? And who can say in what subtle ways they have been affected, each in his or her own way?

However, as a result of Ethel's devoted interest, and the attention of her relatives and friends, the children have borne up well, and the trauma has probably been minimized.

ꟿ ꟿ ꟿ

Her second goal is to keep alive the ideals of her dead husband.

Ethel's first official public appearance after the assassination was at the dedication of the District of Columbia Stadium in Washington, which had been renamed the Robert F. Kennedy Memorial Stadium.

The first party invitation she accepted was to a fundraising affair in Southampton, Long Island, in support of Cesar Chavez, leader of the Mexican and Filipino agricultural workers who were striking against the California grape growers. "Remember," she told the two-hundred-and-fifty chic guests, "my husband marched with

Cesar." He did, in a union procession in March 1968, marking the end of a twenty-five-day fast Chavez had undergone to dramatize the plight of the grape pickers. Bobby Kennedy had identified strongly with Chavez's struggle.

In the fall of that year, she journeyed to the Bedford-Stuyvesant section of Brooklyn, New York, a black ghetto area as bad as any in the nation, for the dedication of Superblock. Two years before, crumbling, rat-infested tenements stood on the garbage-strewn street. Now it was an attractive residential area on a traffic-free plaza in a parklike setting. Superblock was one of the projects begun two years before by a private corporation set up by Robert Kennedy when he was the junior Senator from the State.

These things she will always do. Lem Billings explains:

"She knows she represents Bobby's memory. She realizes what an important part of history Bobby was, and she is dedicated to seeing that people, all people, know the kind of person he was."

The single most important means of perpetuating Kennedy's ideals is the Robert F. Kennedy Memorial, headquartered in a small suite of offices on the ground floor of a three-story brick building on Jefferson Place in Washington. Ethel comes here frequently to confer with Fred Dutton, the executive director.

The memorial, set up by Ethel and other members of the family and friends, is not a place nor is it a foundation to finance worthwhile social projects. Rather, it sets up task forces and—as Ted Kennedy described it—"carries on his concern, compassion and interest in the unmet needs of our country."

The memorial has created "action fellowships" for outstanding young people who are assigned to work all across the country in the kind of community projects closely identified with Robert Kennedy.

The first batch of Fellows was named in 1969. Most were in their mid-twenties, many of them young professionals. All were assigned to work on subsistence stipends for poverty organizations that could not otherwise afford the full-time assistance of a professionally trained specialist.

Half of the group represented minority groups, including six blacks, four Mexican-Americans, two Indians, and four second-generation Oriental Americans. Four were women. Some typical assignments:

Louis C. Baldanza, age twenty-four, from Garfield, New Jersey, appointed to Mexican-American Unity Council in San Antonio, Texas, to develop a housing project.

David C. Bellows, age twenty-five, from Little Silver, New Jersey, appointed to Commission on Religion in Appalachia, headquarters in Knoxville, Tennessee, to develop consumer and producer co-ops throughout the Appalachian region.

Duane T. Bird Bear, twenty-one-year-old Hidatsa Indian from Mandaree, North Dakota, assigned to the United Scholarship Service headquartered in Denver, Colorado, to work with Indian college students.

David Ho, thirty-one-year-old Chinese-American from New York City, assigned to work fulltime with the Chinese Youth Council.

Jonathan Shils, twenty-three-year-old sociologist and student leader at Columbia where he was associate director of the Afro-American Studies Institute, assigned to Greene County, Alabama, to serve as an administrative assistant to newly elected black public officials.

Carl L. Shoolman, twenty-five-year-old lawyer from

Rochester, New York, assigned to the Center for Black Elected Officials in Tougaloo, Mississippi, to work with newly elected black officials throughout the state.

Marian Moses, thirty-three-year-old registered nurse, who has taught clinical nursing, supervised a large nursing staff in a metropolitan hospital, and directed research for the Kaiser Research Institute in California. She is assigned to Cesar Chavez to develop a health-services program under the supervision of the Farm Workers, and to recruit a medical staff to work with Cesar Chavez.

Roger M. Dunwell, twenty-five, from Poughkeepsie, New York, a lawyer assigned to the United Farm Workers in San Juan, Texas.

Miss Dorothy Foster, twenty-year-old black teacher from Tuscaloosa, Alabama, to develop experimental black studies curriculum for tutorial projects administered by NAPA (Newark Area Planning Association).

Gerald M. Clifford, thirty years old, Oglala Sioux Indian from Pine Ridge, South Dakota, assigned to the American Indian Leadership Council in Oglala, South Dakota, to develop and coordinate educational programs for Indian young people on reservations.

Robert Cross, twenty-eight-year-old black organizer from Newark, New Jersey, to work fulltime with the North Jersey Community Union to develop a support and training structure for a community health program.

Other task forces created by the memorial include:
A Lawyers Project—thirty-five attorneys in private practice provide free legal assistance to ghetto and rural poverty groups;
A Citizens Communication Center to improve commercial radio and television coverage of public problems with special attention directed to local coverage as it

affects minority groups. The center assists church, labor and other civic organizations in their relationships with local broadcasting outlets;

The Robert F. Kennedy Journalism Awards, annual prizes for the best coverage of the problems of discrimination and poverty;

Community Development, which organizes teams of businessmen, corporate lawyers, bankers and others to assist minority groups in the economic development of their areas. These specialist teams will help a group acquire or create a profitable business, large or small, in urban areas that can best benefit from such economic stimulation.

On June 6, the day after Bobby died, Mrs. Gertrude Claflin, an Indian woman living on the Allegany Reservation in New York State, visited by the Kennedys in 1967, wrote a moving letter to Ethel, expressing sorrow for the people who had not known Bobby as poor Indian families saw him—"good, kind, loving, compassionate." The woman added that Indians envied Mrs. Kennedy because she had known Bobby as no other person did and loved him as no other could. And they loved him too, the woman wrote, though loving a public official was strange, almost unheard-of for Indians. They loved him because they had faith in him: "We trusted him."

Ethel read that letter, and many like it that come to her. They strengthen her resolve to pursue Goal Number Two.

❧ ❧ ❧

Inevitably, comparisons with the woman who married Bobby's older brother and, in the end, suffered the same tragedy, have come up from time to time in this book. There is one other that must be made as we conclude Ethel's story.

Unlike Jackie, who was granted a unique opportunity

to serve mankind but chose not to take it, Ethel will continue to be a growing force for good.

History has known few women more admired, even
honored, than Jackie was by America and the world after
Dallas. She had been unforgettable during those four
agonizing days beginning with the assassination of the
President and ending with his burial at Arlington. She
displayed not only courage and a queenly dignity, but
a sense of history and the ability to plan and act under
the most severe stress. For it was she who drew up the
extraordinarily detailed specifications for her husband's
funeral.

Jackie had been thrust by events, and her own in-
domitable character, into a position of great power. America almost revered Jackie for what she did and how she
acted. Had she wished, she could have led the American
people on any constructive crusade leading to a better
life, furthered any cause or project, social or artistic.

But her commitments were elsewhere.

And so she became for many Americans an object of
intense interest still—but only as a jet-setter on top of
the social pyramid, no longer a national heroine.

One might argue that any individual, even Jackie, is
entitled to make her own choices and lead the kind of life
she prefers. But the question arises: If any of us is granted
the power to be of great service to mankind, do we have
the moral right to reject the call?

Ethel contrasts sharply. In the last half of the 1960s,
her heart opened to an understanding of injustices—the
plight of the blacks, the Indians, the Mexican-Americans,
the unskilled factory hands, the field workers, the poor,
the disabled. With Bobby, and through him, all this became real to her, though she had been born, like Jackie,
into a world of wealth and special status.

With Bobby, Ethel developed an identification with anybody who was hurt, especially children, and this will continue for the rest of her life. While the probability is that no political group would ever persuade her to run for public office, she will work for social change in her own way. For she has taken the torch from Bobby, and it will not drop from her hands.

ABOUT THE AUTHOR

A native New Yorker, Lester David was educated at New York University and at Columbia, earned a master's degree and was almost en route to an instructorship in English literature at an eastern college when he was diverted to journalism. During World War II, he was managing editor of *The Stars and Stripes,* the soldiers' newspaper, and later served on the city desk of the Brooklyn *Eagle.* Since 1950, he has had two books published, contributed to numerous others and written more than 850 articles for well-known periodicals. He lives in Woodmere, New York, with his wife and two daughters, Margery and Susan, both students at Northwestern University.